Manet to Matisse

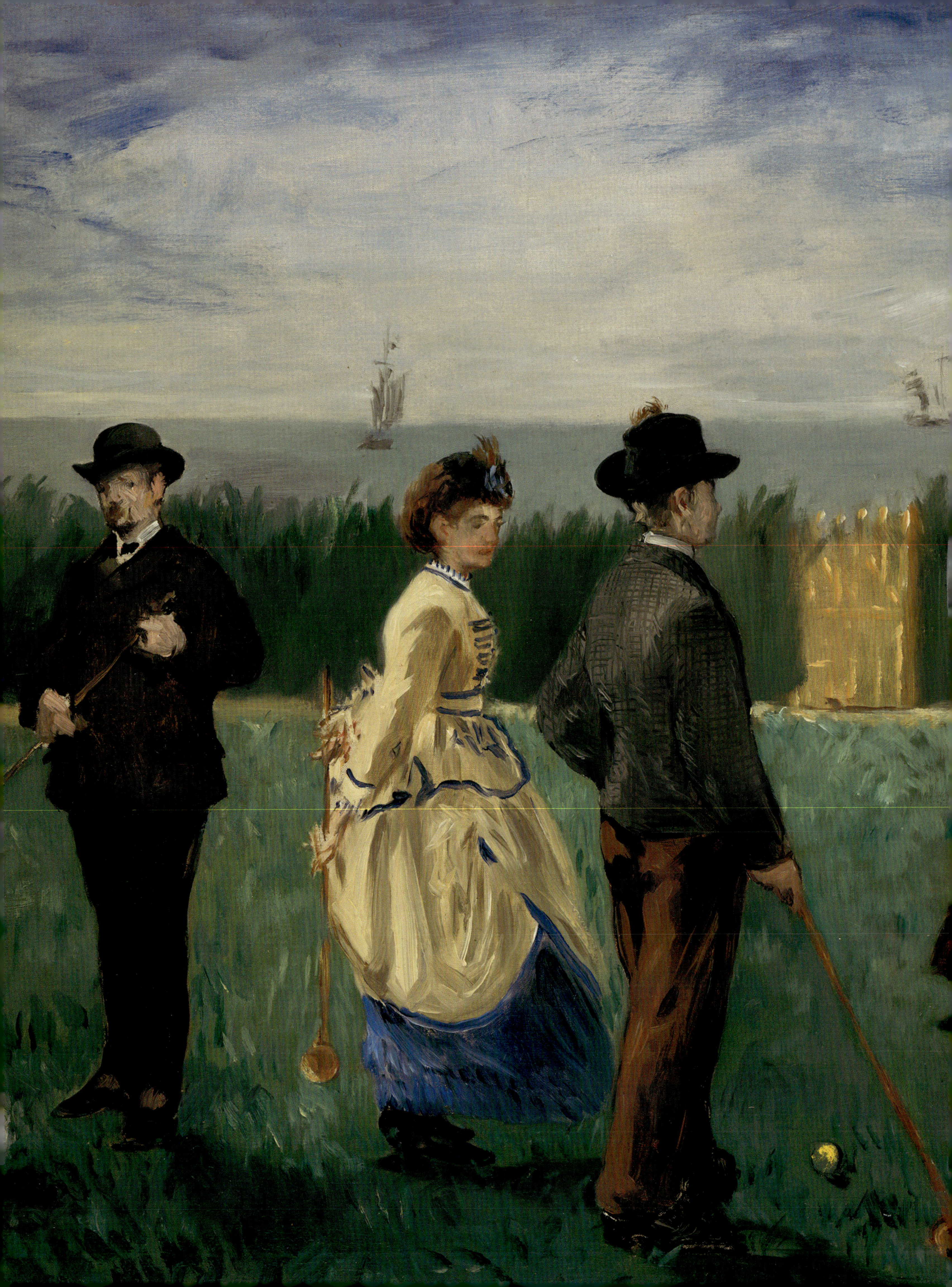

Manet to Matisse

Impressionist Masters from the Marion and Henry Bloch Collection

Richard R. Brettell and Joachim Pissarro

The Nelson-Atkins Museum of Art
Kansas City, Missouri

The publication of the catalogue has been funded by the H & R Block Foundation. Published on the occasion of an exhibition held at The Nelson-Atkins Museum of Art from June 9 to September 9, 2007

Library of Congress
Cataloging-in-Publication Data
Brettell, Richard R.
Manet to Matisse: impressionist masters from the Marion and Henry Bloch collection / Richard Brettell and Joachim Pissarro.
p. cm.
Includes index.
ISBN 978-0-942614-35-0 (hardcover : alk. paper)
ISBN 978-0-942614-36-7 (softcover : alk. paper)
1. Impressionism (Art)—France—Exhibitions. 2. Post-impressionism (Art)—France—Exhibitions. 3. Painting—Private collections—United States—Exhibitions. 4. Bloch, Henry W.—Art collections—Exhibitions. 5. Bloch, Marion H.—Art collections—Exhibitions. I. Pissarro, Joachim. II. Nelson-Atkins Museum of Art. III. Title.
ND547.5.I4B745 2007
759.4074'778411—dc22 2007001994

Distributed by University of Washington Press
PO Box 50096
Seattle, WA 98145–5096
www.washington.edu/uwpress

Cover: Gustave Caillebotte, *Boat Moored on the Seine at Argenteuil (Bateau au mouillage sur la Seine, à Argenteuil)*, c. 1884 (see cat. 13)
Frontispiece: Édouard Manet, *The Croquet Party (La partie de croquet)*, 1871 (see cat. 1)
Page 8: Alfred Sisley, *Rue de la Princesse, Winter (La rue de la princesse, l'hiver)*, 1875 (see cat. 10)
Page 18: Pierre Bonnard, *The White Cupboard (L'armoire blanche)*, 1931 (see cat. 29)
Page 28: Paul Cézanne, *Quarry at Bibémus (Carrière de Bibémus)*, 1895–1900 (see cat. 23)

Project Director and General Editor: Simon Kelly
Editor: Suzanne Kotz
Proofreader: Laura Iwasaki
Indexer: Candace Hyatt
Designer: Zach Hooker
Photographers: Louis Meluso and Jamison Miller
Color separations by iocolor, Seattle
Produced by Marquand Books, Inc., Seattle
www.marquand.com
Printed and bound by CS Graphics Pte., Ltd., Singapore

Contents

Foreword

The opening of the spectacular new Bloch Building is the most significant event in the history of The Nelson-Atkins Museum of Art since its opening in December 1933. This momentous occasion is being marked by special exhibitions that signal the aspirations and values of Kansas City and the Nelson-Atkins. What better, then, that two achievements bearing the Bloch name should come together in mutual celebration? Nothing could be more fitting to this occasion than the first-ever public exhibition of the splendid collection of French Impressionist and Post-Impressionist paintings built so lovingly over the past three decades by Henry and Marion Bloch. Their willingness to share this remarkable collection with the public demonstrates their life-long generosity to the arts and to the community, a generosity that has been reflected in Henry's twenty-three years of service as a member of the Museum's board of trustees and as its current chairman.

As one who has watched the collection grow, I can say that the Blochs have considered each new addition with a rare and admirable modesty. While the deliberations have been as relentlessly rigorous as any, each has rested on a caring appreciation for the expressive qualities of the work. No matter by which master or on what subject, the paintings in the Bloch Collection share a common attribute. Aesthetically and emotionally, they are all approachable. They repay quiet visual conversations with straightforward invitations to return often to enjoy the sublimity that makes them so special.

While each painting is a great or memorable example of an artist's achievement, each also registers the personal sensibilities of Marion and Henry Bloch. This catalogue will help readers and visitors to the exhibition to extend their own reach into that very special private realm where the collectors' sensibilities meet those of the artist. At this level, collecting itself becomes an art, one clearly mastered by Henry and Marion with care and affection.

My first and deepest words of thanks must go to the collectors themselves, Henry W. and Marion H. Bloch, for their liberal willingness to share their collection through public exhibition upon the momentous opening of the Bloch Building. The making of the exhibition itself has demanded total commitment from numerous participants, and to each of them I extend sincere gratitude. Ian Kennedy, Louis L. and Adelaide C. Ward Curator, European Painting and Sculpture, initiated the project and contributed an engaging introductory essay for the accompanying catalogue. Ian also selected the authors of the catalogue, and I am sure that all its readers will applaud his choice of Richard Brettell as lead author of the individual entries and principal essayist. The lively tone of the entries belongs to Dr. Brettell, whose sparkling language and intellectual vigor flow easily from a rare convergence of native talent and passion for his subject. It was Dr. Brettell who persuaded Joachim Pissarro, Curator, Department of Painting and Sculpture, at the Museum of Modern Art, New York, to join the writing team, and certainly the catalogue is much the richer for the insights we find in Pissarro's well-crafted entries.

Since joining the Nelson-Atkins as Associate Curator of European Painting and Sculpture, Simon Kelly has ably served as the curatorial leader of the project, developing a conceptual framework for the exhibition, editing and producing the catalogue, designing the installation, and planning accompanying programs.

As is our practice, a team of specialists joined the project at the outset, bringing the energy and expertise needed to realize our ambitions. Steve Waterman, Director of Design, and Rebecca Young, Manager of Exhibition Design, provided a handsome installation. Theirs was a pioneering effort that transformed untested space. Lou Meluso, Manager, Imaging Services, has earned his stripes by expertly handling the mountains of imaging issues related to the project. From beginning to end, Cindy Cart, Curator of Exhibitions Management, and Elly Miles, former Department Assistant, kept every strand of this complex effort in perfect, productive order. MacKenzie Mallon, current Department Assistant, diligently saw that catalogue deadlines and organizational requirements were met. Lara Kline, Manager, Marketing and Communications, and Scott Stuart, Media Relations Officer, mounted an effective media campaign to make the world at large aware of this wonderful exhibition.

We are fortunate to enjoy the incredibly magnanimous support of the H & R Block Foundation. Everyone who sees and enjoys this exhibition and catalogue can appreciate the thoughtful generosity of the foundation and its board of directors, chaired by Henry Bloch. They are exemplars of enlightened corporate philanthropists investing in the community.

MARC F. WILSON
Menefee D. and Mary Louise Blackwell Director/CEO
The Nelson-Atkins Museum of Art

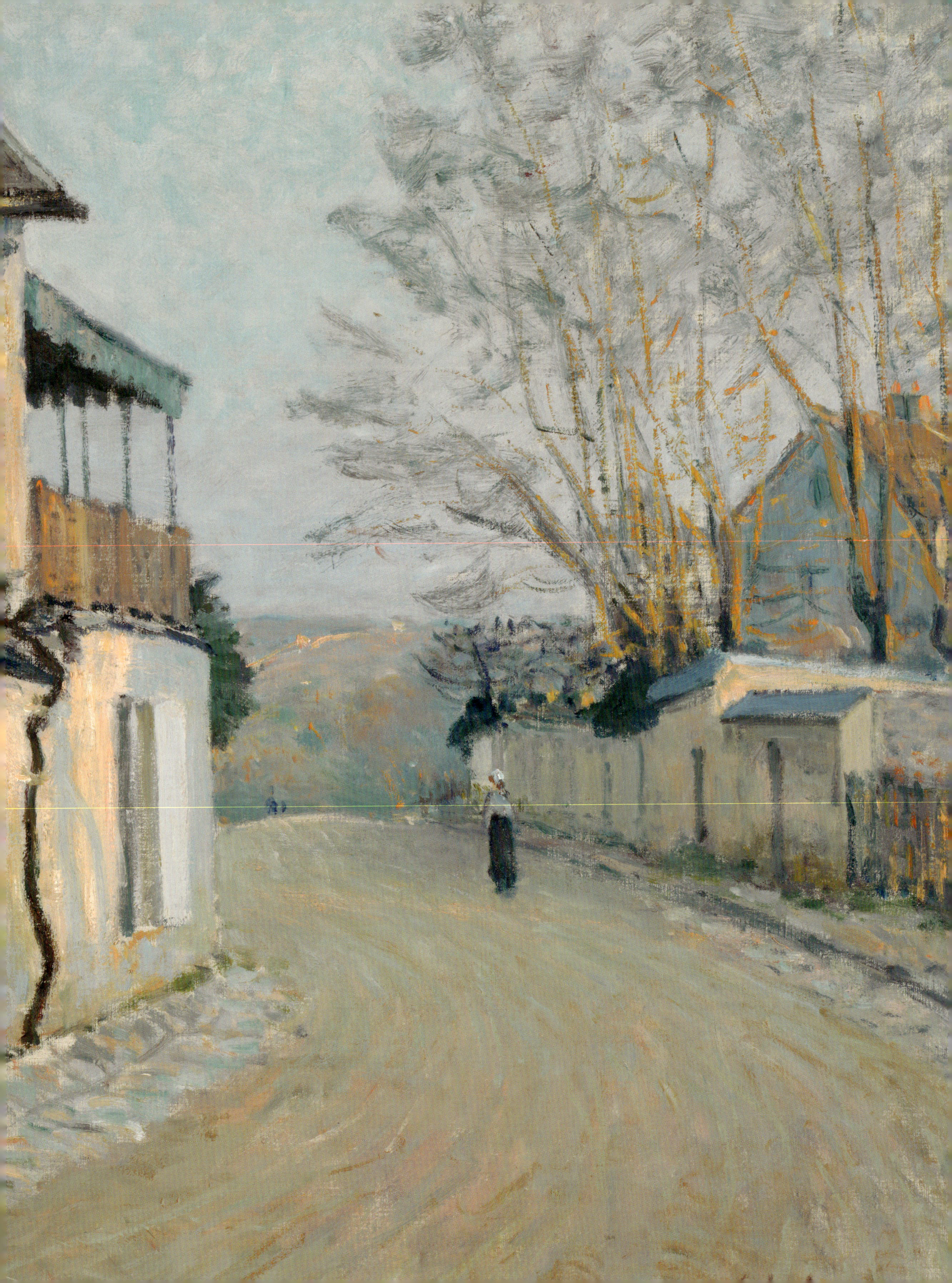

The History of the Bloch Collection

The Marion and Henry Bloch Collection of Impressionist and Post-Impressionist paintings is one of the choicest of its kind left in private hands in the United States. Many of the most discerning collectors—past and present—have made little claim to deep expertise, and Marion and Henry Bloch are no exception (fig. 1). Henry has been heard to describe the collection as "a bunch of pretty pictures," and in a thank-you note to the Wildenstein gallery for a French catalogue of a Paris exhibition, he wrote, "While I couldn't read a word of it, I nevertheless found it most interesting"! The art historian or museum curator better versed in the French language must ask: would he or she have put together a better collection given the means and opportunity? It is doubtful the answer would be yes. Success in business and as a collector demands many of the same qualities. One needs the courage and agility to seize the main chance but also sufficient caution to avoid precipitate errors of judgment and the patience to wait for the right opportunity. Collecting demands confidence and the flexibility to both take advice and learn from mistakes. Above all, it requires a love of art, which can work as powerfully on the quieter as on the most extroverted of enthusiasts. No one who has visited their residence can doubt the passion for art shared by Marion and Henry Bloch, however unostentatiously expressed, or the essential role the pictures on their walls play in their daily lives (figs. 2 and 3). The Blochs have always been prepared to lend, but selectively; as Henry once observed, "We are not a museum."

The instinct for quality that propelled the Blochs' collecting was at all times supported by experts in the field, whether dealers and auctioneers, other private collectors, or museum professionals. Most prominent among the Blochs' advisers was Ted Coe, director of The Nelson-Atkins Museum of Art from 1977 to 1982. Coe was raised in Cleveland surrounded by a distinguished family collection of Impressionist paintings. Thus the Blochs saw him not just as an expert but as a fellow collector. In Kansas City, he remains legendary, not only for the way in which he inspired collectors in general, but for the Impressionist works he obtained for the Nelson-Atkins. Among the Blochs' other advisers, Gary Tinterow, Engelhard Curator of Nineteenth-Century, Modern, and Contemporary Art at the Metropolitan Museum of Art, stands out. They also consulted the dealer Susan Brody and members of the Nelson-Atkins staff, notably the former curator of European paintings Roger Ward.

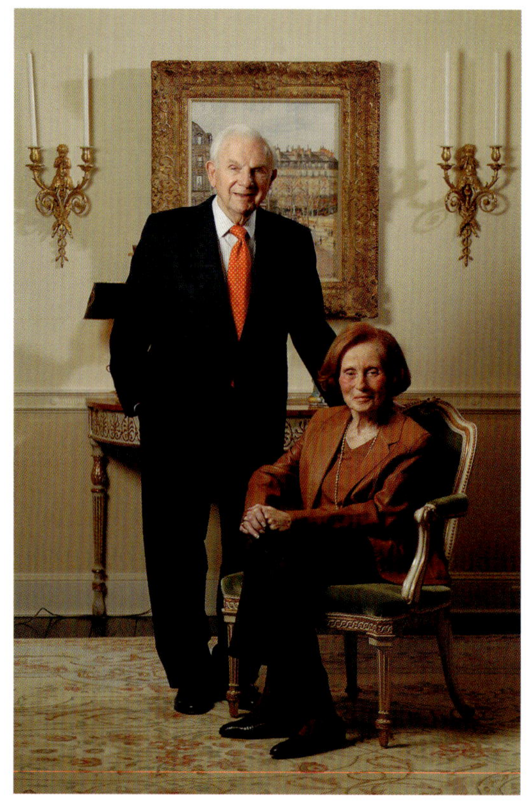

FIG. 1 Henry and Marion Bloch

The first painting of consequence to be acquired by the Blochs was an Old Master, a landscape by Jacob van Ruisdael. Their first Impressionist painting, dipping their toes in the water, was a small but pretty Renoir, *Woman Leaning on Her Elbows* (cat. no. 16), which they purchased from Knoedler's in 1976 and still own. Another Renoir, the pastel *The Flowered Hat* (cat. no. 17), followed the same year, bought from the Herring brothers, who later sold the Blochs one of their Lautrecs, *Jane Avril Looking at a Proof* (cat. no. 26). In the 1980s the tempo quickened, and the Blochs were frequent visitors to Wildenstein and Company in New York, so often the first port of call for the new and ambitious collector. Here they acquired a small Vuillard, *Woman in a Red Dress* (cat. no. 28); Bonnard's *The White Cupboard* (cat. no. 29); and Pissarro's *Banks of the Seine at Port Marly* (cat. no. 6), a classic Impressionist work of 1871.

The first Pissarro to be acquired by the Blochs was one of the artist's later Paris views, *Rue Saint-Honoré* of 1898 (cat. no. 8), which had been part of the great Impressionist collection formed by the actor Edward G. Robinson. Another work with a stellar American provenance, this time the Havemeyer collection, was Monet's *Snow at Argenteuil* (cat. no. 9), bought in 1988 from Susan Brody, from whom the Blochs acquired one of their greatest pictures, Gauguin's Brittany landscape *The Willow Tree* (cat. no. 22). From the Lefèvre Gallery in London they purchased a crystalline late Manet still life, *White Lilacs in a Crystal Vase* (cat. no. 2). In 1986,

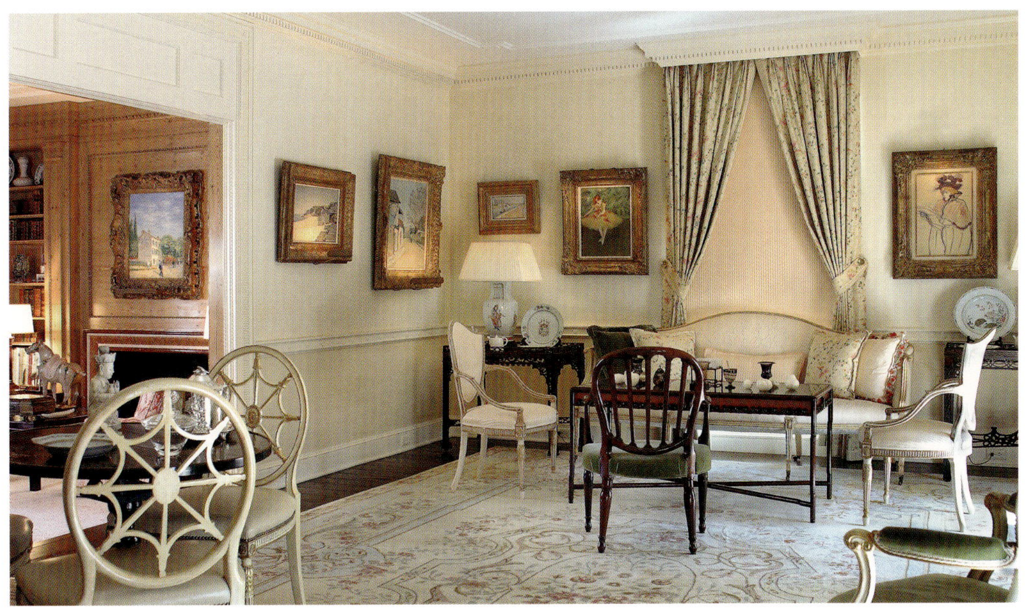

FIG. 2 Interior, house of Marion and Henry Bloch

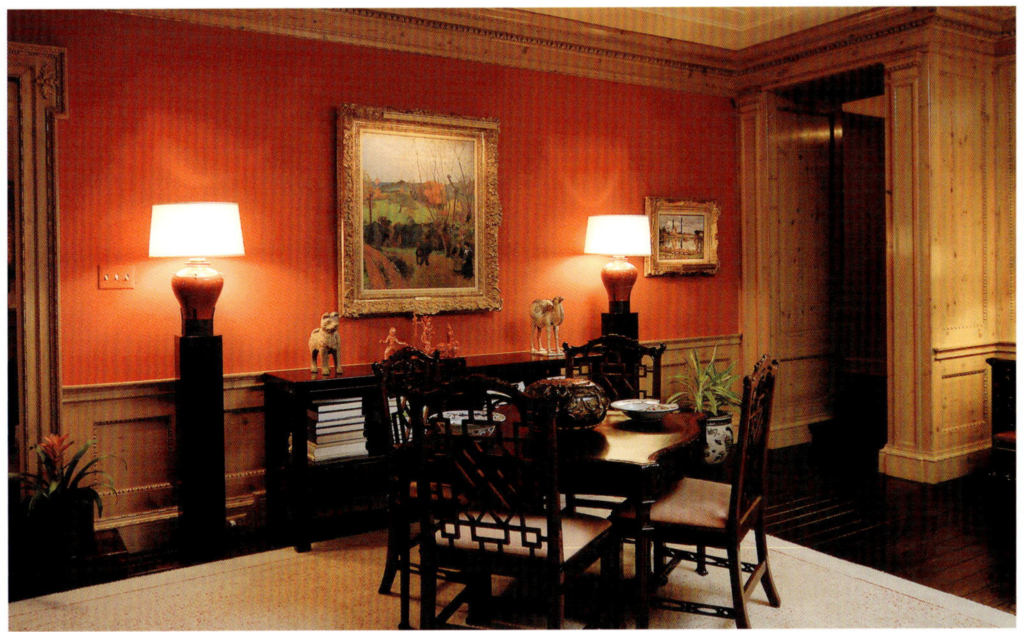

FIG. 3 Interior, house of Marion and Henry Bloch

from the De Bestegui collection, they bagged the rarest of prizes, Manet's *The Croquet Party* (cat. no. 1), a small-scale, moody masterpiece showing the artist's friends and family uneasily juxtaposed on a blustery day by the sea. Further dealer purchases in the 1990s included Signac's *Portrieux, The Bathing Cabins, Opus 185* (cat. no. 20) from Richard Feigen, Redon's *The Green Vase* (cat. no. 27) from Thomas Gibson, and Berthe Morisot's *Under the Orange Tree* (cat. no. 18) from Susan Brody.

Buying from a dealer allows time to consider one's purchase. The pace is quicker when bidding in the auction salesroom, but here, chiefly at Christie's and Sotheby's in New York, the

Blochs were still well up to the mark. Their first auction purchase in 1979 was a major one, Van Gogh's *Restaurant Rispal at Asnières* (cat. no. 21), after which there was a break until 1985, when they bought Caillebotte's *Boat Moored on the Seine at Argenteuil* (cat. no. 13), followed the next year by Matisse's *Woman Seated before a Black Background* (cat. no. 30). The Blochs have always taken great trouble with frames, acquiring them, when existing ones needed upgrading, from Guttmann in New York and Paul Mitchell in London. In the case of the Matisse, they chose from Mitchell a restrained and classical French frame from the Louis XIII period. The Blochs' next major auction purchase, in 1987, was Cézanne's *Quarry at Bibémus* (cat. no. 23). Several more works were acquired from the salesroom in the 1990s, including, from Sotheby's, the Degas bronze *Grande Arabesque* (cat. no. 15) and the Seurat study *Channel at Gravelines* (cat. no. 19), and, from Christie's, Cézanne's *Man with a Pipe* (cat. no. 24) and Pissarro's *Chestnut Grove at Louveciennes* (cat. no. 7). The Pissarro, a well-known work from the Lewyt collection, was their last and most recent acquisition.

When any collection is discussed, the question inevitably arises, often whispered behind the collector's back, whether mistakes were made. In the Blochs' case little comment is necessary, since mistakes are something Henry is quite happy to admit. No collector is without regret for missed opportunities, and it would be platitudinous to list those here, but as Henry ruefully confesses, he should not have been persuaded to let go of his great Monet, *Houses of Parliament*. However regrettable, this is scarcely the first time a collector has followed the wrong advice. Henry is also sorry that he did not buy many other wonderful paintings, but, he explains, they did not want their house to look like a museum, and they were offered "so many, so fast."

When the Blochs were told that the Museum wanted to show their collection to celebrate the opening of the new building bearing their name, Henry suggested that we display his collection with the Impressionist and Post-Impressionist works from the Nelson-Atkins. This was a most civilized idea and, in today's world, unusually self-effacing. The Museum felt, however, that the public might prefer to see the collection on its own, allowing visitors to make a more personal association between the works of art and their owners. Whichever idea was best, Henry latched onto an important point: his collection and that of the Nelson-Atkins complement each other most instructively. Under the terms of the William Rockhill Nelson Trust, established in 1915, the Museum could purchase no work by an artist who had been dead less than thirty years. This may have benefited the Old Master and nineteenth-century collections, but it meant the Museum had no Picasso or Matisse paintings, and other significant gaps exist in its earlier twentieth-century holdings. In the present exhibition, the Blochs' charming and incisive Matisse, *Woman Seated before a Black Background*, at least partially redresses the balance, as does the masterly Bonnard, *The White Cupboard*. As Richard Brettell speculates in this catalogue, Bonnard's painting could reflect the artist thinking of Mondrian, so dominating is its grid of horizontals and verticals.

Like Matisse, Lautrec is a pivotal artist unrepresented in our galleries, so the opportunity of seeing the Blochs' spirited study *Jane Avril Looking at a Proof* along with the early Lautrec watercolor *General Séré de Rivières* (cat. no. 25) is doubly welcome. Indeed, *Jane Avril* was

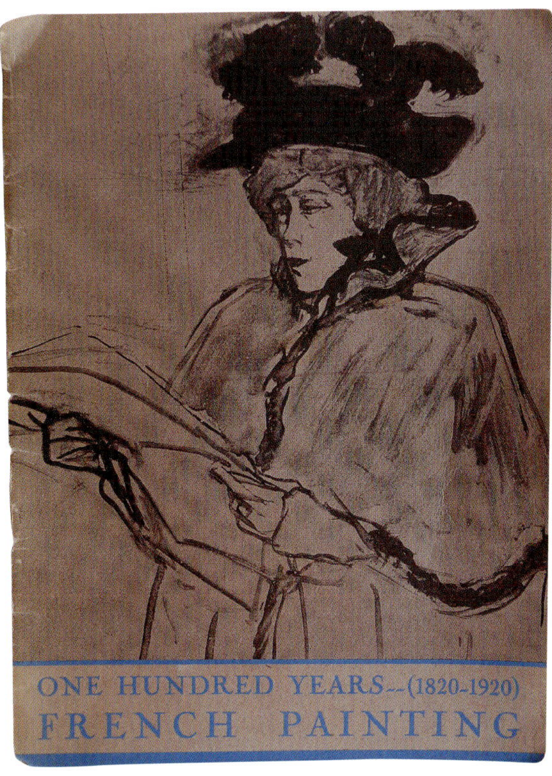

FIG. 4 Catalogue cover featuring Henri de Toulouse-Lautrec's *Jane Avril Looking at a Proof* (cat. no. 26), from a 1935 exhibition at The Nelson-Atkins Museum of Art

featured as the cover illustration (fig. 4) for the catalogue of the first exhibition of French paintings, held in 1935, at The Nelson-Atkins Museum of Art (then known as the William Rockhill Nelson Gallery of Art and Mary Atkins Museum of Fine Arts). Generally speaking, however, there are fewer gaps in our late-nineteenth-century than early-twentieth-century holdings. In the case of Pissarro, the three Bloch pictures in the exhibition can now be compared to four in our own collections. Together, they give a fairly thorough overview of the artist's career, and especially helpful in this regard is the Blochs' *Rue Saint-Honoré*, since we have no late urban scenes. Pissarro's mainstream Impressionism of the 1870s, already represented in the Museum by *The Garden of Les Mathurins at Pontoise* (1876) and *Wooded Landscape at L'Hermitage* (1879), is supported by the Blochs' *Banks of the Seine at Port Marly* (1871) and *Chestnut Grove at Louveciennes* (1872). *Banks of the Seine at Port Marly* shows the structural rigor that also informs, in more Cézannesque and abstract fashion, our *Wooded Landscape at L'Hermitage*. The same applies to *Chestnut Grove at Louveciennes*, where the armature of the bare branches is reinforced by the shadows of more trees beyond the picture field. One can see why this painting, which has a tougher and more austere composition than most in the collection, might have appealed to the Blochs. The light is clear but also soft, drawing out rather than suppressing the muted colors of winter in a way that is remarkably similar to the winter light in Kansas City, and different from the harder, more metallic sunlight in the eastern states at this season.

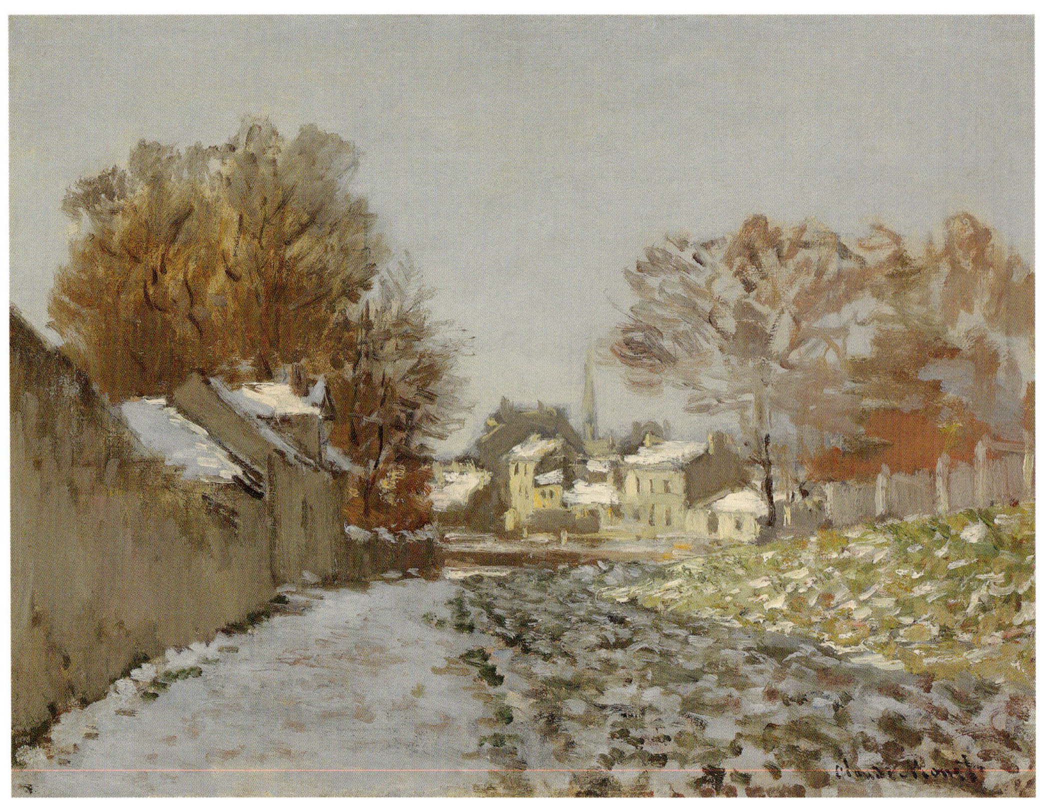

FIG. 5 Claude Monet, *Snow at Argenteuil (Neige à Argenteuil)*, 1874–75, oil on canvas, 19¾ × 26¾ in. (50.2 × 68 cm). Collection of Marion and Henry Bloch

The gentler art of Sisley is also well represented in the Bloch Collection. The Nelson-Atkins has an attractive winter scene of the Seine at Billancourt, but the two Bloch Sisleys, *Rue de la Princesse, Winter* of 1875 (cat. no. 10) and *The Lock of Saint-Mammès* from the middle of the next decade (cat. no. 11), are arguably somewhat stronger examples. The Bloch family possesses Armand Guillaumin's *Landscape, Île de France* (cat. no. 12), one of that artist's best works. The encroachment of open country by urbanization or, as here, heavy industry was a theme of particular interest to late-nineteenth-century artists and novelists, perhaps because it served as a metaphor for the social change facing the old agrarian way of life in the rush to modernity.

The Museum already has two important winter scenes by Claude Monet, *View of Argenteuil—Snow* and the celebrated *Boulevard des Capucines*, with which the Blochs' *Snow at Argenteuil*, also from circa 1874–75, makes an informative threesome. The Bloch Monet (fig. 5) is one of the artist's subtlest evocations of winter, with the snow just beginning to melt, unlike the museum's Argenteuil scene (fig. 6), where it lies thick and fresh. Monet readily admitted his debt to Boudin, his early mentor, and the Museum's late *Port of Deauville* by Boudin is now joined on view by the three Boudins in the Bloch Collection: a second Deauville harbor (cat. no. 5), the earlier and classic *Trouville Beach Scene* of 1874 (cat. no. 4), and a rare, early pastel of a beach scene from circa 1865 (cat. no. 3).

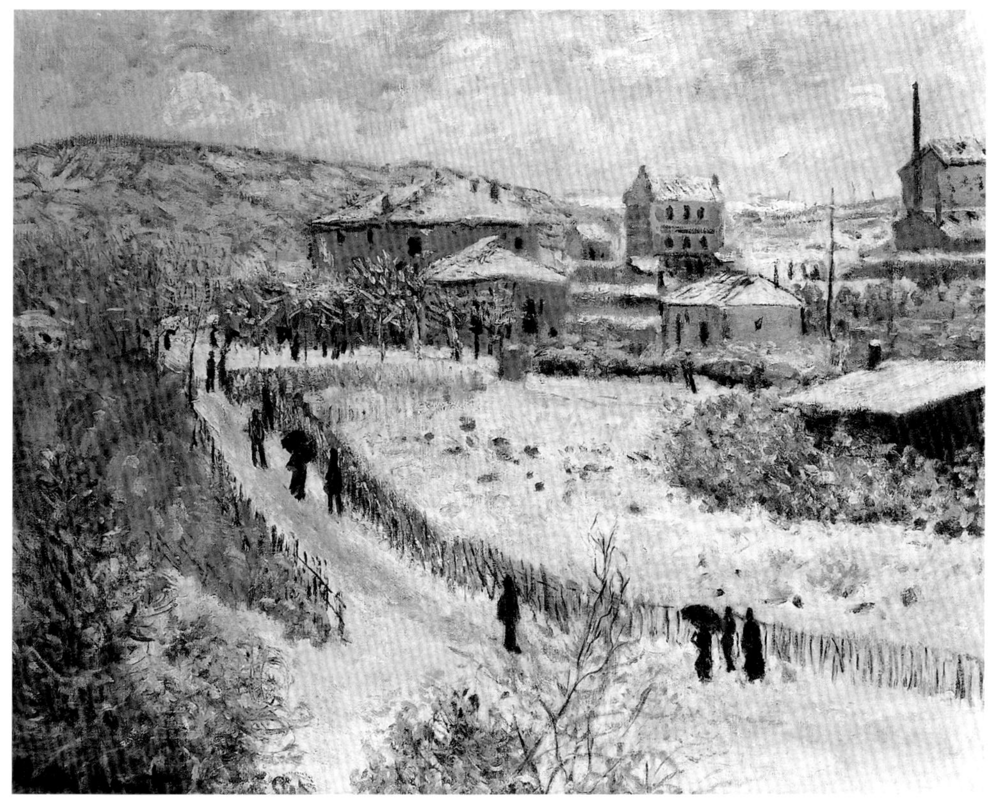

FIG. 6 Claude Monet, *View of Argenteuil—Snow*, 1874–75, oil on canvas, 21½ × 25⅝ in. (54.6 × 65.1 cm). The Nelson-Atkins Museum of Art, Kansas City

The Museum currently possesses only one painting by Manet, a portrait of the precociously flirtatious Lise Campineanu. As Manet himself observed, his oeuvre looks better when seen as a whole, and the presence in the exhibition of the Bloch *Croquet Party* and *White Lilacs in a Crystal Vase* gives us a better chance of appreciating this point. The Museum's Renoir portrait of the young Paul Haviland, one of our most frequently requested loans, has functioned as a kind of pendant to the Manet portrait. Now it has company in the two Renoirs from the Blochs, *Woman Leaning on Her Elbows* and *The Flowered Hat*.

Two outstanding Degas pastels owned by the Nelson-Atkins, *Little Milliners* and *Ballet Rehearsal*, have been infrequently exhibited, but in the new installation they will be shown more often on a rotating basis. The Blochs' pastel by Degas, *Dancer Making Points* (complemented by their *danseuse* in bronze) is smaller and simpler but of the same quality. It is bold in the placement of the fragile figure against the bare floorboards and in the complementary contrast of the orange trim of her tutu with the floriated green backdrop. The exceptionally fine *Daydreaming* by Berthe Morisot is another pastel belonging to the Museum which we intend to exhibit more often, now joined on view by the Blochs' equally good Morisot, *Under the Orange Tree*.

In addition to the trios of Sisley, Manet, and Degas, the exhibition permits us to enjoy further trios of Cézanne, Van Gogh, and Gauguin. The Bloch Cézannes, *Quarry at Bibémus* (fig. 7) and *Man with a Pipe*, which is almost an extract from the Barnes Foundation *Card Players*,

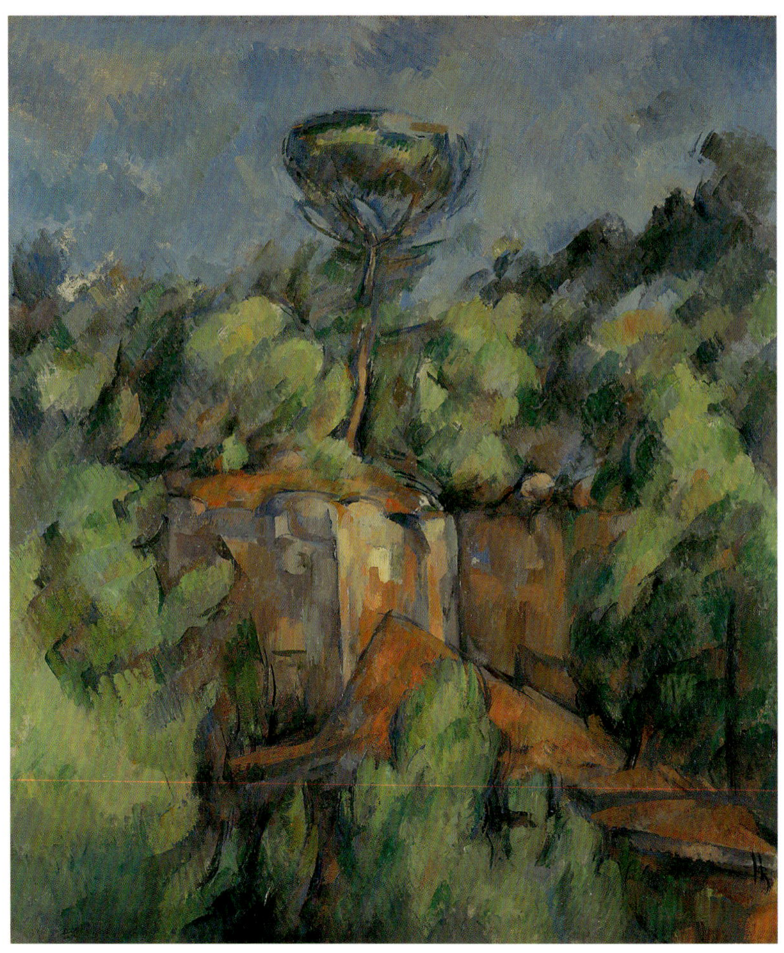

FIG. 7 Paul Cézanne, *Quarry at Bibémus (Carrière de Bibémus)*, 1895–1900, oil on canvas, 25¾ × 21½ in. (65.5 × 54.5 cm). Collection of Marion and Henry Bloch

complement our own slightly later *Mont Sainte-Victoire* (fig. 8). With the presence of the Blochs' *Restaurant Rispal*, three major phases of Van Gogh's work can be admired: the earthy style of the *Potato Eaters* in our *Portrait of Gysbertus de Groot*, the Impressionism of the Paris period in the Bloch painting, and the Expressionism of the artist's last years in our widely admired *Olive Orchard*. The Blochs' magisterial Gauguin, *The Willow Tree*, painted in Brittany in 1889, can be contrasted with our Brittany landscape, which Gauguin made in 1894 during a brief return from the South Seas. The Bloch landscape perhaps wins out as more truly Breton, since the tropical tinge of the Museum's makes it hard to decide whether one is in Brittany or Tahiti.

Finally we come to Seurat and Divisionism. The Museum's only Seurat, a study for his *Bathers at Asnières* (National Gallery, London), has great power despite its small size. An appropriate companion is now on view in the Blochs' *Channel at Gravelines*, Seurat's study for a larger picture in the Indianapolis Museum of Art. Compared to the strong colors and broad brushwork of the earlier Nelson-Atkins painting, this is a typical late Seurat in its cooler palette and more rigorous pointillism. It nonetheless retains something of the spontaneity of an Impressionist *coup d'oeil*. Signac's pointillist *Portrieux, The Bathing Cabins, Opus 185* in the Bloch Collection

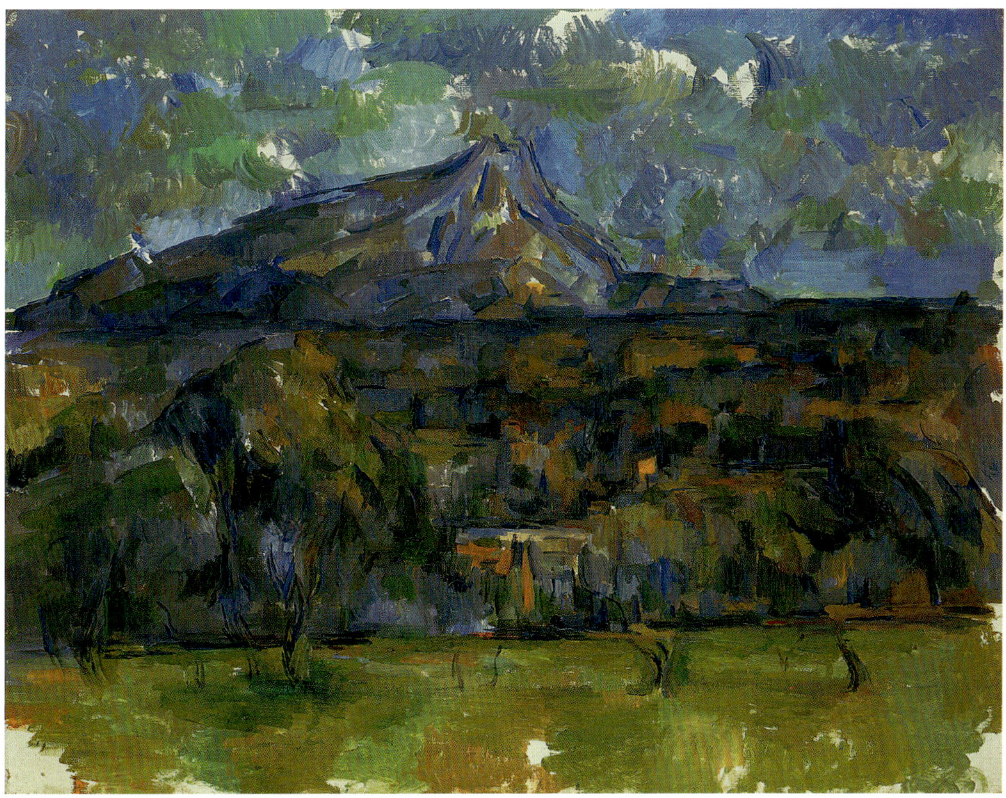

FIG. 8 Paul Cézanne, *Mont Sainte-Victoire*, 1902–6, oil on canvas, 25⅛ × 32⅛ in. (63.8 × 81.6 cm). The Nelson-Atkins Museum of Art, Kansas City

complements the Museum's slightly more decorative *Chateau Gaillard*. Closer to the more rigorous Divisionism of Seurat himself, the Bloch picture admirably conjures up the silence of a deserted beach under the fresh light of the early morning sun.

Is it still possible to put together a collection of this caliber now, in the early twenty-first century? Guest author Richard Brettell's answer is possibly yes, but at prohibitive cost. The collection with which it best compares is perhaps that of Ailsa Mellon Bruce now at the National Gallery in Washington. The Bruce collection, larger and more varied than that of the Blochs, shares the same gentle serenity and feeling of private enjoyment on a domestic scale. Kansas City is a conservative town, and its citizens look before they leap; they are not an impulsive brood. But when they decide to do something ambitious, they generally do it extremely well. The Bloch Collection, like the outstandingly good new Bloch building, fits right into this pattern, adding a new richness to the cultural landscape of Kansas City that will surely inspire generations to come. In this exhibition we celebrate this achievement, of which the Blochs should be justly proud.

IAN KENNEDY
Louis L. and Adelaide C. Ward
Curator of European Painting and Sculpture
The Nelson-Atkins Museum of Art

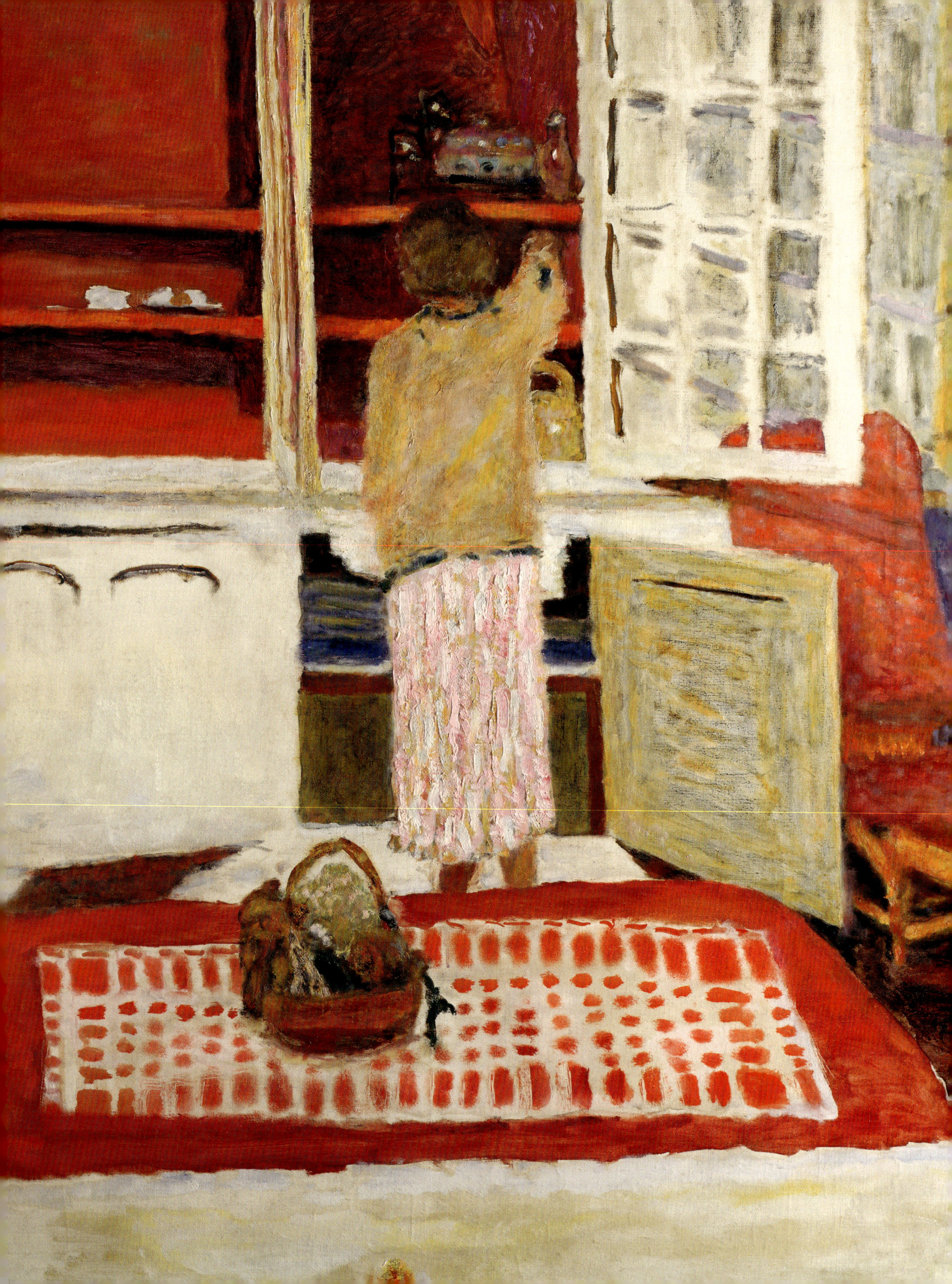

Domestic Artifice

Art Collecting and Modern Bourgeois Life

Late in 1876, the great Impressionist painter Gustave Caillebotte took it upon himself to organize the third Impressionist exhibition, to be held in Paris in April of the next year. At the time Caillebotte was working on one of his largest paintings, the masterpiece *Paris Street; Rainy Day* (Art Institute of Chicago), whose sheer scale suggests that he painted it for the immense public galleries of the official Salon or another large-scale venue. Yet, when Caillebotte secured gallery space for the 1877 exhibition (he paid the rent himself), he chose a large apartment in an upper-middle-class building in an expanding residential neighborhood. His strategy—and it was a radical one at the time—recognized that the most important future clients for Impressionist paintings would be the nouveaux riches, men and women who had made their money in industry, retail, publishing, and financial speculation. These people, whom the French call the "bourgeoisie," rather than those with hereditary wealth or family roots in the old aristocracy, were the natural constituency for the completely nouveau riche artist, whose paintings celebrated bourgeois life in the city, its suburbs, and the more distant beach resorts and casinos built for modern urbanites.

The apartment Caillebotte rented was located in the recently built area surrounding the new Paris Opera House, near the large boulevards and department stores for which the city was increasingly being recognized throughout the world. Few historic monuments existed in this utterly modern part of Paris, and life in its *quartiers* was aggressively modern and forward looking. In the elegantly proportioned living room, dining room, drawing room, bedrooms, and hallways of this empty apartment, Caillebotte and his colleagues Pissarro, Monet, Degas, Renoir, Sisley, Morisot, and Cézanne arranged their paintings to suggest their suitability as decor for the domestic spaces of wealthy urbanites. Landscapes and urban genre scenes were appropriate for the rooms where one received visitors or sat before and after meals. Dining rooms could be easily decorated with still-life paintings, informal portraits, or domestic genre scenes. Private spaces such as bedrooms and corridors were natural places for smaller-scale paintings as well as pastels, drawings, and prints. Caillebotte installed his immense *Paris Street; Rainy Day* canvas in the large living room, where its life-size figures so dominated the space that they appeared almost to walk directly into it. Caillebotte thereby became the first important artist to connect art directly to the private spaces of the urban middle class rather than to public life.

This link between modern bourgeois domesticity and art is, in the end, the most important aspect of Impressionist aesthetics. And, as a marketing strategy, it proved to be brilliant, for most of the greatest collectors of Impressionist and modern painting in the nineteenth century were not aristocrats or landed gentry; they were men and women who had earned their own money. Publishers, postal officials, opera singers, factory owners, department store magnates, bankers, real-estate speculators, jewelers, fashion designers, doctors, actors, writers, dentists, bakers, restaurant owners, lawyers, professors, and capitalists throughout the economic scale—these were the purchasers of Impressionist art. The very idea of this most bourgeois type of modern painting is that a work of art is a commodity to be bought and sold individually, making its possessor an "owner" rather than a "patron." Hence, modern art was made for the market rather than on commission. When Caillebotte or Monet or Renoir made a painting, they did so, most often, without a particular client in mind. Indeed, as we have learned in recent years, even a good many Impressionist portraits were painted as "advertisements" to secure future commissions rather than to fulfill specific requests. (Degas's only commissioned portrait was refused by its sitter, Mme Dietz-Monin, and shown, as if to spite her, in an Impressionist exhibition with the title *Portrait after a Costume Ball* [Art Institute of Chicago].)

Although the early histories of Impressionism are filled with stories of the financial and critical struggles of the artists, they were, in fact, almost all financially successful within their lifetimes, effectively becoming precisely the kind of people for whom they made their art. And, after somewhat more than a generation of study, we now know a good deal about the purchasers of Impressionist and modern painting. Anne Distel's magisterial 1989 study of the early French collectors proves that they were, almost without exception, nouveaux riches, and from the patterns of sales, we also know that several bought works of art as hedges against the ups and downs of the financial markets—selling them as commodity assets when stock or property markets fell. The same can be said for the American, British, German, Dutch, Russian, and Scandinavian collectors of Impressionism and later modern movements.

These utterly modern "commodity collectors" can be divided into two types. The first group purchased works in quantity less for the decoration of their domestic spaces than as tradable

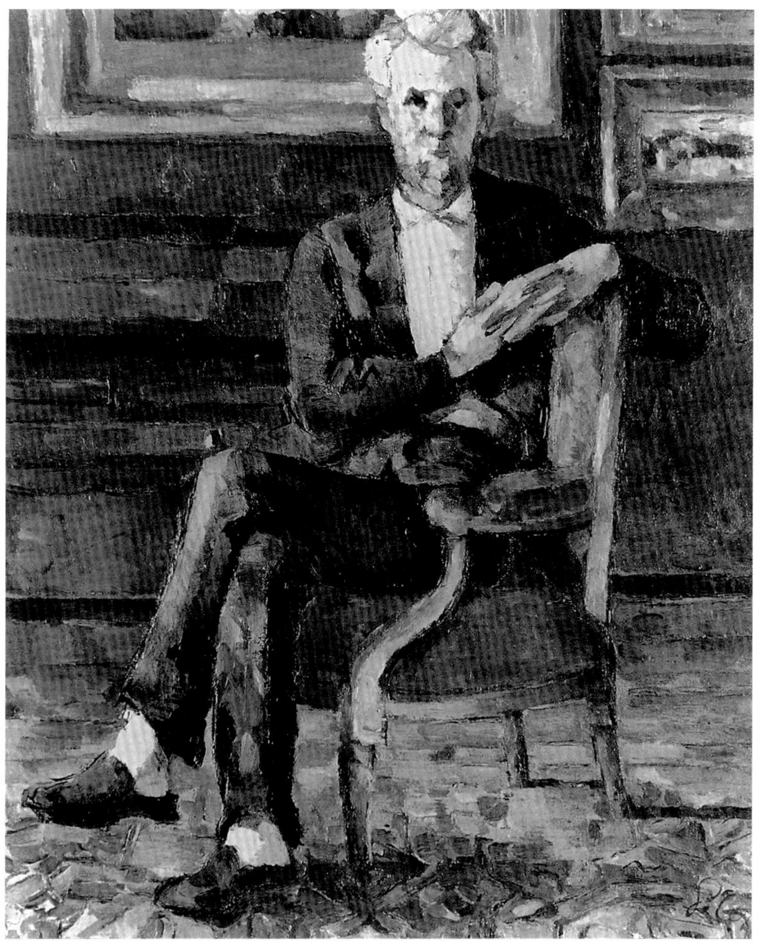

FIG. 9 Paul Cézanne, *Victor Chocquet*, 1877, oil on canvas, 18⅛ × 15 in. (46 × 38 cm). Columbus Museum of Art, Ohio, museum purchase, Howard Fund

assets. Indeed, certain capitalist collectors created more than one collection, selling when markets were advantageous and then forming another. The second type of collector was—and is—in the majority: men and women who bought works of art to decorate their homes and apartments, adding works as their fortunes increased and occasionally upgrading, but holding the works of art to a small enough number to fit comfortably on their walls. These collectors most often owned between eight and forty works, depending on their means and the scale at which they lived. They tended to buy occasionally rather than habitually, taking as much pleasure from the protracted negotiations necessary for private transactions as from the works themselves. It is to this group of collectors that the Blochs belong.

Perhaps the earliest representations of the "domestic" collector are Paul Cézanne's and Auguste Renoir's wonderful portraits of their first major patron, Victor Chocquet. He worked in the French customs service but his wife had a small income, and he became the earliest major collector of both artists. Cézanne represented the middle-aged man sitting in a recently made but luxurious Louis XV–style armchair, set on an oriental carpet in front of a wall filled with paintings in substantial gilt frames (fig. 9). Renoir, by contrast, allowed Chocquet's upper

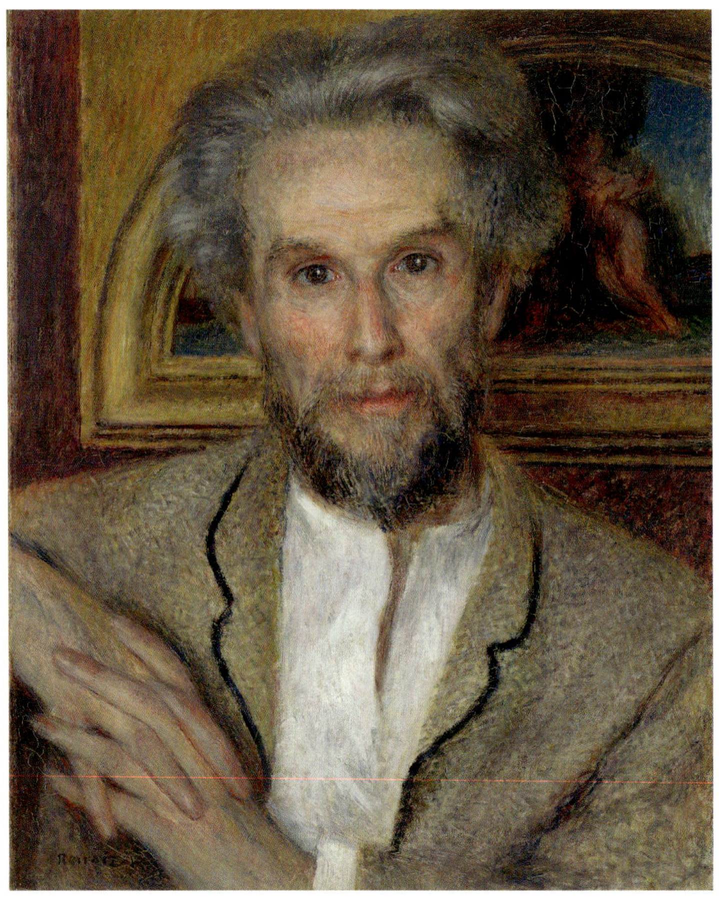

FIG. 10 Pierre-Auguste Renoir, *Victor Chocquet*, c. 1875, oil on canvas, 20⅞ × 17⅛ in. (53 × 43.5 cm). Fogg Art Museum, Cambridge, bequest of Grenville L. Winthrop

body to fill the picture surface, juxtaposing his head and hands against a single framed work of art—in this case a prized work by Delacroix in the collector's possession (fig. 10). In each case, Chocquet's identity is that of an art collector—we have no idea from the painting whether he is married or single, and neither artist gives us a clue to his profession. He is, in a sense, defined as a connoisseur or, as the French preferred to say in the nineteenth century, an *amateur*, who derived more of his life's meaning from his art collection than from religion, family, friends, or employment.

The number of such collectors that have emerged since the mid-1870s, when the Chocquet portraits were painted, until the present is in the hundreds. Few large modern cities in Europe and America are without several serious collectors of modern art who keep their works at home for personal enjoyment. We know that even in France this kind of collecting was not limited to Paris, and one can find evidence of private collectors of domestically scaled modern art in many of France's regional cities. The businessman Félix-François Depeaux (1853–1920), part of whose extensive collection of Impressionist works was given to his hometown museum in Rouen, is one example among many. If we cast our net wider to include Germany, Austria, Great Britain, the Netherlands, Scandinavia, Romania, Hungary, Poland, and Russia, the number of such collectors begins to mount. Yet it is important to say that this kind of collecting remained—even in Paris—a mark of distinction. This is because, from the early 1890s onward, modern works of art were either difficult enough to appreciate or expensive enough to appeal only to a minority of collectors. The men and women who collected them well were—in every community—rare, in spite of the fact that there were hundreds of them collectively in the Euro-global world.

Collecting of modern art by the bourgeoisie came to the United States quite early. By the 1880s the great Impressionist dealer Paul Durand-Ruel had established a gallery in New York, and it is scarcely original to say that most Americans with serious incomes and ambitions traveled abroad with some frequency by the same date. Works by Monet, Degas, Pissarro, Manet, and others could be found in private collections in Boston, New York, Chicago, and Philadelphia by 1890, and, within fifty years, scarcely an American city of any size was without a collector of modern French painting. Clearly Caillebotte's introduction of Impressionist art into the domestic sphere of the *haute-bourgeoisie* worked out well. By the 1960s and 1970s, New York dealers and museum curators actually referred to certain types of work by Sisley, Monet, Renoir, and Cassatt as "Park Avenue paintings." They fit so well into a particular kind of upper-class interior that they had become almost clichés.

The sheer success of Caillebotte's innovation should not dissuade us from recognizing both its brilliance and its aesthetic importance. To begin with, the artists themselves utterly accepted the strategy and produced their best works for this targeted clientele. And, equally important, the collectors and the dealers they patronized with regularity became a highly critical and selective market for the artists, often goading them to produce works in a consistent fashion and, in some cases, to shift styles when their oeuvre had ceased to appeal. This is particularly true of American collectors, who, from Louisine Havemeyer and Bertha Honoré Palmer through Albert Barnes and John Quinn to Paul Mellon and John Hay Whitney, had a profound effect on the market, using their financial clout and critical acumen in equal measure to elevate the quality of paintings.

Perhaps the earliest book in English to treat this new system of artistic production fairly is Cynthia and Harrison White's *Canvases and Careers* (1965), a study less of the art than its production, distribution, exhibition, and evaluation. For the Whites, it was the dealer/critic system of sales and evaluation that was the stuff of modernism. The role of governmental institutions weakened with respect to the visual arts, and the private sector aggressively took their place. Yet, for all its successes, the dealer/critic system is utterly dependent on a large—if well-managed—group of collectors with the capital and the desire to participate. Buying a painting for one's home had become, by 1900, a rarified commercial act in which a sort of personal intimacy developed between dealers and their buyers. These men and women shared superb meals, visited each other's houses, exchanged holiday greetings, and even vacationed together. And, when traveling in Europe or America, a shared dealer meant an instant invitation to the home of another fellow collector. Hence, acts of aesthetic judgment were at once private and shared by other men and women with similar interests and tastes.

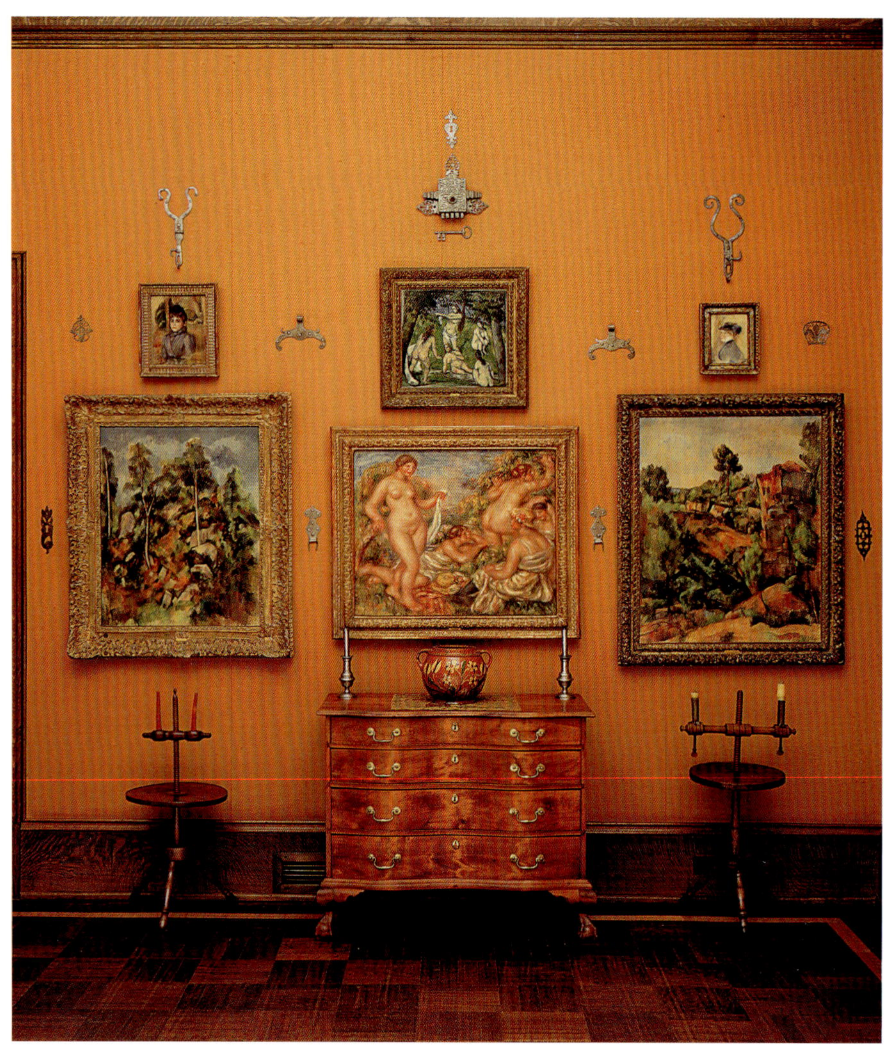

FIG. 11 Gallery VIII, south wall, Barnes Foundation, Merion, Pennsylvania. (For a discussion of the Cézanne landscape on the right, see cat. no. 23)

Certain of these collectors—one thinks of Bertha Honoré Palmer, Albert Barnes, Chester Dale, Paul Mellon, or Norton Simon—became such addicted buyers of art that their collections became much too large for their home (or homes), forcing them to sell, store, or share works with family or, more often, art institutions (or, in several cases, to create their own institutions). All of the earliest public museums or galleries of modern art were, in fact, large private collections that had, in effect, outgrown their domestic function. Hansen outside Copenhagen, Osthaus near Essen, Shchukin and Morozov in Moscow, Barnes near Philadelphia (fig. 11), Phillips in Washington, Kröller-Müller in rural Holland, Clark in Williamstown—all of these "private" institutions have their roots in precisely the kind of personal domestic collecting that Caillebotte envisioned in 1876.

Domestic collecting has persisted to this day in the United States, and there are signs that it is far from over, in spite of the almost prohibitively high prices for Impressionist and modern paintings. Even secondary or tertiary cities like Memphis, Denver, Nashville, Portland, and

Santa Barbara have collectors with at least two rooms of paintings by significant Impressionist and modern artists, and the situation in major cities is equally strong. Los Angeles, San Francisco, Seattle, Dallas, Houston, St. Louis, Atlanta, Miami, Minneapolis, Cleveland, Chicago—all these cities have more than one collector of Impressionist and modern painting whose domestic environment is dominated by works in the manner envisioned by Caillebotte.

Collecting of this type at once liberates and confines its practitioners. The liberation comes from the large quantity of works produced for this market, allowing the collector a wide range of choices (though this is less true as time goes on). The limitations are less the budget of the collector—though, of course, a factor—than the character of the rooms in which the collection is to be housed. Most of the important apartments on New York's Upper East Side and most of the well-placed houses of the urban bourgeoisie have at least three major rooms—the living room, the dining room, and a library or family room. Filled with furniture and objects, these spaces are increasingly the realm of professional decorators or architects, who work with collectors to choose fabrics, furniture, decorative objects, and the like. Even the largest of these rooms is dominated more by furniture and architectural features—doorways, windows, and fireplaces—than by works of art, which, by the sheer fact of their participation in this environment, must "fit in." Questions of scale, palette, texture, and imagery play as important a role in the selection of a painting for a room as do authenticity, quality, rarity, and condition. Seasoned visitors to collections of this type know instantly when they enter a room which aspects of a work of art are most important to the collector.

In the United States, a carefully crafted aesthetic for these domestic rooms was established over the past century. It favors English and American eighteenth- and early-nineteenth-century furniture (often with lacquered cabinet pieces for accent), Chinese or Japanese ceramics and decorative objects, Asian and Middle Eastern carpets, comfortably ahistorical upholstered furniture, and subtly patterned fabrics for accent pillows and wall panels. With the addition of seasonal flowers and discreet stacks of illustrated books, these interiors are made current. We see these patterns in the apartment and country houses of the Havemeyers, the Mellons, the Whitneys, the Rockefellers—to recall the most prestigious of names—but similar interiors can be found in the homes of a wealthy Englishman near Amarillo, a cotton merchant in Memphis (fig. 12), a computer technology heiress in Dallas, a television producer in Los Angeles, a personal products innovator in suburban Chicago, an automobile magnate in Detroit, an oilman in Houston, or a textile queen in San Francisco. These environments—often more alike than different, belying the disparities among their owners of region, religion, and social origin—can be linked through a common source. From the time of Paul Mellon onward, the London market for French painting and decorative objects has been as important for Americans as that of Paris, linking vanguard French painting to the comfortable interiors associated with English wealth, both landed and otherwise.

For most of these collectors, modern French painting stretches from Manet through Matisse, including Impressionism, Post-Impressionism, the Nabis, and the Fauves. Missing in almost

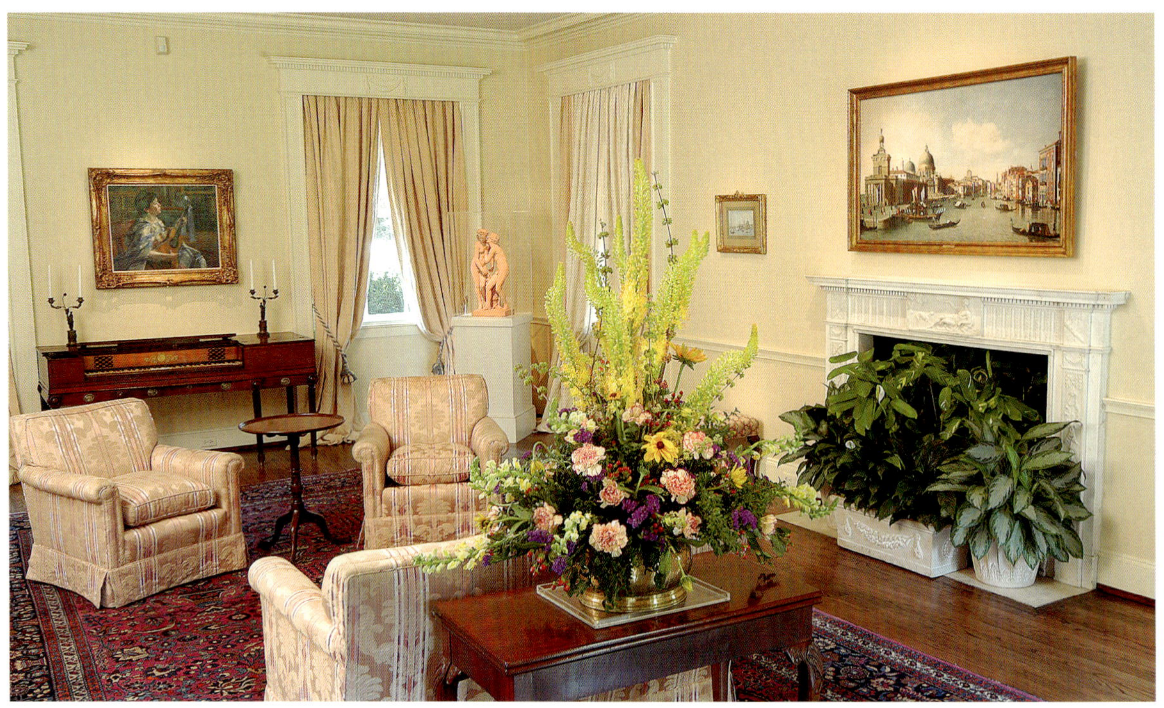

FIG. 12 Living room of Hugo and Margaret Dixon, Dixon Gallery and Gardens, Memphis

every case is Cubism, Dada, Surrealism, or abstract painting, either constructivist or neoplastic. One finds few works by Mondrian, Ozenfant, Duchamp, or Ernst in these houses, and Picasso's work is usually represented—when it is—with his pre-Cubist oeuvre or the neoclassical paintings and drawings of the 1920s. "Modern," in these cases, means the colorful representation of modern life rather than radical experiments in style. Although the art in these collections challenged conventional norms at the time it was made, it no longer inspires rage or disgust in contemporary viewers. Now associated enough with a common cultural and aesthetic experience, such collections can easily be shared with friends and family as well as with numerous professional visitors from the trade, museums, and universities.

Since World War II, when American art museums joined with their European counterparts to mount important exhibitions of modern art, private collectors have been pressed to share their riches with the public by lending to prestigious temporary shows. Whether monographic exhibitions, careful re-creations of landmark historical exhibitions, or groupings of works by style, date, or imagery, these scholarly gatherings have often allowed both the collector and the public to measure their works against others of the same type. Private collections experience a relative fluidity as works are moved, reconsidered, and often replaced as a result of frequent physical shifts. When the Manet or the Monet or the Cézanne is gone for a year, one must deal creatively—and often expensively—with the space on the living room wall!

What is most important about these private collections—and the Bloch Collection is at the very top of the list—is that, by the very nature of their domesticity, they can be found throughout the world. There are country houses in South Africa, apartments in Buenos Aires, houses and apartments in Tokyo and Osaka, suburban residences in Mexico City, and even hidden houses and apartments in Cairo and Kuwait City that belong to the world because of their carefully calibrated mix of modern painting, European furniture, Asian decorative arts, and Middle Eastern carpets. This magical mixture is, in a sense, as important to Caillebotte's—and the Impressionists'—idea of painting as the paintings themselves. When these works of art are viewed as an essential element of a global bourgeois life, then their painters have succeeded in their task of modern pictorial embodiment. The dinners, café concerts, dances, ballets, country walks, river scenes, restaurants, and private interiors represented by these artists lend deeper historical significance to contemporary life than any work by de Kooning or Koons.

The Bloch Collection is among the finest pictorial ensembles of its type ever formed in America, and the competition is significant. Remarkably, it was formed in the past thirty years—not at the turn of the century or in the 1930s or 1950s, when such a project was financially easier and major works more readily found. This very fact proves that the project of domestic bourgeois modernism instigated by Caillebotte in 1876 is far from dead. The devotion of the Blochs to their collection, as well as their wider philanthropic interest in their community, is more like that of Louisine and Horace Havemeyer, Duncan Phillips, Paul Mellon, Sterling and Stephen Clark, Walter Annenberg, and Walter Paley than the cash-out-high collectors who dominate the Impressionist and modern market today. Throughout their adult lives, the Blochs have shared their paintings with friends and family. Now, in this inaugural exhibition of the remarkable new building named in their honor at The Nelson-Atkins Museum of Art in Kansas City, they are sharing their entire collection for the first time with their city and their nation. We should all be deeply grateful to them.

Richard R. Brettell
Margaret McDermott Distinguished Chair, Art and Aesthetics
University of Texas at Dallas

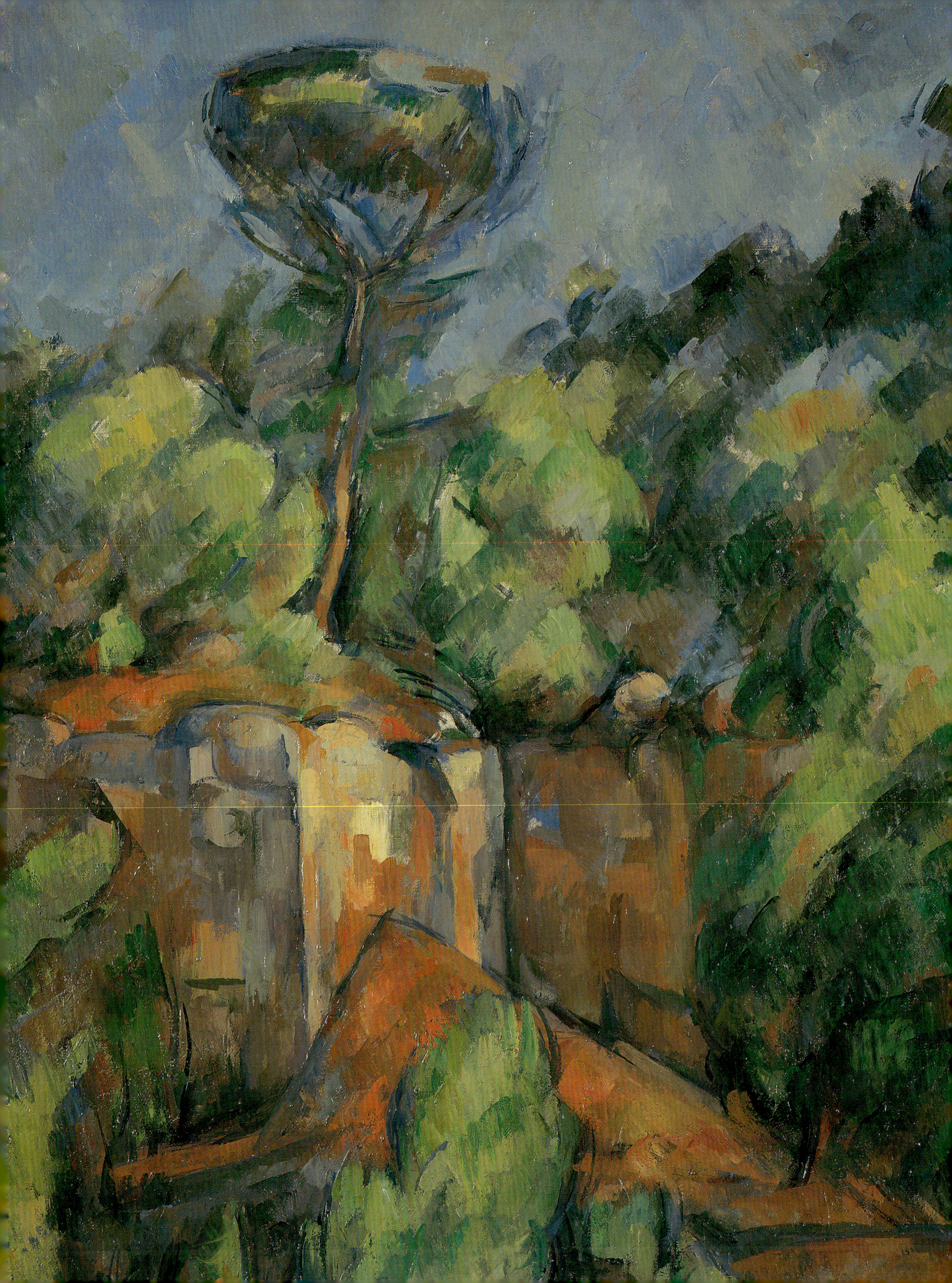

The Collection

Édouard Manet

French, 1832–1883

1. *The Croquet Party (La partie de croquet)*, 1871

Oil on canvas, 18 × 28¾ in. (46 × 73 cm); signed lower right: *Manet*

Édouard Manet was the acknowledged leader of French avant-garde painting in the 1860s. His submissions to the official Salon, whether rejected or accepted, were prime fodder for critics, novelists, and social commentators, and by 1865 his name was almost a household word in Paris. Perhaps for that reason, the paintings from that decade have dominated Manet studies, while the final dozen years of his career have received less attention. The two Manets in the Bloch Collection fall into this later period, and their interpretation raises questions about the artist's intentions at a time when the young Turks, the Impressionists, increasingly came to push Manet from his pedestal as the leader of modern art. Manet made *The Croquet Party*, the earlier of the two, at a critical point in his career. The later work, a still life of lilacs (cat. no. 2), painted in the last years of his life, is a meditation on art and human mortality.

The Croquet Party is a somewhat puzzling and inscrutable painting in that the visible narrative and its immediate historical context seem at odds. At first glance we see a mundane society game—croquet—played by a group of five figures on a lawn. What we actually perceive, however, is clouded by what we sense but cannot see: the physical and psychological suffering that Manet was enduring at the time. We propose a date for this picture of August 1871, when, according to biographer Adolphe Tabarant, Manet's doctor recommended that he take a vacation because of virtual "nervous collapse."[1] Recently some scholars have argued for pushing the painting's date into 1872,[2] but Tabarant's observations point to the earlier year. Indeed, the interpretation offered below hinges on the painting having at least been begun in the late summer of 1871.

That year was possibly the toughest of Manet's life. The Franco-Prussian War had ended in the siege of Paris, and French defeat was followed by civil war when a revolutionary government, the Commune, seized power in the capital. Military force soon suppressed the rebellion, but the siege itself brought great deprivation and famine to the city. On January 28, 1871, the French government sent notice of its capitulation to the Prussian government. Manet, who had remained in Paris, received this news with great relief, given that throngs of people were literally dying of starvation. He quickly sent word to his family that he was alive and, on February 12, left Paris to meet them in southwest France, at Oloron-Sainte-Marie. His wife found him as thin as a wire and in terrible shape, as he virtually had not eaten for weeks.

Manet soon returned to Paris and, on his doctor's advice, went to Boulogne-sur-Mer for a rest. It was there that he executed *The Croquet Party*. The painting shows the lawn of the

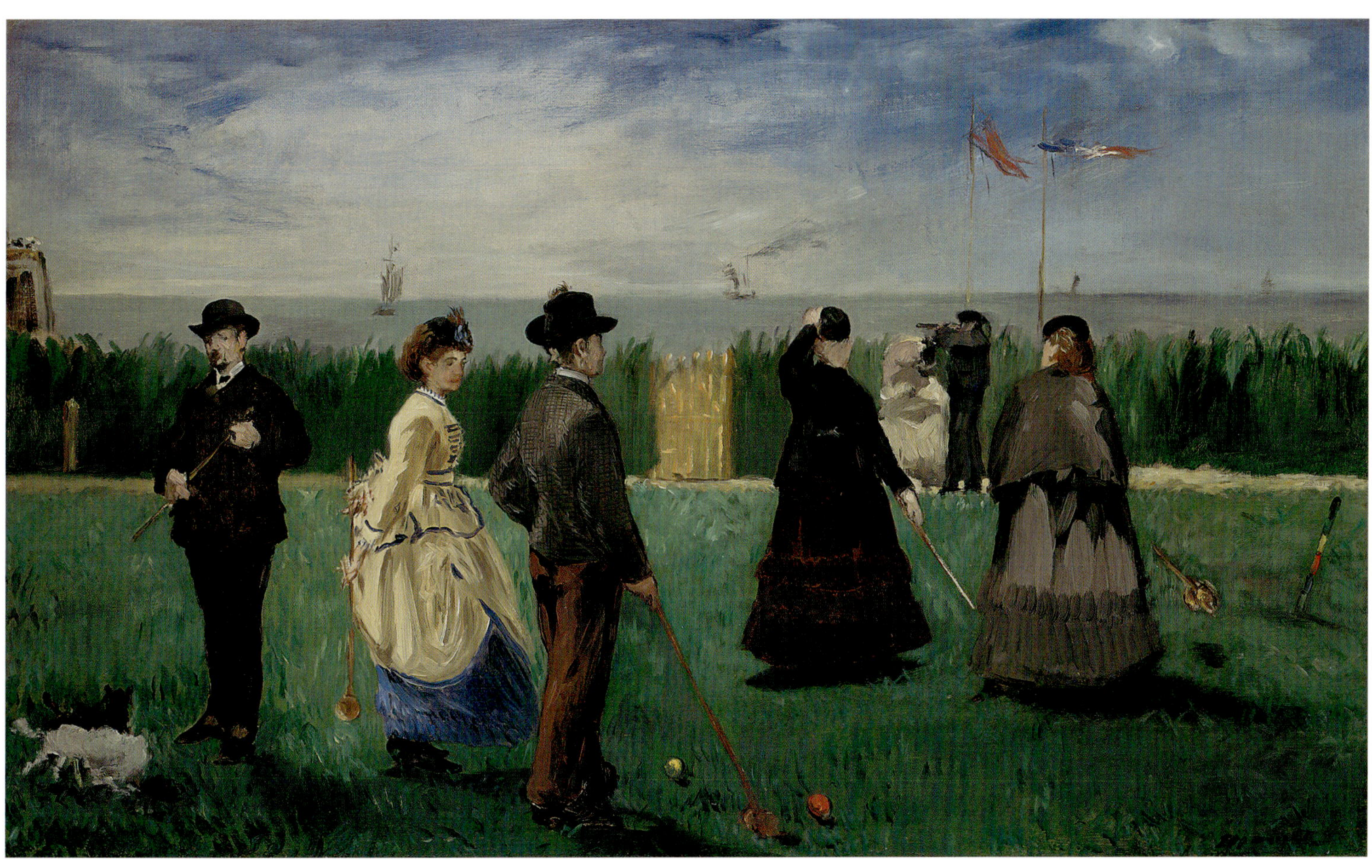

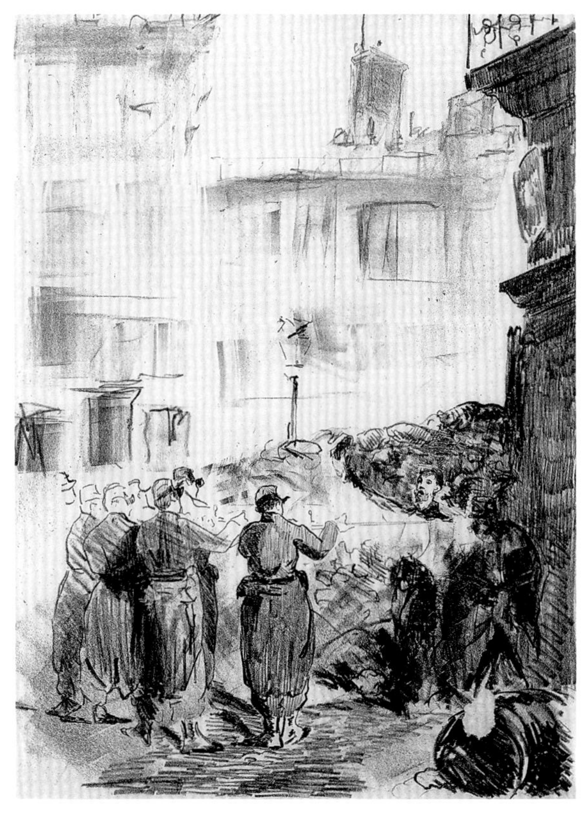

FIG. 13 Édouard Manet, *The Barricade (La barricade)*, 1871, lithograph, 18⅛ × 13⅛ in. (46 × 33.2 cm). National Gallery of Art, Washington, Rosenwald Collection

famous casino on the sea front, and the croquet game brings together (from left to right) Paul Roudier (Manet's childhood friend), Jeanne Gonzalès (sister of Eva Gonzalès), Léon Leenhoff (Manet's stepson), and two unidentified friends. In a sketchbook in the Louvre there are four rapid drawings for the figures (inv. nos. RF 30409–30412); the painting, however, was probably made not outdoors but in the calm of the studio. The canvas could be interpreted as a sign of the artist's relief at being reunited with family and friends with whom he could once again enjoy life, but there are darker undertones. It was probably executed at the same time as two lithographs, *The Barricade* (fig. 13) and *The Civil War* (National Gallery of Art, Washington), that provide striking testimony of Manet's firsthand experience of the war and its gruesome aftermath. The contrast between the prints and *The Croquet Party* suggests deep conflicts in Manet's view of the world at the time.

At first it is hard to fathom the gap between this depiction of the bourgeoisie playing a society game and images of the fighting, chaos, and violence that had recently ravaged Paris. But it is that very gap the painting seems to address. There is nothing accusatory in this work; it simply speaks of the unspeakable. Like a veneer spread over recently experienced horrors, the composition is slightly tense, staged, and artificial. Like so many Manets, the painting resists obvious interpretation. His work retains a certain opacity that cannot be broken down into semantic propositions, and Manet himself said very little about the meaning of his pictures.

The Croquet Party clearly owes a good deal to Monet's masterful *Garden at Saint-Adresse* of 1867 (fig. 14), which had impressed Manet when he saw it four or five years earlier in Frédéric Bazille's studio. The flagpoles, the boats on the horizon, the garden by the sea, and the parallel structure of horizontal bands are all reminiscent of the Monet. Corresponding with the slightly threatening mood, a stiff breeze seems to keep the players slightly detached from the game. The woman to the right raises her mallet to strike the ball, and Léon Leenhoff and Jeanne Gonzalès, in the left foreground, await their turn to play. Leenhoff, however, seems to look beyond the game, as if his mind is on other things, despite the attitude of Gonzalès beside him, who seems to try to engage him in conversation.

To the far left is Manet's childhood friend Paul Roudier (whose legs the painter had used as a model for the actor Philibert Rouvière in an 1865 painting; National Gallery of Art, Washington). He too appears detached, although he is the only figure who seems to acknowledge us as spectators. Next to him two animals, possibly dogs, are scrapping in the grass. Like some of the human figures, they ignore the game, immersed in their own squabbles. This seemingly

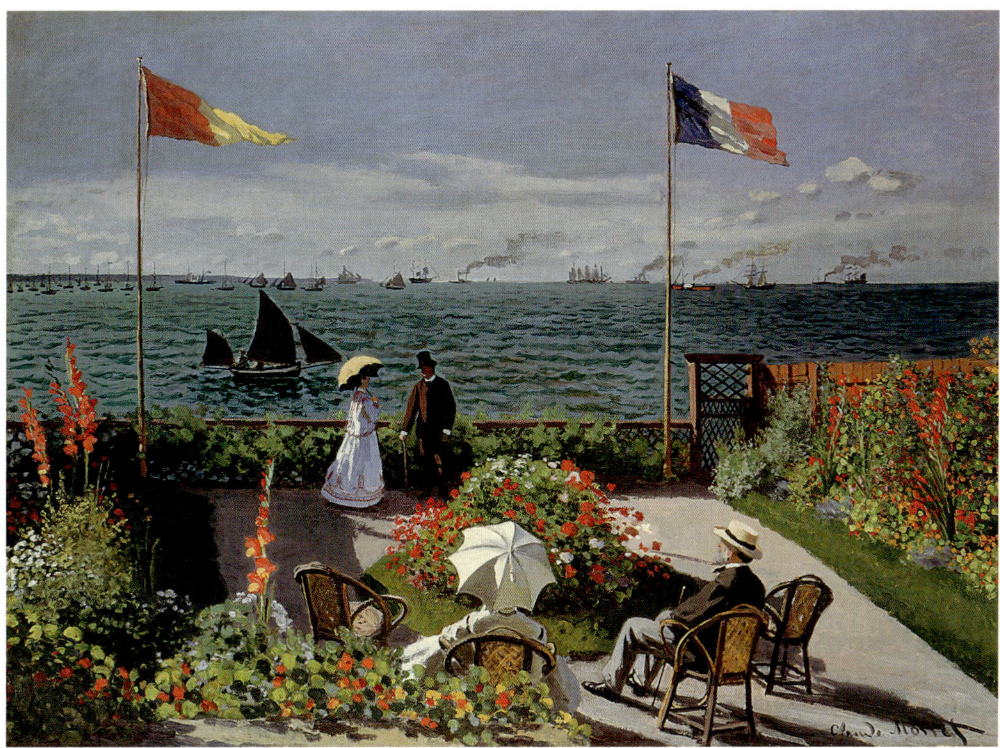

FIG. 14 Claude Monet, *Garden at Sainte-Adresse*, 1867, oil on canvas, 38⅝ × 51⅛ in. (98.1 × 129.9 cm). Metropolitan Museum of Art, New York, purchased with special contributions and purchase funds given or bequeathed by friends of the Museum, 1967

nonchalant painting of a game between friends turns out to be a somewhat perplexing representation with overtones of alienation, detachment, and even estrangement. The players are not wholly absorbed in what they are doing; they are at odds with each other and with their surroundings. In this respect *The Croquet Party* is like a play by Samuel Beckett, and herein lies its profound modernity.

A final element to note is the wind, which blows so stiffly through the flags that one of them streams out horizontally. The strong breeze is also apparent in the pose of the woman in black, who holds her hat to prevent it from flying off. The game thus appears to be played against the odds, either those of recent history or of inclement weather. Nobody seems to care who wins or loses, and the subject might be an attempt on the artist's part to find a moment of serenity or equilibrium against the dark background of recent events. The strength of this painting lies in the way Manet contained these different forces and generated meaning from their uneasy coexistence.

—JP

NOTES

1. See *Une correspondence inédite d'Édouard Manet: Les lettres du siège de Paris, 1870–1871*, ed. Adolphe Tabarant (Paris, 1935), p. 35.
2. See Juliet Wilson-Bareau and David Degener, *Manet and the Sea* (Philadelphia, 2003), p. 135, where it is dated circa 1872.

Édouard Manet

French, 1832–1883

2. *White Lilacs in a Crystal Vase (Lilas blancs dans un vase de cristal)*, 1882 or 1883

Oil on canvas, unlined, 22⅛ × 13¾ in. (56.3 × 35 cm); signed lower right: *Manet*

Édouard Manet stoically endured excruciating pain during the last year of his life as he suffered from the effects of tertiary syphilis and the severe treatments ordered by his doctor. He died, after a month in bed, on April 30, 1883, having painted his last work, a floral still life like the Bloch painting, on March 1 of that year. Almost all of Manet's last paintings were simple floral still lifes painted in one or two sittings on prestretched, fine linen canvases. Twenty of these survive, and they, among the many paintings in his oeuvre, have elicited some of the most moving and important commentary from critics and historians. Unlike the layered and multisourced masterpieces of his early years or even the enigmatic urban paintings from the last decade of his life, the floral still lifes are among the most direct paintings in the history of art.

Confined to his home and, often, to his room, Manet was visited by only his few closest friends, many of whom brought the various fresh flowers he loved. These were arranged simply in glass and crystal containers, set on a table, and painted on canvases small enough to be easily controlled by the sick artist. The flowers included roses, lilacs, carnations, clematis, pansies, and pinks—some from a florist and others from one of several gardens owned by his friends. Occasionally the blossoms were combined to form a varied arrangement (fig. 15). Just as often, flowers of one species and color were shoved into water in a clear vase. Clarity and simplicity are the hallmarks of these paintings, which defy any attempt to burden them with symbolic or theoretical meanings. Emblematic rather then enigmatic, they are almost defiant in their simplicity.

In interpreting these works as late paintings, one can make several observations. First, they make no stylistic or technical advances but rely on the abundant painterly skill that Manet had practiced for three decades. Second, they make no attempt to be serious or complex, thus departing from the kind of twilight mystery seen in the famous late paintings of Titian, Rembrandt, Hals, Goya, Constable, and Turner. Indeed, at least one of them was a gift to a lady who visited Manet, suggesting that they were his final offerings to his friends as much as his response to their floral gifts. Their most obvious quality is effortlessness or ease, and the contrast between this and Manet's own pain and difficulty is a large part of their meaning.

Eight of the twenty paintings include lilacs, a complex bloom on a flowering shrub that bursts forth in March or early April and signals the arrival of spring in northern France. Lilacs are most often pale purple, lavender, or pink, and the white flowers preferred by Manet are rarer. Unlike other flowering shrubs such as pussy willow and forsythia, lilacs cannot be forced to bloom in a

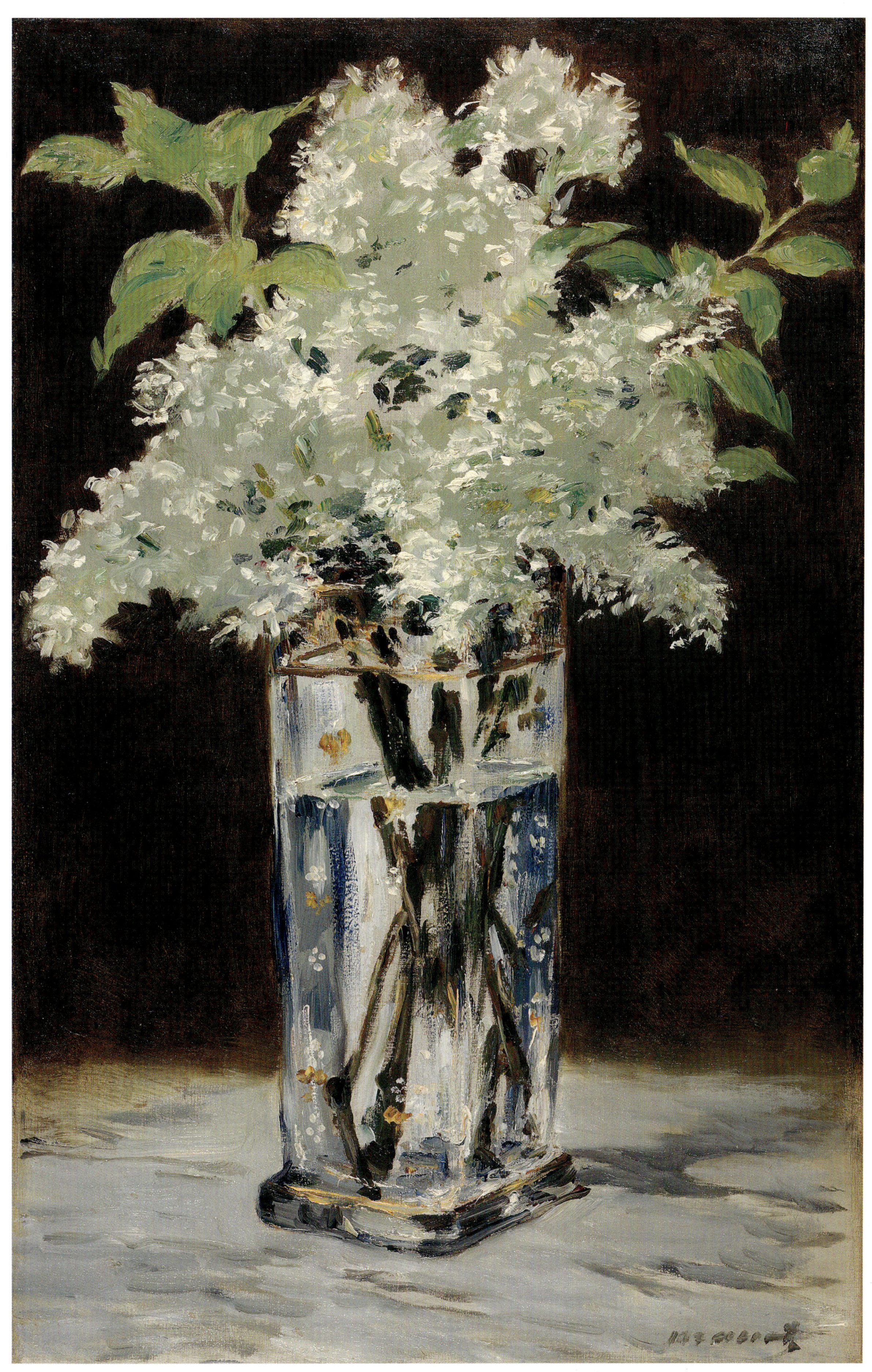

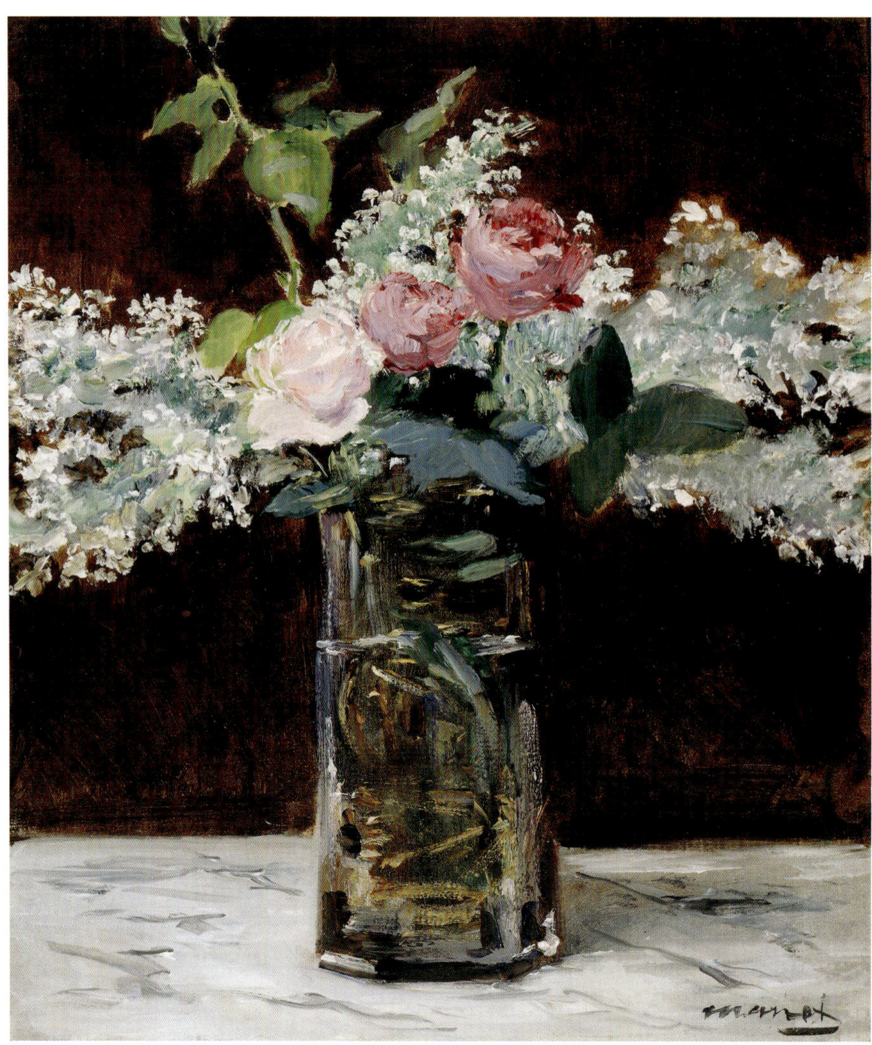

FIG. 15 Édouard Manet, *Vase of White Lilacs and Roses*, 1883, oil on canvas, 22 × 18⅛ in. (55.9 × 46 cm). Dallas Museum of Art, The Wendy and Emery Reves Collection

hothouse and were thus available to Manet for only a brief period. This very fact suggests that the lilac paintings were perhaps made in the early spring of 1882. Of the eight works with lilacs, only three contain no other type of flower, and the Bloch Manet is one of these. The other two (one of which is seen in fig. 16) are painted on slightly wider canvases than the Bloch picture.

The Bloch still life is a marvel for its miraculous condition. Unlike many works by Manet in institutional collections which have been relined and restretched, this one survives on the original canvas and stretcher with no interference except simple cleaning and revarnishing. The linen is so fine that one can see through it when it is held up to the light, and the painting was done in one or, at most, two short sessions. The interplay of the dark brown *ébauche* or underpainting of the background and the trembling white of the flowers animates the painting. Working on a lightly primed surface, Manet painted the area under the flowers a pale celadon gray-green, which acts as a foil for the tiny strokes of pure lead white and mysterious darker green that he flicked onto the surface.

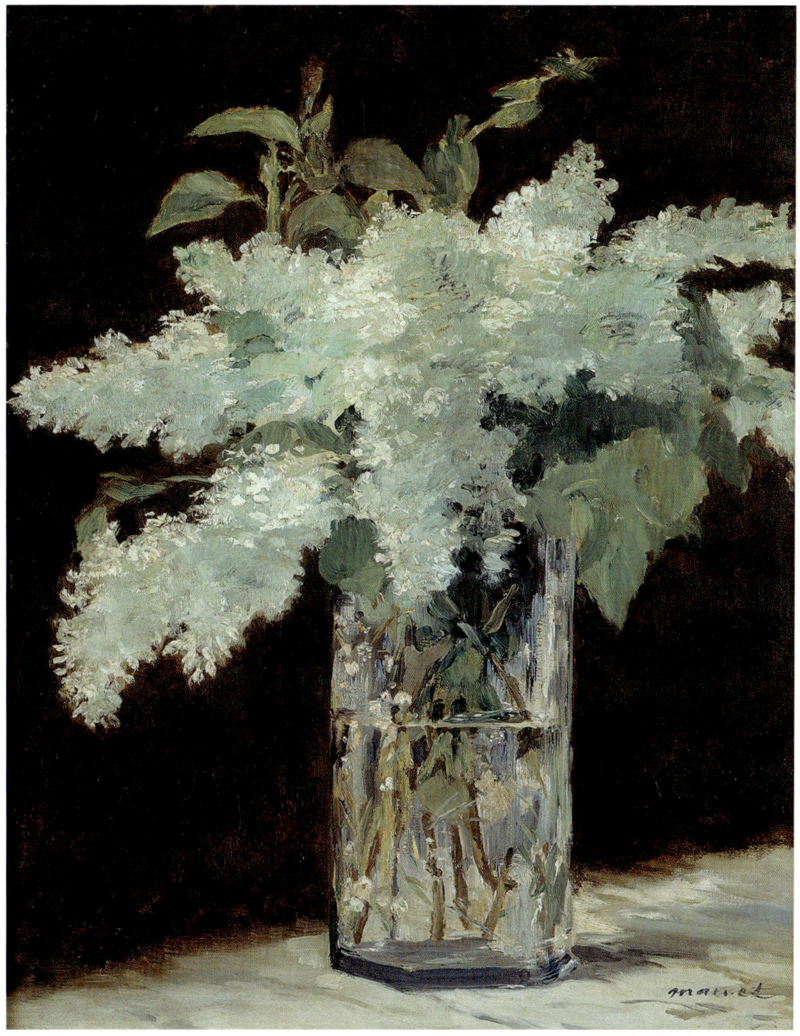

FIG. 16 Édouard Manet, *Lilacs*, c. 1882, oil on canvas, 21¼ × 16⅝ in. (54 × 42 cm). Nationalgalerie, Staatliche Museen zu Berlin

The real miracle of the painting is the representation of the crystal vase, the almost stridently blue water, and the large dark stems of the delicate flowers. Manet used the same vase in at least four other paintings of the group, each time turning it at a different angle, filling it with water to a different level, and placing it on a surface of a different tilt and color. In the Bloch painting, the vase is set at a three-quarter angle on a white marble tabletop, the far edge of which disappears in a blur of brown. Manet simply refuses to let us wander into the picture, and he provides just enough light—and space—so that we believe in the sheer physicality of this "eternal" vase of flowers. The vase itself is far from simple. A heavy crystal square with a solid crystal base, it is decorated with a gilded band at the bottom and a gilded double-patterned band at the top. Its surface is enlivened with regularly applied white enamel dots that dance in a kind of geometric echo of the white blossoms above.

—RB

Eugène Boudin

French, 1824–1898

3. *The Beach (La plage)*, c. 1865

Pastel on paper, 7½ × 11⅝ in. (19.9 × 29.5 cm); signed lower right: *E. Boudin*

4. *Trouville, Beach Scene (Trouville, scène de plage)*, 1874

Oil on wood panel, 8⅛ × 16¼ in. (20.7 × 41.4 cm); signed, dated and inscribed lower right: *E. Boudin Trouville—Aout 1874 à mon* [illegible]

5. *Boats Decorated with Flags in the Port of Deauville (Bateaux pavoisiers dans le bassin, Deauville)*, 1895

Oil on mahogany panel, 10½ × 13¾ in. (25.6 × 35 cm), cradled; signed and dated lower left: *Deauville Aout 95 E. Boudin*

The three small works by Eugène Boudin in the Bloch Collection are, in effect, a retrospective in miniature. Each was made during the summer months of 1865, 1874, and 1895, respectively, and the group shows Boudin's virtuosity in pastel on paper and oil on panel. When the Nelson-Atkins Boudin panel of 1884 (fig. 17) is added to the group, the retrospective is perfectly equilibrated, with one work from each of the four major decades of the painter's career. Boudin was, with Alfred Sisley, the most pure and consistent among the Impressionist landscape painters. Although a little older than most of them, he joined their first group exhibition in 1874 and painted "impressions" of his native region—the Normandy coast of France—until his death in 1898. He began many of his larger paintings outdoors and completed them later in the studio, but a good many of Boudin's freshest and most confident works are the small-scale pastels and paintings made *en face du motif* during August, the traditional French summer month of vacation.

Boudin joined the hordes of urban tourists from both England and France who rented country houses or hotel rooms to take in the sea air. Indeed, the social rituals of sea bathing and sea cures were fashionably new in 1860s Europe. The great French historian Jules Michelet wrote about the curative powers of saltwater and sea air in his best-seller *La mer* (*The Sea*, 1860), and French men and women of several generations followed his lead, flocking in August to the seacoast towns of Deauville, Trouville, Honfleur, and Étretat. The transformation of these communities from tiny, insular fishing towns to fashionable resorts with luxury hotels, shops, restaurants, and casinos occurred between 1840 and 1870, and Eugène Boudin recorded that change with a single-minded intensity.

Each August, Boudin and his family would rent modest hotel rooms in Deauville or Trouville. The painter worked almost undisturbed on the beach because he was as much a seasonal fixture

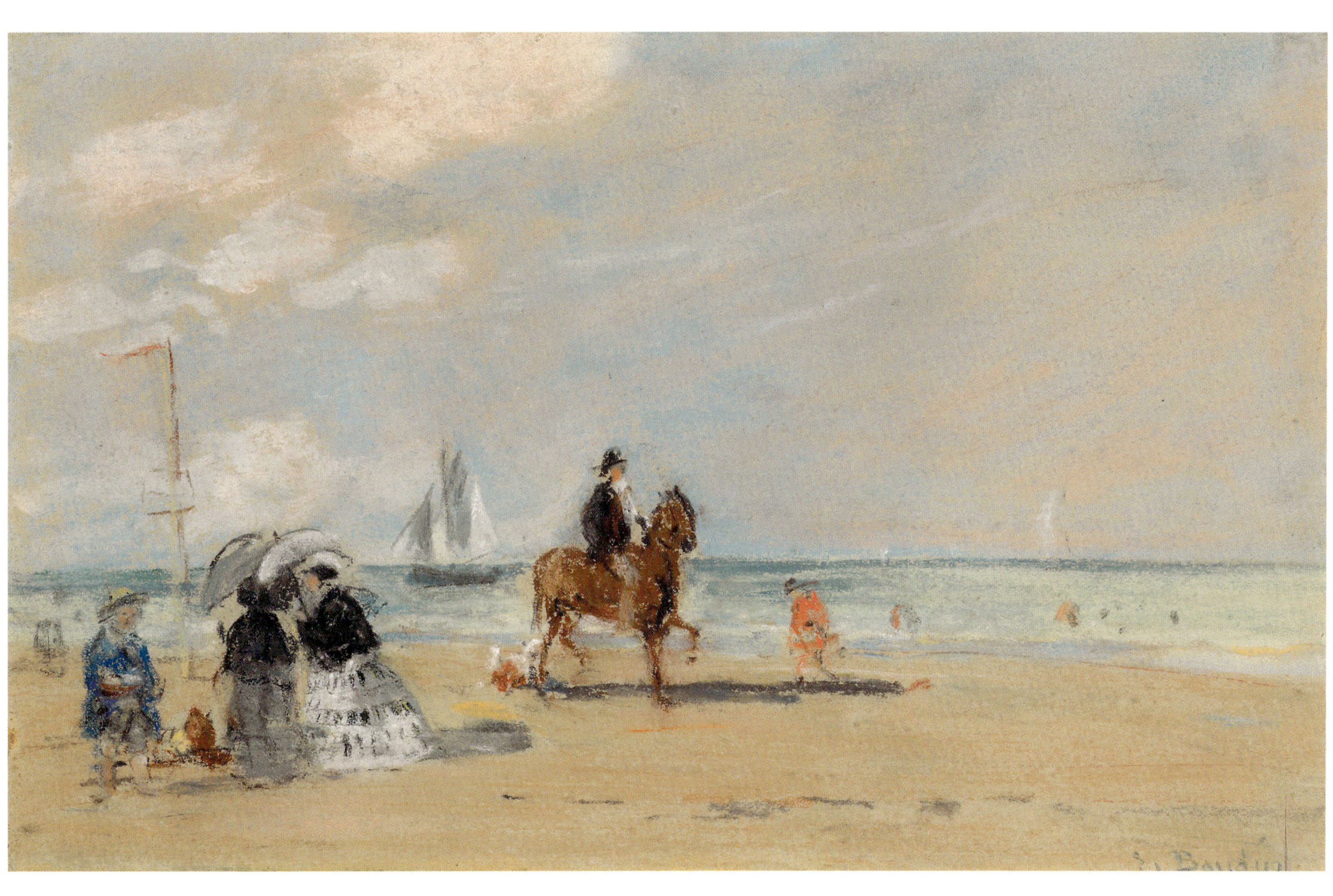

3.

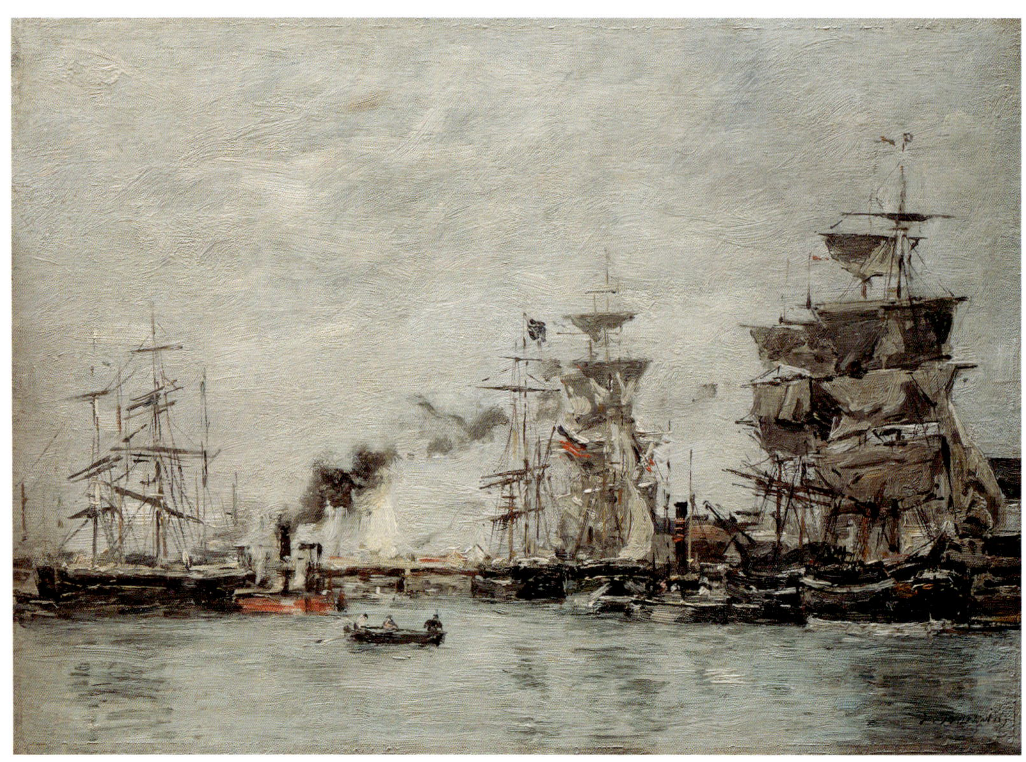

FIG. 17 Eugène Boudin, *The Port of Deauville*, c. 1884, oil on panel, 10⅞ × 13¾ in. (27.7 × 34.9 cm). The Nelson-Atkins Museum of Art, Kansas City

as the swells from Paris. He toiled there so persistently that he succeeded in documenting this famous stretch of sand more carefully than any Impressionist recorded any Parisian boulevard. The ever-changing spectacle of well-dressed urbanites sitting, strolling, standing, talking, playing, swimming, and boating along the sandy Trouville and Deauville beaches becomes, in Boudin's summer paintings, almost cinematic. Certain of the works from these summers are annotated so precisely that we know the very day on which they were made, and, because Boudin so powerfully summarized the movement of drapery, clouds, boats, and portable bathing cabins, his works tell us a good deal more about the actual character of these places than do contemporaneous photographs.[1]

The rarest of the three summer beach scenes in the Bloch Collection is also the earliest (cat. no. 3). Conventionally dated to 1865 and plausibly placed in Trouville, where Boudin spent so many summers, it is among the small number of published pastels by the artist. Unfortunately Impressionist pastels, save for those of Degas, are comparatively understudied, and those of Boudin, though seen with fair regularity in sales catalogues, are almost completely unknown to students of the pastel in France. Robert Schmit's catalogue of Boudin's nearly four thousand surviving oil paintings contains no entries for the pastels, and there is not even a rudimentary census of them, much less a sophisticated study. Yet we know Boudin had used pastel at least since the 1850s, and he encouraged both Monet and possibly even Degas to try the medium to study the skies and atmosphere of northern France. The recent study of Monet's pastels by

James Ganz and Richard Kendall makes clear that Boudin's greatest student used the medium throughout his working life,[2] and it is highly likely that Boudin did as well. The crumbly softness of pastel on paper often made it preferable to oil as a medium for recording the humid atmosphere of the Normandy coast during summer.

The Bloch pastel is wonderfully fresh and survives in a very good state. A slight break in the paper's surface in the lower right indicates that it might have been made on a composite sheet of paper, pasted together either by Boudin himself or, as happened with Degas's pastels, by his framer or art supplier. The composition is at once bold and, for Boudin, unconventional. Most of the pictorial elements are moved to the left, the emptiness on the right being "filled" by the directional pose of the pert man on horseback and the antics of the indistinct bathers in the water. Although signed, the pastel is not dated, raising doubts about the traditional assignment of 1865. Yet we know Boudin did spend that summer in Trouville, where he met and painted with both Courbet and Whistler. It is even possible that this work was among the group of pastels Boudin submitted to the Impressionist exhibition of 1874, whose catalogue lists under number 21: "Two Frames [same number], diverse studies, pastels." Interestingly, Monet submitted seven pastel studies to the same exhibition.

Representations of riders on the shore are rare in Boudin's beach scenes. None of the numerous beach paintings done in Deauville and Trouville in the mid-1860s has a horse and rider. It was, perhaps, the sheer rarity of this sight that prompted Boudin to take up the quicker medium of pastel when he saw the male figure and his horse trotting up the beach. Not until the early twentieth century, when Gauguin made two paintings of riders on the impossibly pink sands of the remote Marquesas islands, would one see this subject again.

Surely a good deal of Boudin's impetus toward modernity as an artist—and a *pastelliste*—must relate to his meeting the great poet-critic Charles Baudelaire in 1859, when the latter devoted a long paragraph to the paintings of Boudin in his review of that year's Salon. Although Baudelaire wrote briefly and admiringly of Boudin's large-scale painting of Brittany in the Salon, he devoted most of his prose, instead, to the freely painted open-air landscape studies in pastel of Normandy, of which he had seen "hundreds" in Boudin's studio. As he wrote about the small studies—each of which was inscribed by the artist with the date, time of day, and conditions of wind and weather—Baudelaire lost himself in a poetic reverie as intense as any he had experienced from art:

> Eventually, as these fantastically shaped and luminous clouds, these chaotic shadows, these immense green and pink forms, suspended and merging with each other, these gaping furnaces, these firmaments of black and violet satin, crumpled, rolled, or torn, these horizons in mourning, or streaming with molten metal—all these depths and all these splendors rose to my brain like a heady drink, or like the eloquence of opium. Rather strangely, in front of this liquid or aerial magic, I did not once regret the absence of man.[3]

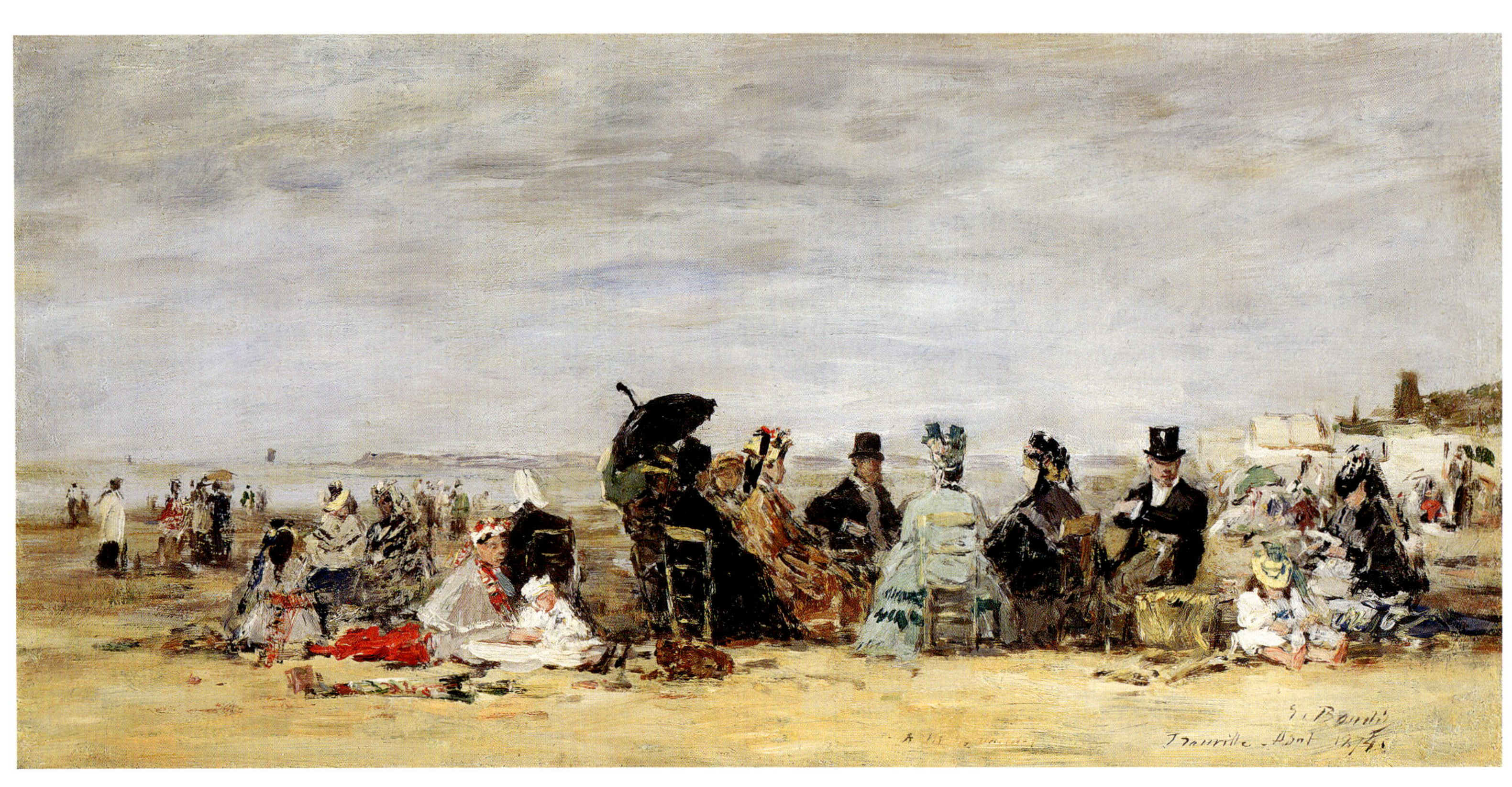

4.

Baudelaire went on to suggest to Boudin that he include his fellow man in his spectacle of nature, and, as the Bloch pastel, made six or seven years later, makes clear, Boudin followed his advice. Throughout the next four decades, the artist described nature's light as it played on crinoline gowns, satin top hats, and flounced bathing costumes with as much finesse as he had represented its effects on the clouds, waves, and sand that Baudelaire transformed into fire and fabric. Indeed, Boudin mastered the setting for his human comedy of manners before he allowed the characters to enter.

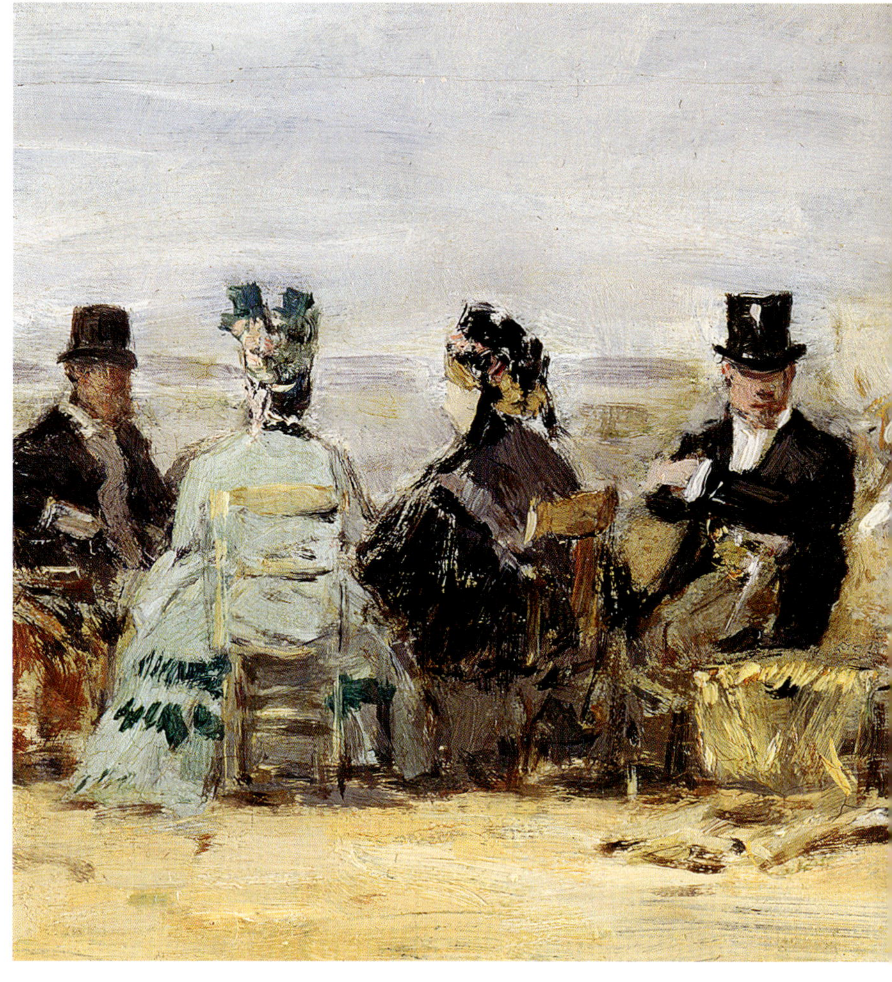

If the Boudin pastel was among the artist's submissions to the 1874 Impressionist exhibition, he must have had it firmly in mind when he returned to Normandy after the exhibition closed in mid-May. When he arrived in Trouville, he executed his usual complement of plein-air oil studies of fashionable Parisians at the beach. Robert Schmit includes eleven panels dated to that summer in his 1973 catalogue raisonné, although the Bloch panel is not one of them.[4] Nonetheless, Schmit readily accepts the authenticity of the Bloch panel (cat. no. 4), which is not only the largest of the group dated to 1874 but one of only four that details the month, in this case August. Three smaller panels from the group were dated on the days they were made—July 26, August 16, and August 26. Interestingly, the Bloch panel was also inscribed—perhaps to its first recorded owner, known from the painting's provenance as M. Bullier. Unfortunately, the name on the painting has been partially effaced and painted over, making it illegible.[5]

The scene represented here is unusual among these summer beach pictures for its inclusion of three well-dressed male figures. Two gentlemen in top hats sit among the beautifully dressed women. The elaborate state of dress almost suggests that the group is about to attend or has just returned from the races. A nursemaid with a small child sits on a beach blanket outside the group to the left, another child is to the right, and one of the gentlemen faces the painter-viewer directly, almost confronting us. It was, perhaps, this powerful figure to whom the shy Boudin inscribed the painting, "a mon [illegible]." Yet the gentleman must not have accepted the offering, because the inscription, once made, was painted over by Boudin himself, creating a conundrum for the scholar. Who was this gentleman? Was he annoyed at having been entrapped without permission by the painter? Does this painting record one of the few direct encounters between painter and subject to interrupt Boudin's placid career?

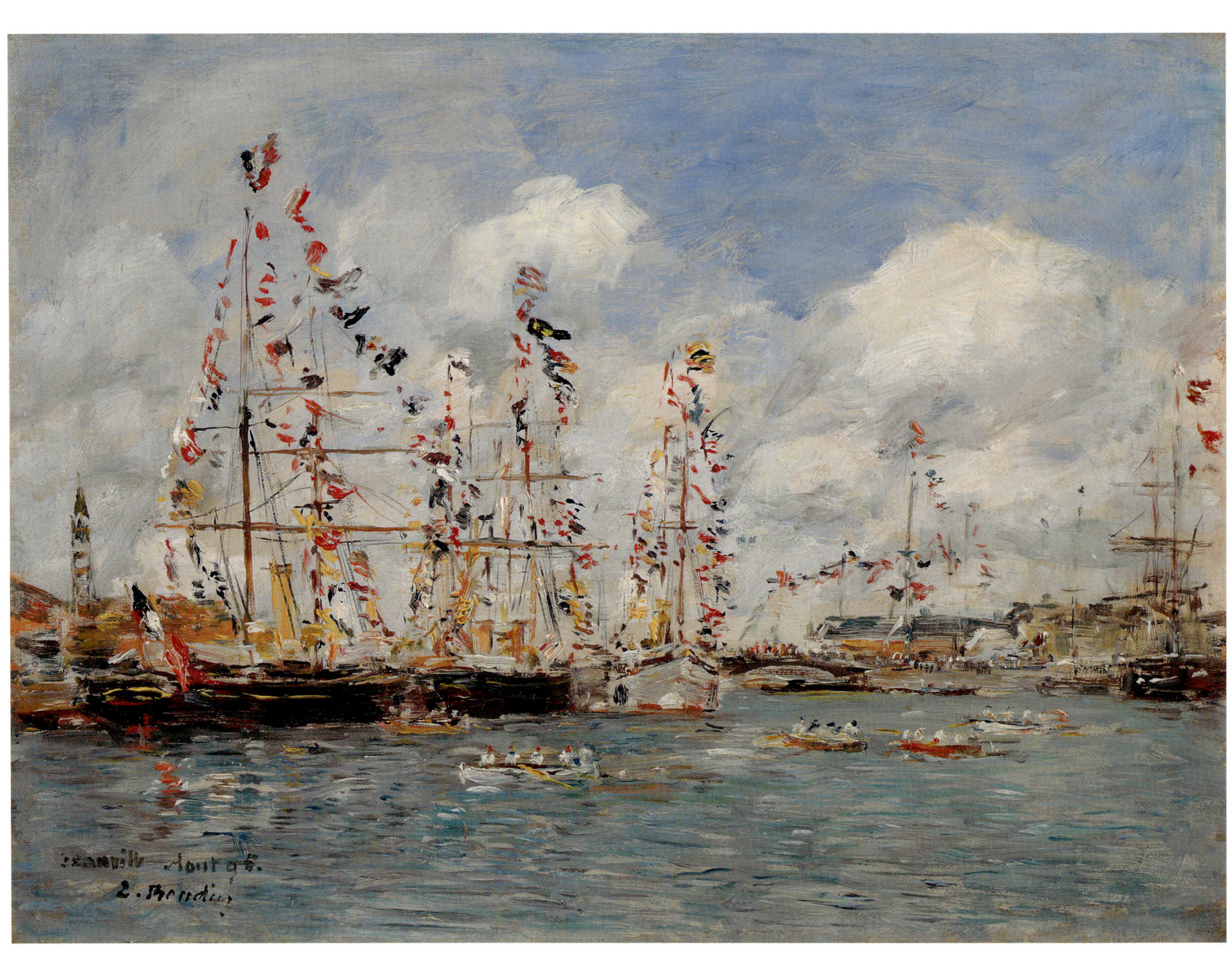

5.

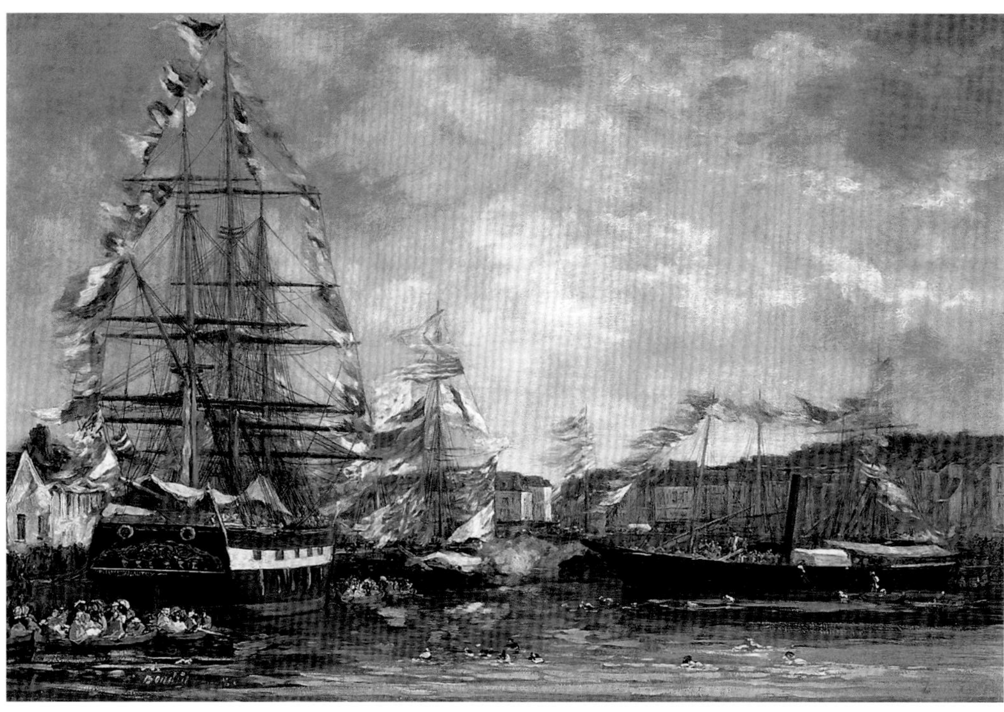

FIG. 18 Eugène Boudin, *Festival in the Harbor of Honfleur*, 1858, oil on wood, 16⅛ × 23⅜ in. (41 × 59.4 cm). National Gallery of Art, Washington, Collection of Mr. and Mrs. Paul Mellon

Boudin chose to paint his plein-air scenes on small wooden panels rather than canvas. In this way he anticipated the practice of Georges Seurat (cat. no. 19), Henri-Edmond Cross, Paul Signac (cat. no. 20), and other Neo-Impressionists. The Impressionists themselves usually recorded scenes of nature on larger canvases. Although Boudin never explained this preference, surely it had to do with the windy conditions of the beaches. It must have been far easier to work on a small panel than on a stretched canvas, which easily could have become a sail in the brisk winds of Normandy. And it would have been much easier to pack still wet panels into a backpack or specially fitted box than to maneuver stretched canvases.

Boudin painted the latest of the three Bloch works (cat. no. 5) in Deauville in August 1895, but Schmit erroneously dated it to 1896. He related it to two similar paintings with signatures and dates that clearly read "96."[6] In the Bloch panel, the inscription "Deauville Aout 95" and the signature were applied at different times, the signature in a darker hue than the inscription. Although this is not the norm for Boudin, there are many cases in his considerable oeuvre in which he inscribed a work of art at its completion but signed it later, when it was purchased by a dealer or collector. The subject of this painting, a group of sailing yachts specially decorated for a festival, can be found throughout Boudin's long career. One of the most splendid early examples is *Festival in the Harbor of Honfleur* of 1858 in the Mellon collection at the National Gallery of Art (fig. 18). Paul Mellon's sister, Ailsa Mellon Bruce, gave another Boudin painting of decorated yachts to the National Gallery (fig. 19) which is virtually identical to the Bloch painting in its massing of the yachts. Unfortunately this vertical panel, while signed, is undated;

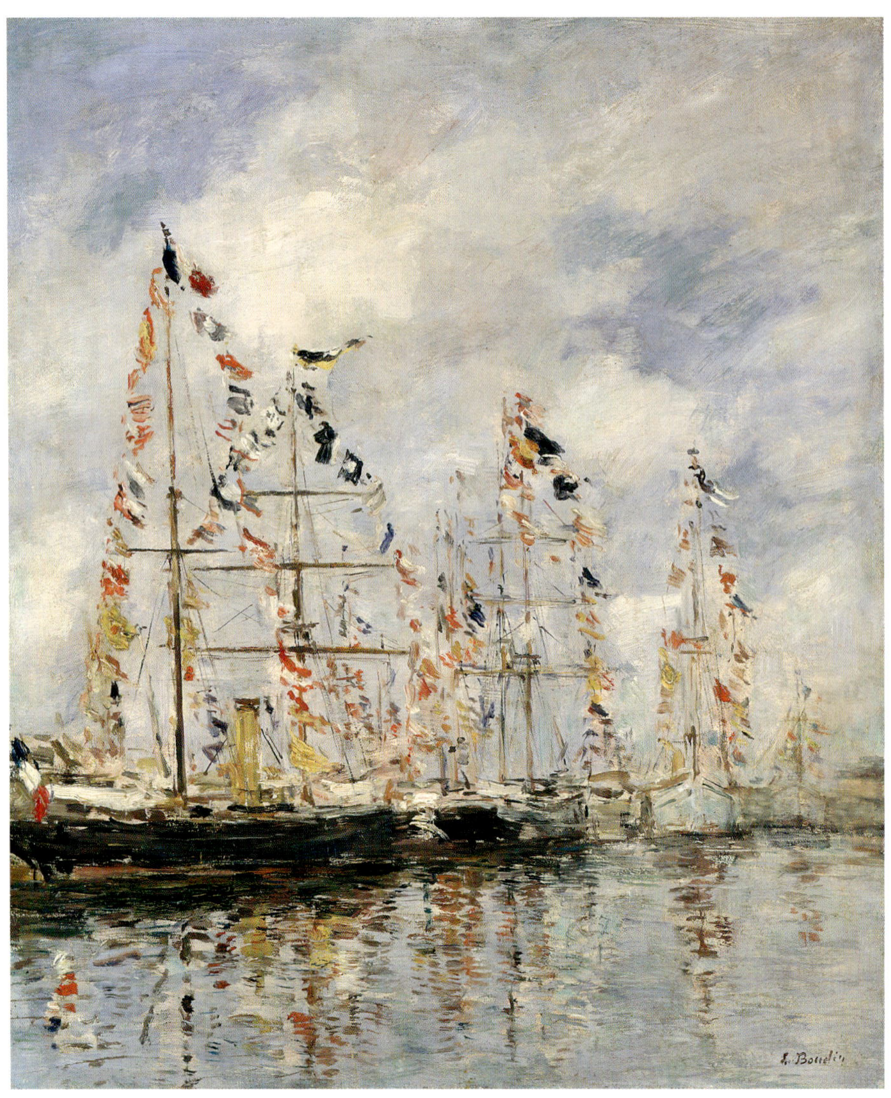

FIG. 19 Eugène Boudin, *Yacht Basin at Trouville-Deauville*, probably 1895–96, oil on wood, 18 × 14⅝ in. (45.7 × 37.2 cm). National Gallery of Art, Washington, Ailsa Mellon Bruce Collection

a later version of the same subject is signed and dated 1897.[7] The Mellon family had a special taste for these paintings, and it is likely that the "private collector, Virginia" listed in the provenance of the Bloch panel was none other than Paul Mellon.

Surviving in a perfect state because it was painted on panel, the entire surface of the Bloch picture quivers with painterly life. Boudin evidently selected the motif for its abundance of small-scale motion—hundreds of tiny flags on the decorated ships twist in the breeze, and the tiny rowers of the foreground boat race move rhythmically. Flickering, quivering movement is the true subject of this charming small painting, which completes a perfect trio of what might be called "direct paintings" by Eugène Boudin.

—RB

NOTES

1. For a succinct discussion of the phenomenon of Normandy beach tourism, see Richard R. Brettell et al., *A Day in the Country: Impressionism and the French Landscape* (Los Angeles, 1984), pp. 273–96.

2. James A. Ganz and Richard Kendall, *The Unknown Monet: Pastels and Drawings* (New Haven, 2007).

3. Charles Baudelaire, "Le Salon de 1859," published in *La revue française* (June 1859), quoted in G. Jean-Aubry, *Eugène Boudin* (London, 1969), p. 231.

4. Robert Schmit, *Eugène Boudin, 1824–1898* (Paris, 1973), vol. 1, pp. 335–37, nos. 938–48.

5. No one by the name Bullier is known to have owned any other work by Boudin, whose collectors have been exhaustively studied by Schmit. Ibid., vol. 1, pp. xlvi–xlix, and vol. 3, pp. cxiv–cxli.

6. Ibid., vol. 3, nos. 3547 and 3552.

7. Ibid., no. 3621.

Camille Pissarro

French, 1830–1903

6. *Banks of the Seine at Port Marly (Au bord de la Seine à Port Marly)*, 1871

Oil on canvas, 12⅜ × 17¾ in. (31.5 × 45 cm); signed and dated lower left: *C. Pissarro 1871*

Camille Pissarro was the oldest and most dedicated of the group of artists associated with Impressionism. Born a Danish citizen in the Caribbean colony of Saint Thomas in 1830, Pissarro came from a distinguished Sephardic Jewish family who spoke French at home and Spanish, English, and Danish in their business. Because of his Danish citizenship, Pissarro could not fight for his adopted France during the 1870–71 Franco-Prussian War, and, for that reason, he took his family abroad to the safety of suburban London. When he returned at the end of the war to Louveciennes, a small town directly east of Paris, he found that the Prussians had used his house as a base of operations. It and many of his paintings had sustained damage. Undaunted, Pissarro took up his brush again with real conviction, creating at least eighteen wonderful paintings dated 1871 in Louveciennes and the surrounding countryside.

While in London, Pissarro spent as much time in museums and galleries as he did making his own works of art. Because the Pissarro family had relatives in England and the painter could speak creditable English, he helped his French friends Monet and Charles-François Daubigny, who also were in exile in London, to cope with the complexities of a foreign capital. Yet the most important aspect of his London sojourn was Pissarro's repeated exposure to the paintings of the great English artists J. M. W. Turner and John Constable, both long dead, whose works were to have such an impact on the Impressionists. Although Pissarro was moved by the achievements of Turner, many of whose works he studied in the original, his aesthetic was much more aligned with that of Constable. Both artists shared a love of the material qualities of natural form and of the corresponding physicality of oil paint itself. Pissarro sought out Constable paintings in the public museums and galleries of London and became, in effect, the first French painter since the 1820s and 1830s to be familiar with the achievements of this supremely English landscape painter. It is possible, for example, that he saw *Dedham Lock and Mill* (fig. 20), which had been acquired in 1857 by the South Kensington Museum (now the Victoria and Albert Museum).

There is no single landscape more akin to those of Constable than the Bloch Pissarro of 1871. The Impressionist's fascination with the mechanics of weirs and locks is exactly analogous to that of his English predecessor, and the wonderfully juicy paint handling in the clouds and foliage is precisely like that of Constable's mature technique. Unfortunately, in his letters Pissarro did not detail which Constables he saw and where, but, from the evidence of a score of 1871–72 paintings, there is little doubt that his exposure to the British artist was prolonged.

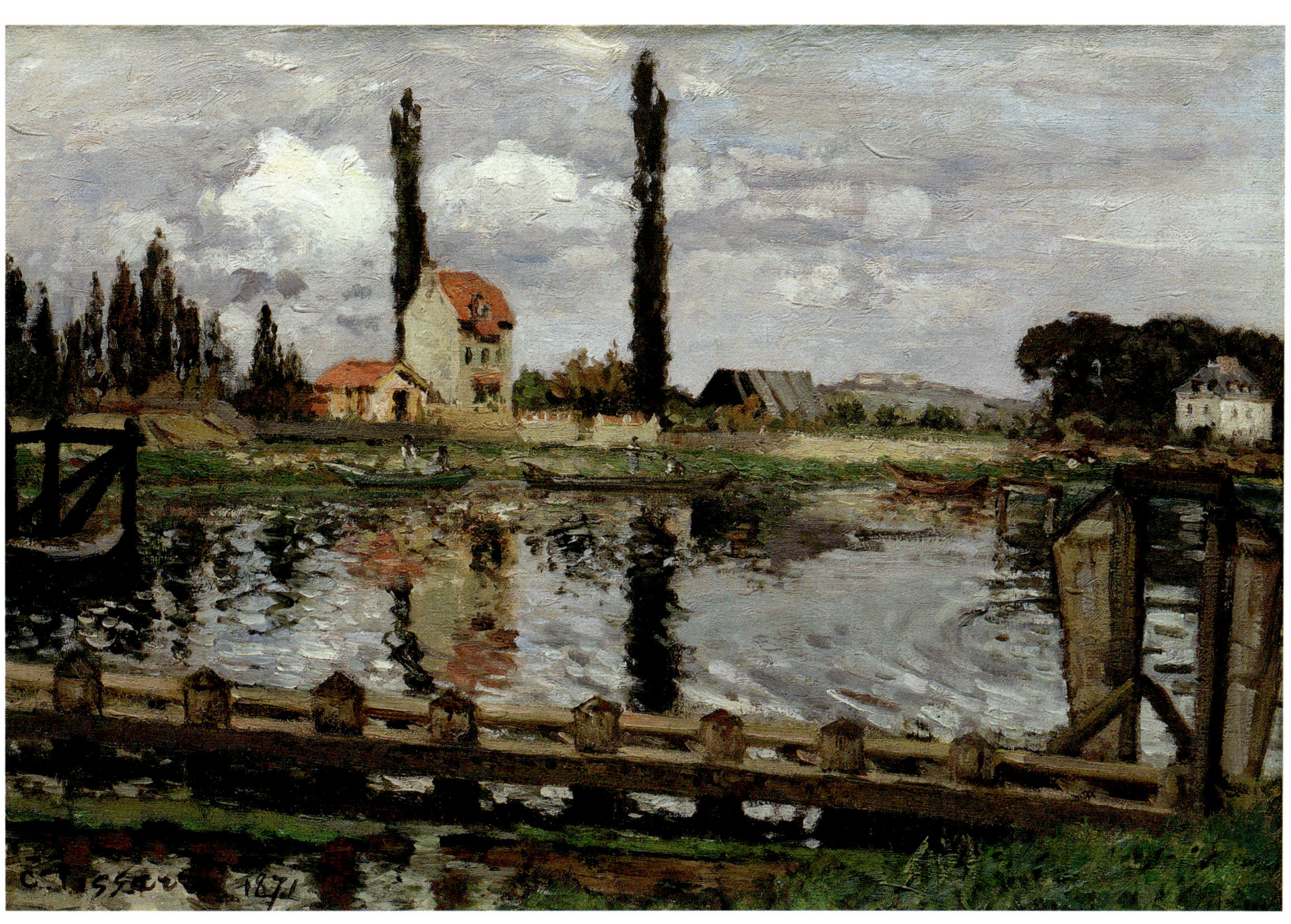

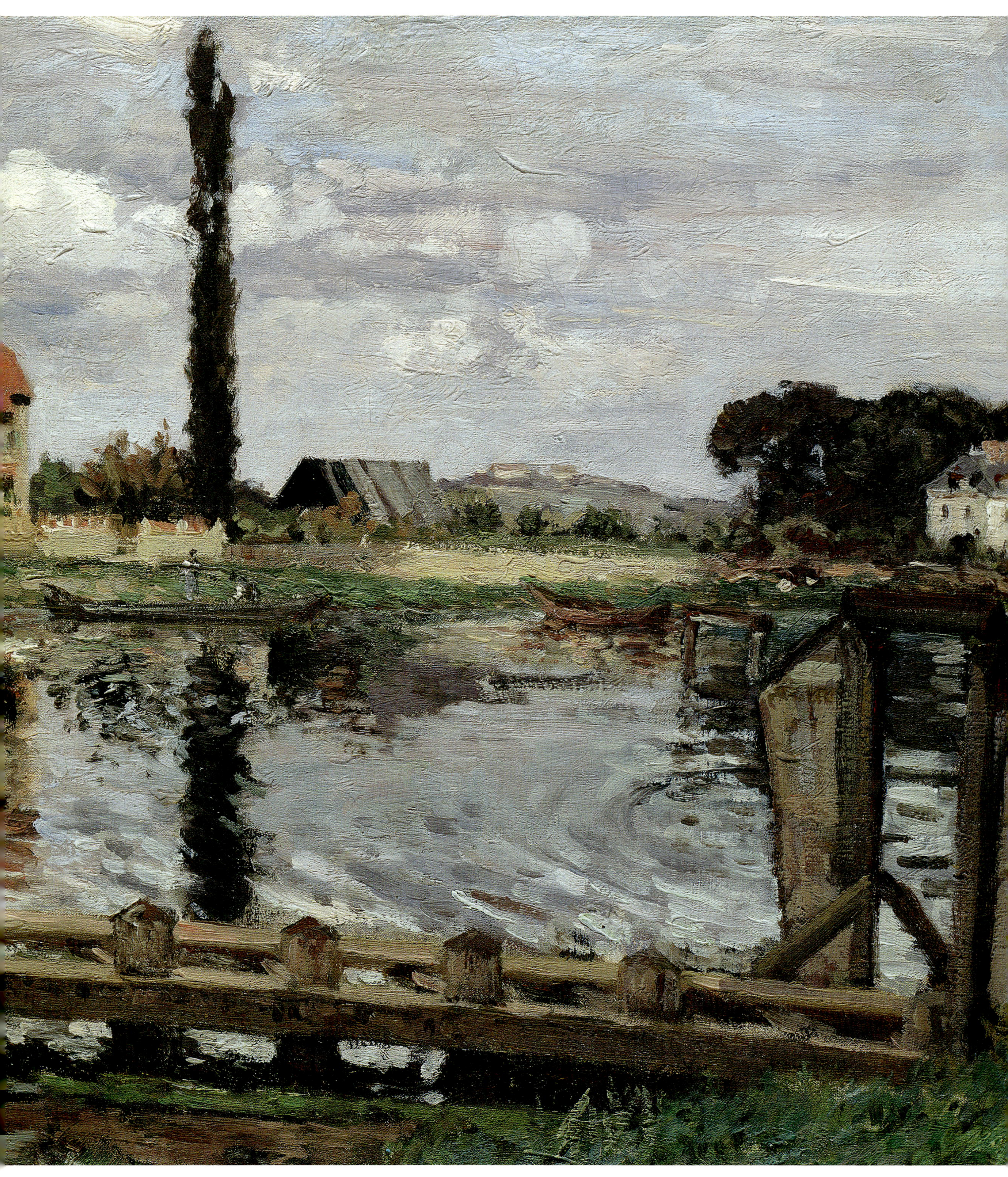

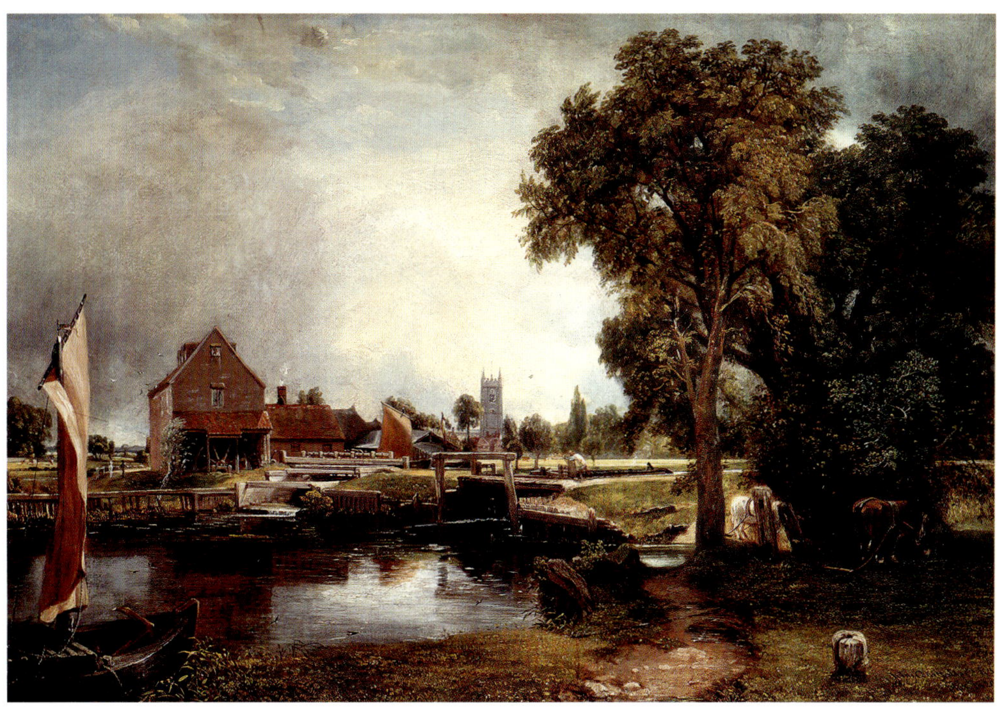

FIG. 20 John Constable, *Dedham Lock and Mill*, c. 1816, oil on canvas, 21⅛ × 30 in. (53.7 × 76.2 cm). Victoria and Albert Museum, London

For his motif Pissarro walked along the Seine's Quay Rennequin-Sualem between Bougival and the downriver town of Port Marly. He looked north toward the long Gautier Island, to the portion of the Seine that had been diverted to provide water for the fountains of Versailles since the seventeenth century and later disciplined against flooding by locks and dams. Sisley also painted in this area in the early 1870s, and one of his works represents the same motif from a different angle.[1] Two inscriptions on the back of the Pissarro painting identify it as "Au bord de la Seine à Port Marly" (banks of the Seine at Port Marly), and this is probably more accurate than its traditional title, *Weir on the Seine at Bougival*. The landscape of this area, with its interlocking village scenes in Bougival, Louveciennes, Port Marly, Marly-le-Roi, and Voisins, was truly the cradle of Impressionism. Here, from 1869 until 1872, all the major landscape painters of the movement lived and worked with real collaborative spirit. Monet was in Bougival, Pissarro in Louveciennes, Sisley in Marly-le-Roi, and Renoir's mother lived in Voisins, a hamlet of Louveciennes, so even the utterly Parisian painter spent a good deal of time in the area.

—RB

NOTE

1. Discussed and reproduced in Joachim Pissarro and Claire Durand-Ruel Snollaerts, *Pissarro: Critical Catalogue of Paintings* (Paris, 2005), vol. 2, p. 173.

Camille Pissarro

French, 1830–1903

7. *Chestnut Grove at Louveciennes (Bois de châtaigniers à Louveciennes)*, 1872

Oil on canvas, 16⅜ × 21 in. (40.6 × 54.4 cm); Signed and dated lower left: *C. Pissarro 1872*

In 1874 Jules-Antoine Castagnary remarked, "Pissarro is sober and strong. His synthesizing eye embraces at a glance the whole scene. He commits the grave error of painting fields with shadows cast by trees placed outside the frame. As a result the viewer is left to suppose they exist, as he cannot see them."[1] This quotation aptly describes the pictorial makeup of many of Pissarro's paintings executed in Louveciennes immediately before and after the Franco-Prussian War of 1870–71. Shadows and structures—intertwined in an ongoing dynamic exchange—constitute the defining elements of these paintings. The shadows disrupt the gentle, quiet order of the rural settings; they seem to determine the whole visual field, energizing the static presence of objects while covering over the entire ground. The innovative *Chestnut Grove at Louveciennes* epitomizes this practice. In it, Pissarro opposed rigidity and movement, weight and immateriality, presence and absence. The shadows point to the immaterial, the perpetually changing and yet unavoidable visual mark of things that stand under the sun. Meanwhile the oaks, the anchoring points of this stellar web of shadows, endow the picture with a perennial substance and monumentality.[2]

In the Louveciennes works, shadows take on the status of a subject matter in their own right. For instance, in *Route de Versailles, Roquencourt*, 1871 (fig. 21), the shadows of trees cross the picture plane horizontally, creating a rigid axis with the straight, vertical trees. In *Chestnut Trees at Louveciennes, Springtime*, 1870 (fig. 22), the shadows are just as unavoidable but function very differently. They appear as amorphous, dancing, scattered echoes of an intricate maze of tree branches and trunks. In the Bloch painting Pissarro achieved something of a synthesis in his use of shadows: they continue to provide structure while also endowing the entire picture with a magnificent sense of movement. Pissarro contrasted the sweeping, twisting hard motion of the trees (which—to our postmodern eye—seems to take on the quality of whirling helicopter blades and an undeniably aerial presence) with the soft, embedded, deep shadows that pull down into the earth while, at the same time, remaining flatly on its surface. This opposition results in a vibrant tension between trees and ground. Paradoxically, the shadows themselves appear to share the same texture as the trees that create them. These immaterial flickering forms take on an extraordinary visual intensity while rooting the trees to the painted surface.

A second contrast compounds the first one: the almost frenzied dynamic of this dance of forms (material or not—but all intensely visual) in the foreground is offset by the quiet, detached

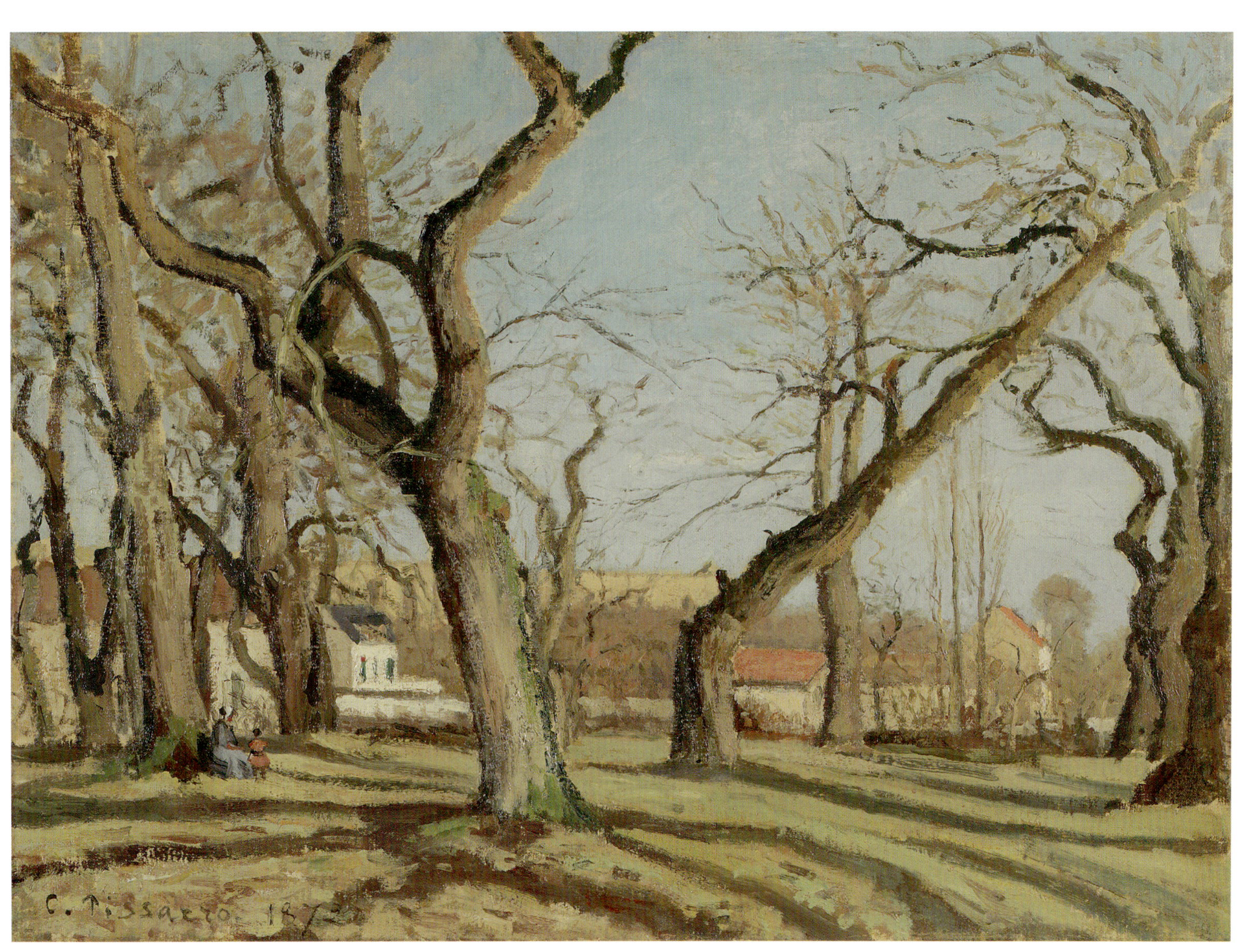
C. Pissarro.

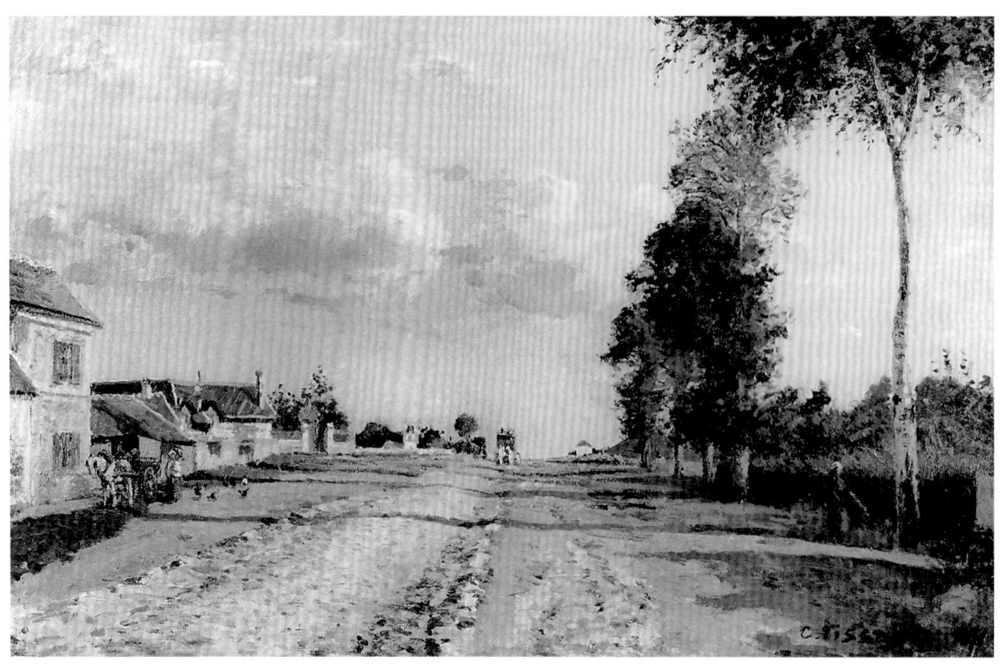

FIG. 21 Camille Pissarro, *Route de Versailles, Roquencourt*, 1871, oil on canvas, 20¼ × 30 in. (51.5 × 76.2 cm). Van Gogh Museum, Amsterdam

rural setting in the background. As one's gaze passes back and forth, this forceful juxtaposition creates a sense of vertigo. The viewer's eye sways around the picture, almost as if he or she has been set in motion. These powerful sets of contrasts finally meet and coexist in the sky. The quiet, clear plane of blue paint and soft pastel hues, punctuated with filaments of white, evokes a quiet and sunny day. At closer examination, however, these poetic harmonies conceal the slightly agitated hand that held the brush and activated the brushstrokes animating the upper surface of the composition.

One of the received ideas about Impressionism is that this innovative movement was all about painting light or atmospheric effects. Here one sees that it may be truer to say the Impressionists painted light insofar as it produced its inevitable countereffect: shadow. Furthermore, one could perhaps say that one of the discoveries of the Impressionists was that light is made visible only through its shadow. While the archetype of the Impressionist vision lies in the play of exquisite silvery patches of light falling on the ground or in freckling light screened through foliage (see, for example, Renoir's later *The Swing* of 1876, Musée d'Orsay, Paris), these paintings by Pissarro attest that the interplay of light patches piercing through foliage was not the only tool for representing atmospheric sensations. Pissarro proposed another method for activating a forceful pictorial dialogue, wherein each element (the shadows and the objects that cast them) is given equivalent importance within the picture field—laying the ground for some key modernist practices.

Finally, this picture seems to deliver an important message. Pissarro's profound and sincere attachment to reality, concreteness, and honesty finds an interesting perspective through his

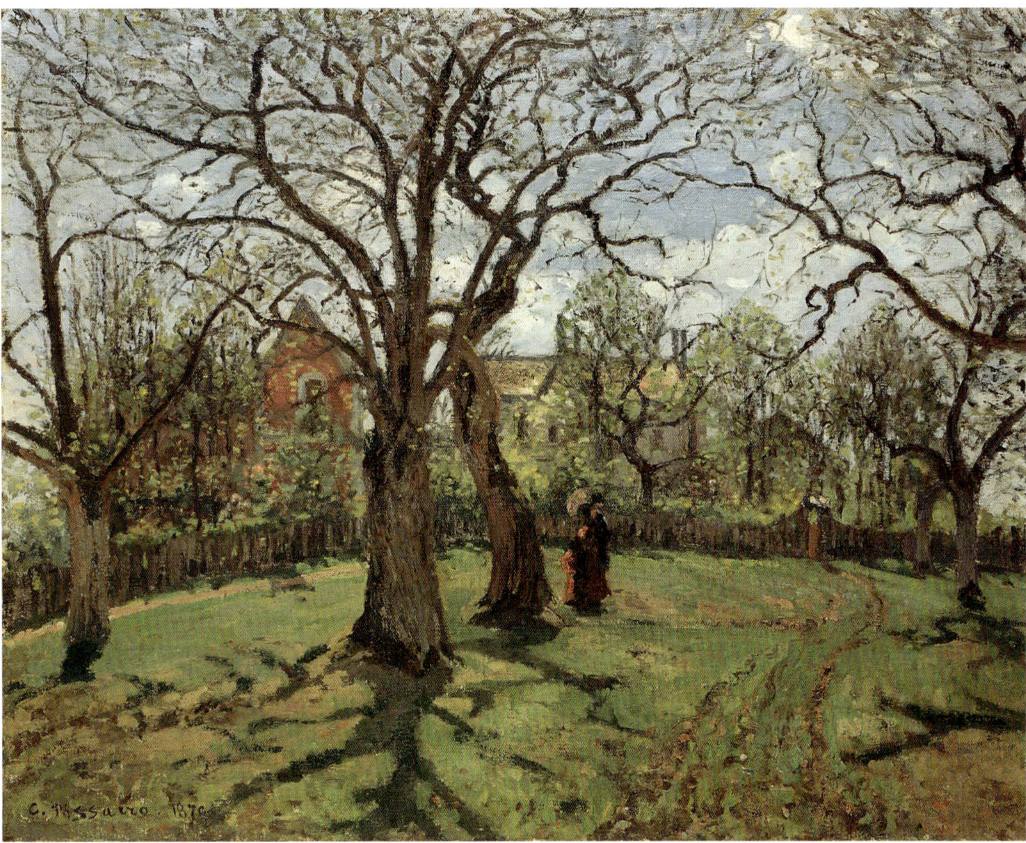

FIG. 22 Camille Pissarro, *Chestnut Trees at Louveciennes, Springtime* (*Châtaigniers à Louveciennes, printemps*), 1870, oil on canvas, 23½ × 28¾ in. (59.5 × 73.0 cm). Museum Langmatt Sidney und Jenny Brown, Baden, Switzerland

treatments of shadows. The Louveciennes works are preeminently Impressionistic in the polymorphic opposition between permanent structures and various transient effects, and this leads to a noteworthy paradox: it is through an extreme attachment to the real that Pissarro produces a configuration of dancing forms which invites the use of metaphors (such as "shadows take on a life of their own") to describe the hinging of the real and the unreal. Thus Pissarro's Louveciennes works—and most notably, among them, the Bloch painting—do not merely offer an immediate precedent for the opening of the Impressionist decade but also, with their serial procedures and symbolism, point toward its end.

—JP

NOTES

1. Review of the first Impressionist exhibition, *Le siècle*, April 29, 1874, translation in *The New Painting: Impressionism, 1874–1886*, exh. cat. (Geneva and Seattle, 1986), p. 138.

2. The author would like to acknowledge the pathbreaking research of Cora Michael in her 2006 dissertation for the Institute of Fine Arts, New York, "'As Much as the Light': The Importance of Shadows in the Art of Camille Pissarro."

Camille Pissarro

French, 1830–1903

8. *Rue Saint-Honoré, Sun Effect, Afternoon (La rue Saint-Honoré, effet de soleil, après-midi)*, 1898

Oil on canvas, 25¾ × 21½ in. (65.5 × 54.5 cm); signed and dated lower right in dark lavender: *C. Pissarro 98*

Pissarro undertook a series of views of the avenue de l'Opéra and the rue Saint-Honoré during the winter of 1897–98. It was a time of drama and sadness in Pissarro's life. His eldest son, Lucien, to whom Pissarro was especially close, was between life and death, having just suffered a major stroke that left him partly paralyzed. Just as Lucien was beginning to recover, another tragedy befell the Pissarros: their third son, Félix, died from tuberculosis. Pissarro himself, now sixty-seven years old, was suffering from a recurrent eye infection that forced him to work indoors from behind a window. Finally, the political situation in France had become intensely polarized around the Dreyfus case: protecting the rights of a French Jewish army officer, falsely accused of treason on the basis of forged evidence, was set against upholding the honor of the French nation and its army. It is amazing, in this fraught context, that Pissarro found enough energy to go on painting. Characteristically, however, he took solace in work. He expressed himself most clearly in a moving letter to the ailing Lucien: "Let us work, that will dress our wounds. I wish you strength, I want you to wrap yourself, so to speak, in art."[1]

Pissarro was already ensconced in a rented room at the Grand Hôtel du Louvre, painting away, when Zola published his now famous article "J'accuse" in defense of Dreyfus (Pissarro would have read it in one of the anarchist newspapers to which he subscribed).[2] Even while Paris was engaged in what Zola termed "a struggle between clarity and obscurantism," the artist was obstinately determined "to paint these Paris streets that people have come to call ugly, but which are so silvery, so luminous, and vital. They are so different from the boulevards. This is completely modern!"[3] Pissarro's hotel overlooked the intersection of the avenue de l'Opéra, just in front of his window, and the rue Saint-Honoré, to his left. The series contains fifteen works divided into three motifs: the rue Saint-Honoré, the avenue de l'Opéra with the Palais Garnier in the background, and the place du Théâtre Français (to the right of the avenue). The rue Saint-Honoré group counts three works: the largest, an afternoon and rain effect, dated 1897 (fig. 23); a morning and sun effect dated 1898 (fig. 24); and the Bloch Collection's afternoon and sun effect, also dated 1898 and the same size as figure 24. All three have vertical formats, whereas the avenue de l'Opéra paintings are horizontal. The verticality of these pictures was clearly dictated by the tall building (higher than the trees and other buildings) at the corner of rue de Rohan and rue Saint-Honoré. It is seen at closer range than any other structure in this series,

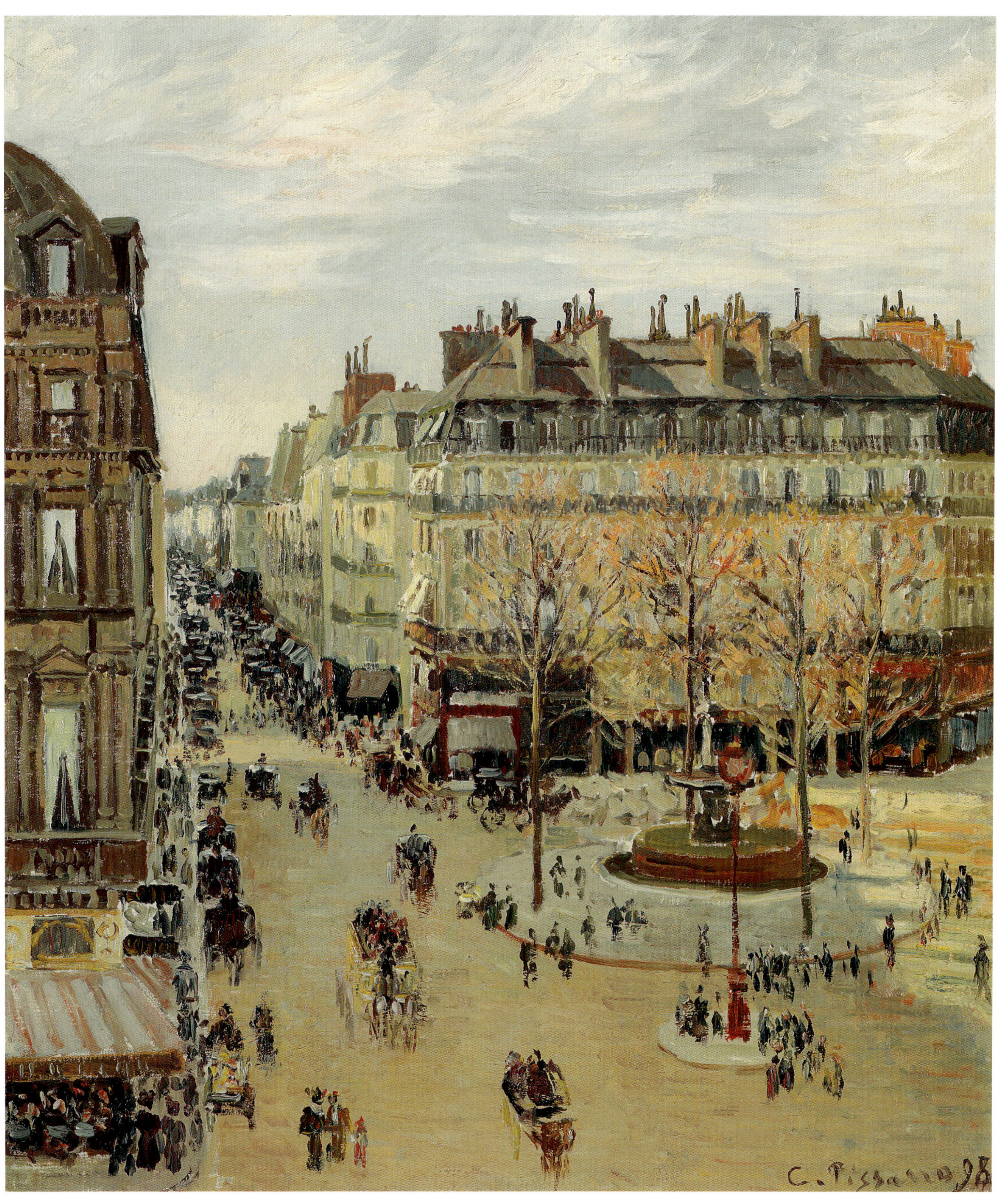
C. Pissarro 98

and Pissarro heightened the effect of verticality by cropping its facade to a narrow band that parallels the left edge of the picture.

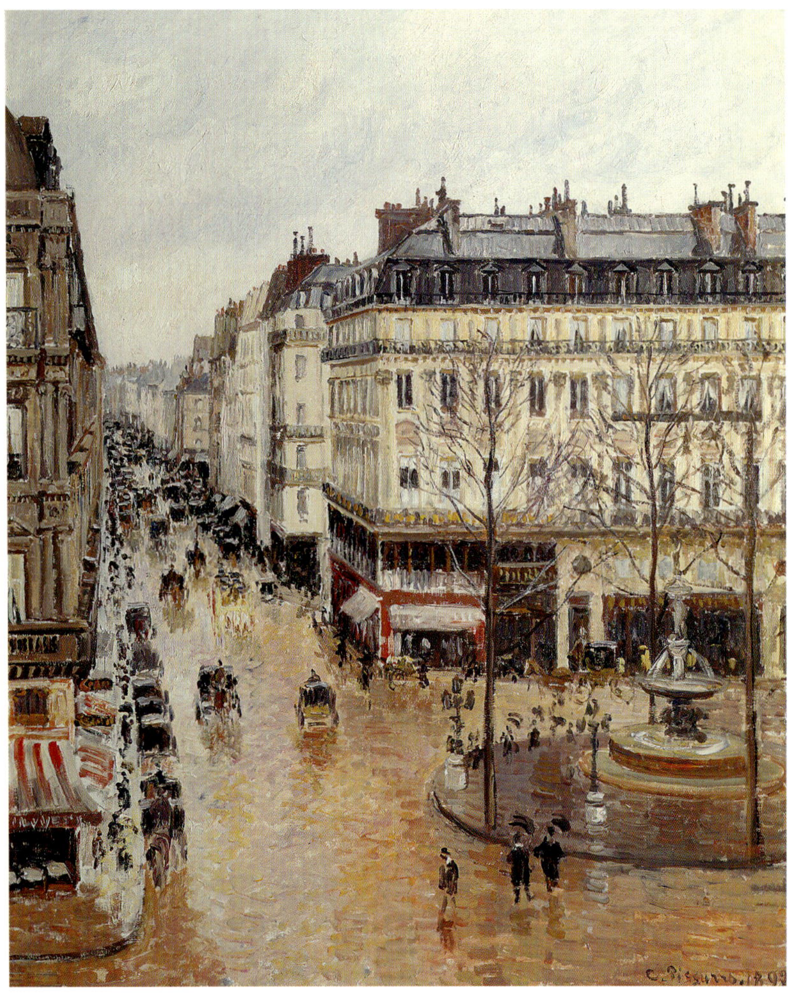

FIG. 23 Camille Pissarro, *Rue Saint-Honoré, Afternoon, Rain Effect* (*Rue Saint-Honoré, après-midi, effet de pluie*), 1897, oil on canvas, 31⅞ × 25⅝ in. (81 × 65 cm). Fundación Colección Thyssen-Bornemisza, Madrid

The paintings in this entire series deal not only with verticality versus perspective—a dichotomy that also best defines the artist's boulevard Montmartre series—but with circularity, metonymically suggested by the round pedestrian island found in every one of these fifteen works. The notion of circularity commands the structure of the series in several ways. Pissarro's compositional tactics proceed from left to right, as though intent on enclosing the circle of the place du Théâtre Français with his gaze. It is significant, in this context, to note that when Pissarro wrote to Lucien about Félix's death, he recommended as a remedy against grief "to wrap yourself . . . in art." The series certainly evokes this effect, wherein the artist seems to envelop himself in art, surrounded by all fifteen works.

The traffic itself (*circulation* in French) also follows the same circular dynamic: it no longer functions according to the orthogonal, orderly pattern observed in the boulevard Montmartre series. Here the traffic moves around sets of roundabouts, building circles upon circles. There is something organic in the way individual components (pedestrians, carriages, omnibuses, wheelbarrows) form sets of patterns all their own—free yet organized, autonomous yet circumscribed. The cycles of light, weather, and seasonal effects gain a new resonance in this particular human context.

An analogy can be drawn between the patient introspection with which Pissarro approached the works of this series and the gradual enlightenment of French society as it uncovered its injustice in the Dreyfus case. It took twelve years for the French judicial administration to fully realize its mistake, and Dreyfus was exonerated only in 1906. In Pissarro's terms, an equivalent mode of reflection is precisely what is needed "for a painter to paint a good picture!"[4] As he worked on the avenue de l'Opéra series, Pissarro explained that he needed to be "looking for elements in which we surround ourselves with our own meanings."[5] It is the same concept he used to describe the self-examination experienced by French society as the Dreyfus case unfolded: "We began to reflect on matters."[6] From this process of reflection comes (hopefully) the knowledge that dissipates prejudice, obscurantism, traditionalism: "Wouldn't it be amazing if a dozen jury members were able to see clearly in this case? Only independent people can see through darkness. One should hope that [the people] will see clearly where one is trying to lead them."[7] As Pissarro points out, the result of this reflection cannot be predetermined: this is what democracy is about.

The metaphors Pissarro used in the corpus of letters he wrote while painting this poignant series correlate to both France's political situation and Pissarro's own pictorial methods. A sentence such as "one cannot see very much" can be read as a metaphor for the political confusion of the time and as a literal description of a fog effect, or of the painting representing that effect. The artist's eye is at the center of a network of significations and concerns that bring together artistic and political matters.

—JP

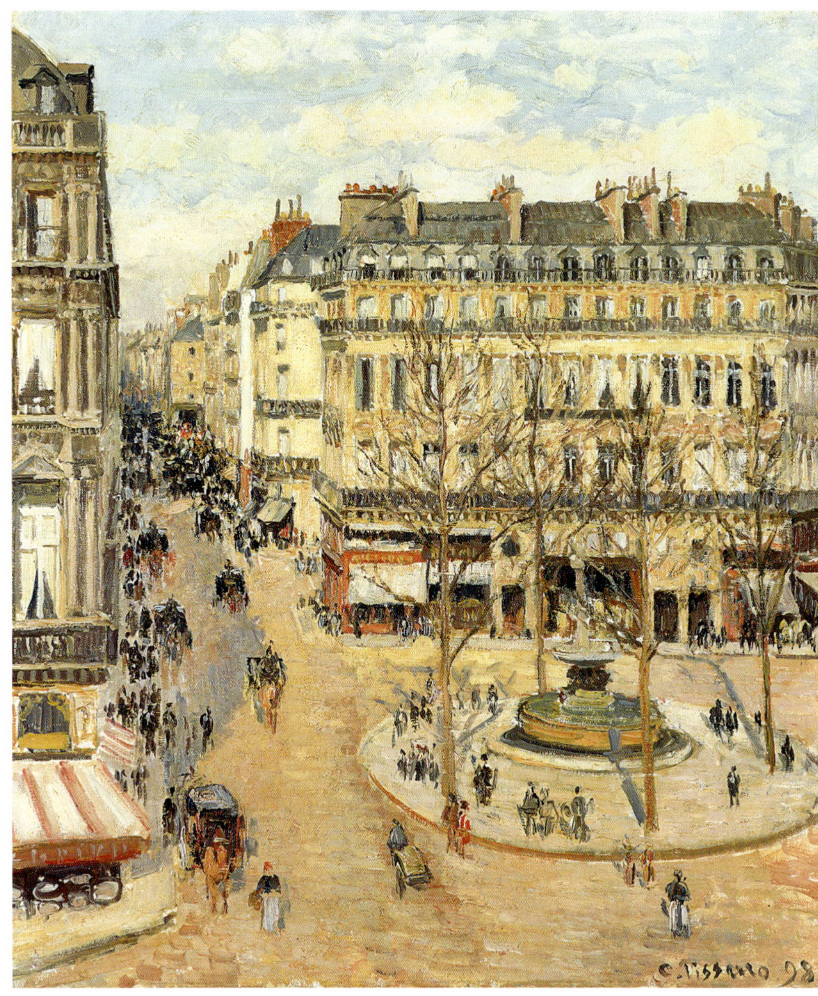

FIG. 24 Camille Pissarro, *Rue Saint-Honoré, Place du Théâtre Français*, 1898, 25⅞ × 21¼ in. (65.5 × 54 cm). The Ordrupgaard Collection, Copenhagen

NOTES

1. Letter to Lucien, December 15, 1897, in *Camille Pissarro: Letters to His Son Lucien*, ed. John Rewald (Boston, 2002), pp. 315–16.
2. For a full discussion of the horrifying street demonstrations in Paris and throughout France, see Pierre Birnbaum, *The Anti-Semitic Moment: A Tour of France in 1898*, trans. Jane Marie Todd (New York, 2003).
3. Letter to Lucien, December 15, 1897, in *Camille Pissarro*, p. 316.
4. Janine Bailly-Herzberg, ed., *Correspondance de Camille Pissarro*, vol. 4, *1895–1898* (Paris, 1989), 465 (author's translation).
5. Ibid., 4: 458.
6. Ibid., 4: 446.
7. Ibid.

Claude Monet

French, 1840–1926

9. *Snow at Argenteuil (Neige à Argenteuil)*, c. 1874–75

Oil on canvas, 19¾ × 26¾ in. (50.2 × 68 cm); signed lower right: *Claude Monet*

With the exception of a small number of figure paintings, portraits, and still lifes, Claude Monet devoted almost his entire artistic life to the landscape. He burst upon the Parisian scene with an important series of large-scale Normandy scenes in the 1860s and continued to paint the landscape of his native France until his death nearly seven decades later. He submitted superb views of Paris and its suburbs to five of the eight Impressionist exhibitions held between 1874 and 1886 and has come to be considered the dominant landscape painter of that hallowed group.

Although winter views exist in the lengthy European landscape tradition, they are a distinct minority. Dutch and Flemish masters were, perhaps, the most enthusiastic proponents of such pictures, but they seem to have been more interested in the skaters who plied the frozen surface of wintry rivers than the landscape itself, which most often serves simply as a background for the human antics they favored. We find snow in the alpine landscapes of the eighteenth-century Swiss artist Caspar Wolff, in the chilly Romantic mountain views of Caspar David Friedrich, and in the occasional landscape by the British master Turner. Even Goya painted snow, but it was not until the Impressionists that the winter landscape took on a new visual poetry. From hoarfrost through snow to broken ice and freezing wind, we experience the full range of winter in the paintings and pastels of Monet, Pissarro, Renoir, Sisley, Morisot, Gauguin, Guillaumin, and even Cézanne.[1]

The single Monet in the Bloch Collection is a masterpiece of winter landscape painting. In looking at it, we feel as if we are trudging along the small snowy path leading to the town of Argenteuil. The snow in the winter of 1874–75 clearly energized Monet as a painter, and no fewer than sixteen snow effects have been linked to that long season. Only five are dated—all to 1875. The Bloch painting is related to an identically composed landscape of somewhat larger dimensions (fig. 25). Purchased from Monet's dealer, Paul Durand-Ruel, in 1890 by Anna Perkins Rogers, this painting was given to the Museum of Fine Arts, Boston, in 1921, making it one of the earliest works by Monet to enter an American museum collection. It represents the landscape in front of the painter's newly rented house in Argenteuil on the rue Saint-Denis. The house was located across the street from the railroad station where Monet hopped the trains to Gare Saint-Lazare in Paris. A small unpaved road on the side of the house led directly to the center of Argenteuil. During the snowstorms of that winter, Monet was mostly housebound,

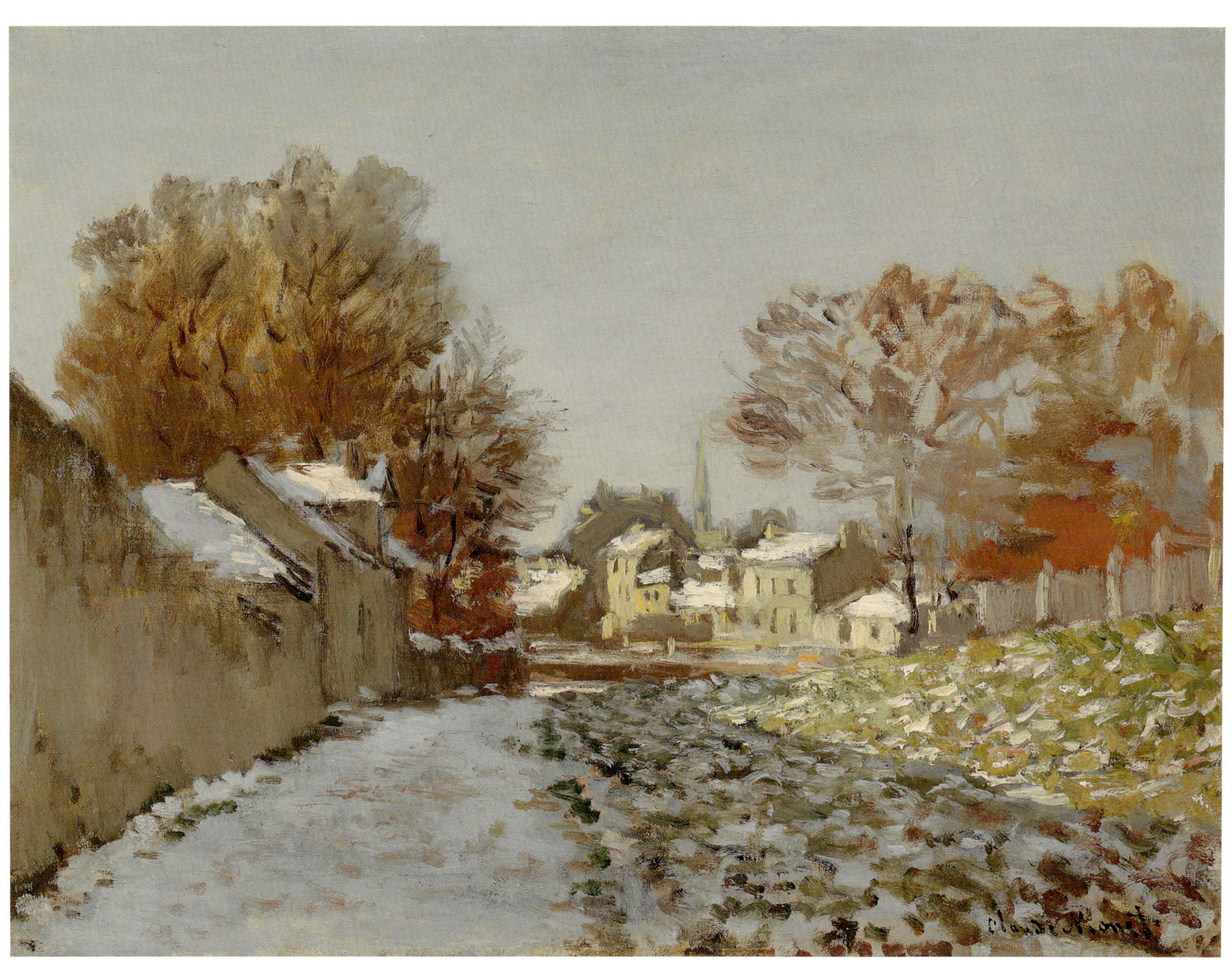

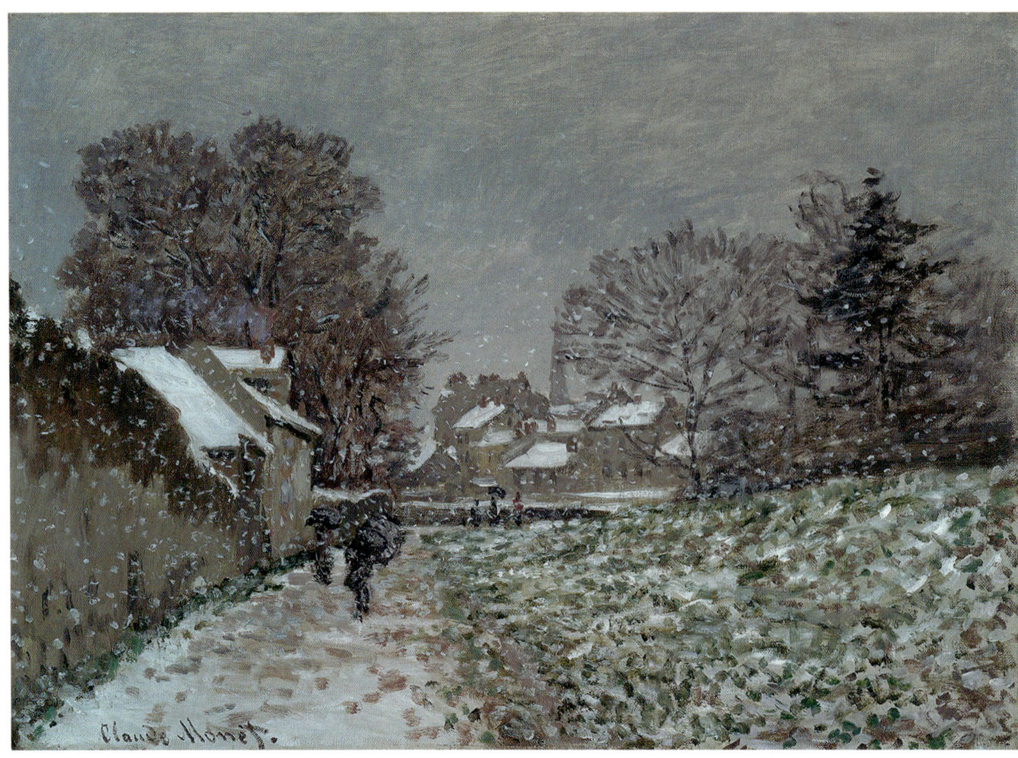

FIG. 25 Claude Monet, *Snow at Argenteuil*, c. 1874, oil on canvas, 21½ × 29 in. (54.6 × 73.7 cm). Museum of Fine Arts, Boston, bequest of Anna Perkins Rogers

painting from his windows. When he did venture into the cold to work briefly on his canvases outdoors, he stayed close to the house. It is perhaps because of the snow and cold that he blocked a virtually identical landscape composition quickly onto two canvases and then completed them independently to create two different landscape effects.

The Boston painting represents the snowstorm itself, while the Bloch painting depicts the landscape after the storm. The snow has been tramped down on the road, but the temperature has risen and the earth has warmed enough so that the snow has begun to melt in the field on the right. Each canvas records with a precision of light, color, and atmosphere the particular climatic conditions of winter in a small town. Monet painted them in two or at most three sessions, and each easily betrays the confident, hasty execution of which he was already considered a master. There were a few other instances in the 1870s when Monet created such compositionally related paintings, and certain of these pairs have identical dimensions. The canvases representing a scene at and after dinner in Monet's dining room; two almost identical windy landscapes painted in Zaandam in 1872; two promenade scenes at Argenteuil, also of 1872; a pair of views of riverboats moored at Asnières of 1873; a pair of chromatically saturated autumn views of the Seine, painted in 1873; two views from Monet's hotel window overlooking the harbor at Le Havre; two startlingly similar views of the Seine at Argenteuil; and two railroad bridges of the same year—all these prefigure the Boston-Bloch pairing discussed here.[2]

The creation of a compositional scaffolding that could be infused with the temporal life of changing light, weather, figures, or boats was clearly a strategy for the young Monet, both before and after what was to be the first Impressionist exhibition, in the spring of 1874. Yet, if this practice held real importance for the painter, he seems not to have communicated it to either his friends or the public. In no case was a pair either sold or exhibited together in Monet's lifetime, suggesting that the method was a kind of shortcut that enabled him to make two paintings more easily and quickly than if he had to reinvent the composition each time. Indeed, "composition" for Monet became a variable in his working method that could be downplayed in his quest for the efficient recording of temporal conditions. These pairs of works in no way prefigure Monet's paintings in series, a deliberate temporal strategy the artist first expressed publicly in the 1877 exhibition of seven paintings of Gare Saint-Lazare, continuing with the 1879 exhibition of one trio and a pair of canvases with the same composition, and reaching a climax in 1891 with the first exhibition of the haystacks.

Although the Bloch painting looks wonderfully controlled and tasteful to us today, it would have been completely shocking to most French bourgeois viewers during the decade of its making. Other artists often made quickly painted sketches and studies, but these were rarely exhibited or sold and most often were considered to be the raw material or research of the artist, of chief interest only to posterity. In painting the Bloch canvas, Monet worked quickly in the cold, setting the major forms of the composition in one working session, using large brushes and a relatively restricted palette. After the paint had dried or become tacky, but still while the effect he sought could be experienced directly, he reworked the canvas with smaller strokes, particularly in the lower right quadrant of the painting. Indeed, Monet deliberately retained the contrast between the virtuoso painterly scribbles that represent the trees and the houses on the left and the smaller overlapping touches of the foreground field; by signing the work in the lower right corner, the painter indicated to us that he intended these contrasts as part of the final, finished work. It was less the rapidity of the painting's execution than Monet's signature that would have shocked contemporary viewers. A painting so apparently sloppy as this could never have been considered "finished" by a conventional artist or art lover, and Monet, by making a fetish of his process, consciously provoked their negative reactions. Indeed the painting was described by Monet himself as a "*pochade,*" a rough sketch.[3]

What is interesting, however, is that many of Monet's earliest collectors bought precisely these highly gestural and apparently unfinished pictures. Both the Bloch and the Boston paintings were purchased during the artist's lifetime, the Boston canvas to form part of the largest group of Monet canvases to be found in any city outside Paris in the nineteenth century and the Bloch canvas by no less than the Havemeyers of New York. Perhaps the most legendary collectors of the late nineteenth century in the United States, the Havemeyers routinely asked the advice of their friend Mary Cassatt, who maintained a friendly relationship with Monet even after the Impressionist group broke up in the mid-1880s. The Havemeyers acquired the Bloch Monet in 1898, undoubtedly with Cassatt's guidance, but it was not part of their bequest to the

Metropolitan Museum of Art. Instead, it remained in the Havemeyer family until a sale in 1930. And, although it has been published several times, this is the first public exhibition of the painting since 1945.

It is worth noting that Japanese art provided a good deal of the aesthetic impetus for the Impressionists in painting snowy landscapes. The poetry of snow has a long and distinguished history in the pictorial arts of Japan—in screens, scrolls, and prints as well as textiles and painted ceramics. The Bloch painting and its Boston mate can be linked to the numerous Japanese prints that represent villages in the snow, and, by including figures in the Boston painting, Monet almost seems to force such links. Every visitor to Monet's famous house in Giverny remembers the painter's large collection of Japanese prints, mostly displayed in his dining room. While he acquired many of these after 1874–75, when he painted the Bloch snowscape, there is no doubt that he was familiar with Japanese prints before he could afford to own them. Particular mention might be made of Hiroshige's *Evening Snow, Kambara* of 1830–34, from his suite of prints *Fifty-three Posting Stations to Tokaido*.

—RB

NOTES

1. Some of the most beautiful of these winter landscapes were recently gathered for an exhibition organized by the Phillips Collection in Washington. The cumulative effect was a revelation for anyone who doubts the poetry of coldness. See Charles S. Moffett et al., *Impressionists in Winter: Effets de Neige* (Washington, D.C., and London, 1998).
2. These works are, respectively, Wildenstein 129 and 130, 177 and 178, 222 and 223, 269 and 270, 290 and 291, 296 and 297, 311 and 312, and 318 and 319. See Daniel Wildenstein, *Monet, or the Triumph of Impressionism*, 4 vols. (Cologne and Paris, 1996).
3. See John House, *Monet: Nature into Art* (New Haven and London, 1986), pp. 162, 167–68, and 242 n. 40.

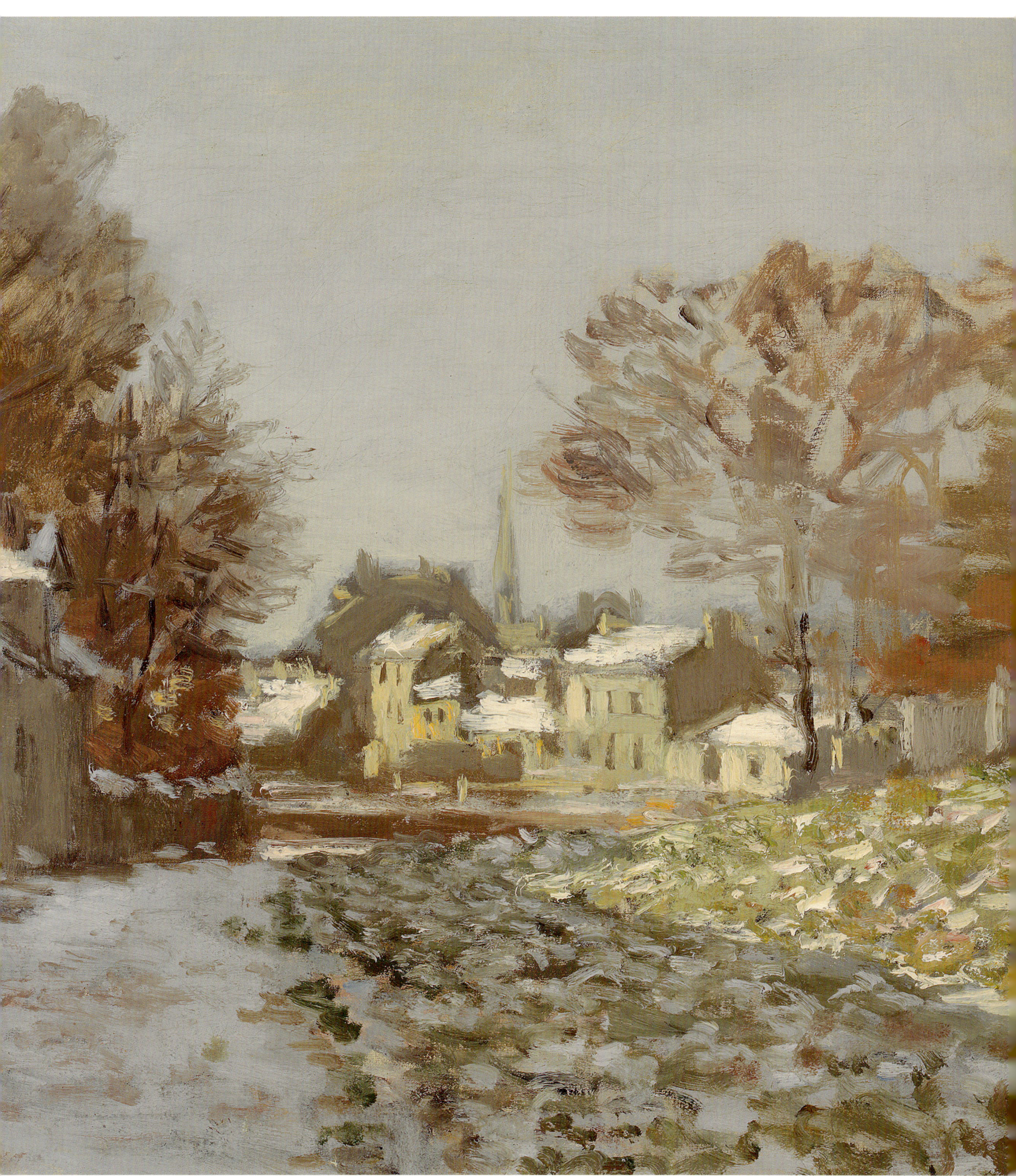

Alfred Sisley

French, 1839–1899

10. *Rue de la Princesse, Winter (La rue de la princesse, l'hiver)*, 1875

Oil on canvas, 24 × 19⅝ in. (61 × 50 cm), glue-lined; signed and dated lower right: *Sisley 75*

Alfred Sisley's very name tells us that he was not quite French, in spite of the fact that he spent all his life in France, spoke the language like a native, was a French citizen, married a Frenchwoman, and raised his children there. Sisley's parents were English citizens living in Paris, actively involved in the import-export of luxury goods between England and France. Hence Sisley was completely bilingual and effectively bicultural as a youth and young man, with a real knowledge of English landscape practice and culture, both of which had a profound effect on his French Impressionist colleagues. As a painter, he has always been considered a secondary artist—too pure and too shy to be compared to the greater genius of Monet, Renoir, or even Pissarro. The latter, whose friendship with Sisley was lifelong, described himself and Sisley as "in the line of Impressionists," by which he meant that neither was at the front of that line. Yet Sisley's commitment to outdoor landscape painting was unwavering, and he never suffered the profound stylistic and pictorial crises that were of such importance in the careers of Monet, Renoir, and Pissarro.

Most connoisseurs of Impressionism rate Sisley's work in the early and mid-1870s at the very top of Impressionist landscape production. He was, in those years, fully equal to Monet, Pissarro, and Renoir, sometimes surpassing them in the sheer pictorial purity of his works. Rarely did he work on a large scale, preferring modestly scaled canvases that were easy to transport and to complete within a few sittings. For him, the unity of the effect was more important than ambition of scale, and, as a direct result, his works are wonderfully suited to furnished domestic interiors. It is for this reason that the majority of Sisley's surviving paintings remain in private collections.[1] And, of the works in major museum Impressionist collections, most were acquired through gift rather than actively sought out by a curator or director. In this way, Sisley is a quiet, discreet artist.

The Bloch Sisley is a masterpiece. On the left it represents a distinctive, even quirky building, which Sisley painted at least two other times in the early 1870s. This building has now been conclusively identified in the hamlet of Voisins as 2, rue de la Princesse, where Sisley lived with his wife and two children from 1871 to early 1875.[2] The Bloch canvas can be placed last in the sequence of three paintings that Sisley made of the house. The earliest (fig. 26) was painted in the late summer or early autumn of 1872 or 1873. The second is dated 1874 and represents a view of the house from the opposite direction and under snow (private collection). The Bloch

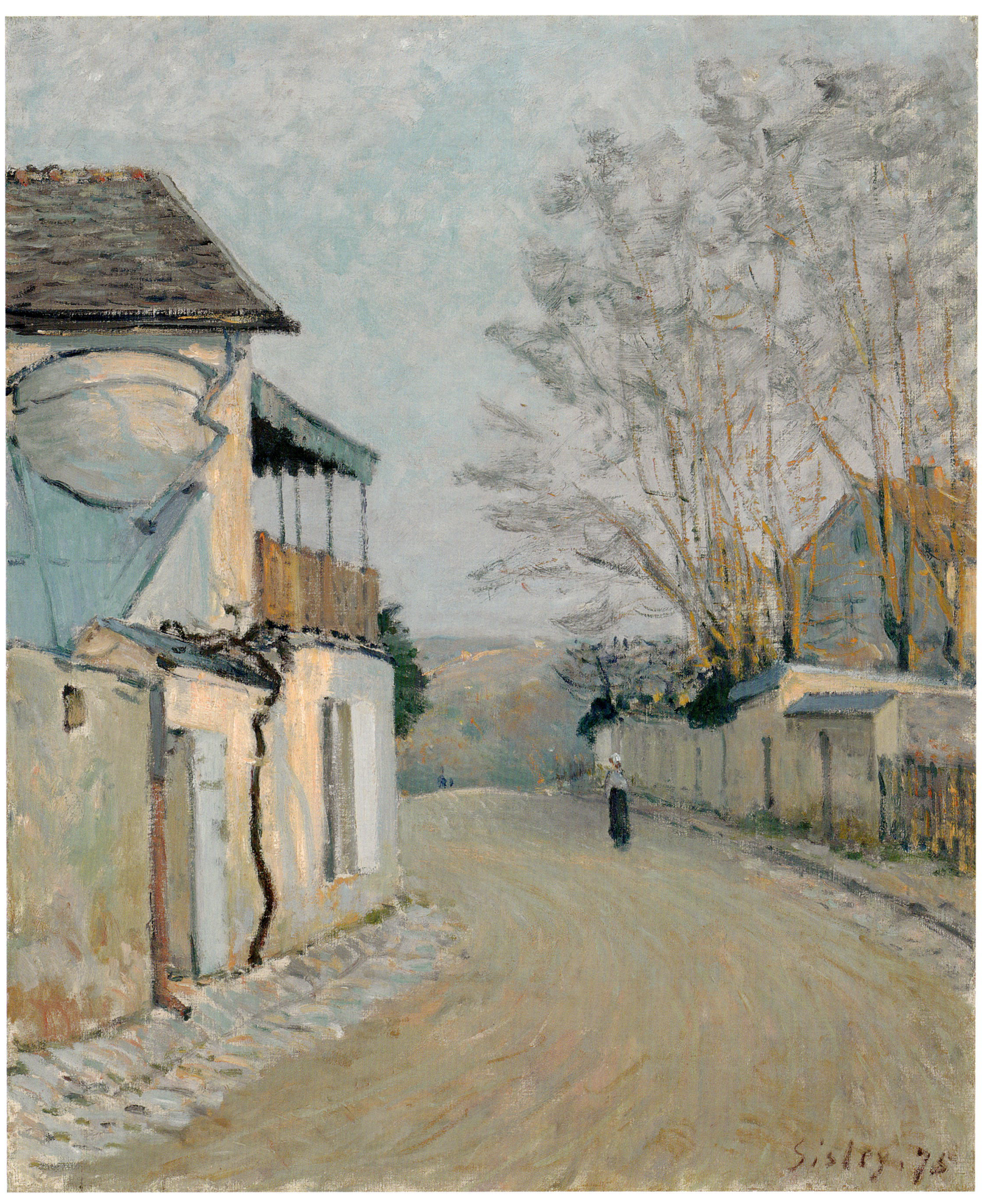
Sisley. 75

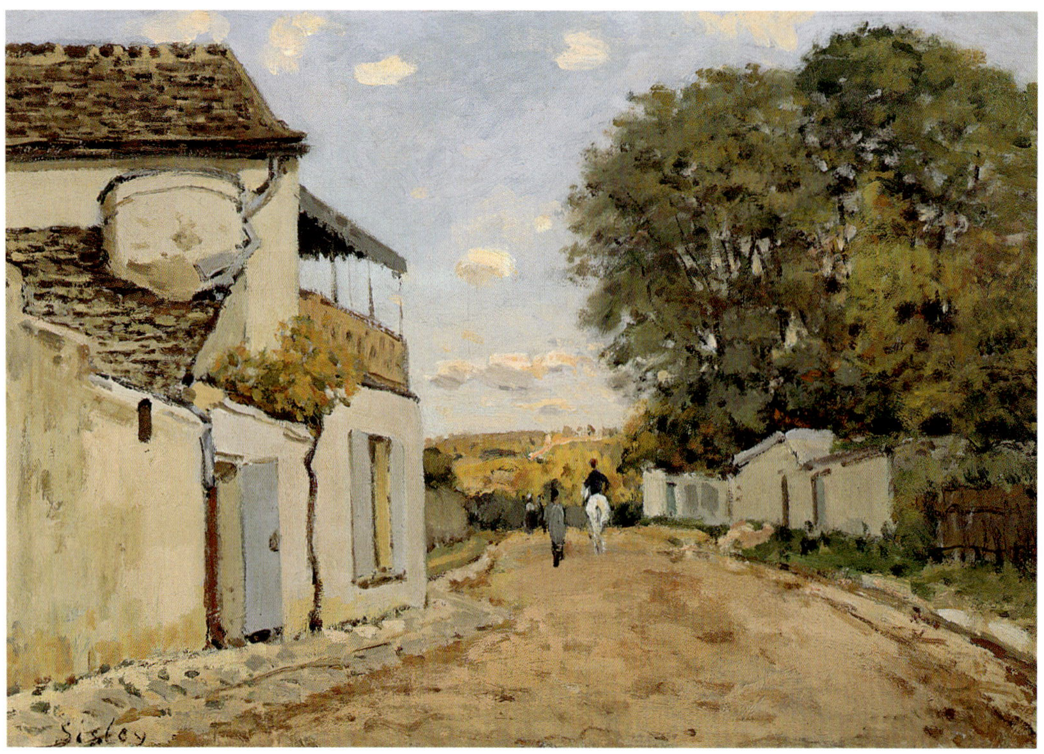

FIG. 26 Alfred Sisley, *Street in Louveciennes (Rue de la Princesse)*, 1872–73, oil on canvas, 15 × 21¼ in. (38 × 54 cm). The Phillips Family Collection

painting, dated 1875, is the last. It was made either in the early morning during a heavy hoarfrost or after a light dusting of snow; it may even have been painted after the major snowstorm of 1874–75 which Monet, Pissarro, and Renoir had also painted (cat. no. 9). Sisley, perhaps, dated the picture as a kind of souvenir of the house, which he and his family would leave for another rented house in nearby Marly-le-Roi in late February or March 1875.

Of the three paintings, the Bloch is technically the simplest and, thus, the most accomplished. In making it, Sisley sought to entrap an effect that is among the most fleeting in nature—when a faint powdering of snow or a heavy frost clings to natural forms, just before being melted by the morning sun. The entire painting is a dialogue between the pale eggshell blue of the morning sky and the wonderful pink and apricot undertones that embody the warmth the sun will bring to this frozen landscape. The pinks and other delicate warm tones can be found in greatest abundance in the subtly painted road in the foreground, while the blue suffuses the white stucco of the house itself and, of course, the sky. The quiet assurance of the painting is complete, and, as we study it, we are hard-pressed to find something we would change. Only in the area beneath the second-story roof of the house does Sisley confound us with a series of lines that seem to swoop and curl for no clear purpose. Yet, when we compare this passage to the analogous area in the Phillips painting, it is perfectly clear that its awkwardness is based on an actual feature of a vernacular building, and Sisley here represents a cistern.

The success of this painting was recognized by two of the greatest connoisseurs of Impressionism—the art critic Théodore Duret, who included a photograph of it in his 1939 *Histoire des peintres impressionistes*, and John Rewald, the towering historian of the movement, who reproduced it in the first (1946) and subsequent editions of the definitive *History of Impressionism*. With Monet's Argenteuil winter scene in the Bloch Collection (cat. no. 9), we can appreciate two canonical Impressionist landscapes, both painted in the same winter, possibly after the same storm, in unconscious homage to each other.

—RB

NOTES

1. Sisley's paintings have been catalogued by François Daulte, *Alfred Sisley: Catalogue raisonné de l'oeuvre peint* (Lausanne, 1959).
2. See Mary Anne Stevens, ed., *Alfred Sisley* (London and New Haven, 1992), pp. 118–19.

Alfred Sisley

French, 1839–1899

11. *The Lock of Saint-Mammès (L'écluse de Saint-Mammès)*, 1885

Oil on canvas, 15 × 21½ in. (38 × 55 cm); signed lower right: *Sisley. 85*

Of all the Impressionists, Alfred Sisley faced the greatest struggle and hardship in his life. He died in abject poverty, virtually unrecognized. Ironically, he was one of the few Impressionists who remained faithful to the technique, practice, and idiom of the movement throughout his career. Still neglected, or even omitted from mainstream art history, Sisley merits renewed and deeper consideration as an artist. An example of this surprising disregard is that Sisley has yet to be fully acknowledged as the pioneer in early modern art of painting in series. The concept of the series, that is, painting the same motif under constantly changing circumstances (light, weather, climate, time, movement), is usually associated with Monet and his Haystack series. This important breakthrough in the representation of reality began paving one of the highways to modernism and found its prolongation, a century later, in the works of such masters as Roy Lichtenstein, Andy Warhol, and Donald Judd. It can be argued that Sisley set this pictorial innovation in motion.

Sisley was painting particular sets of landscapes in series by 1880—nine years before Monet began his haystacks. He had moved to the village of Saint-Mammès, southeast of Paris, at the confluence of the Seine and the Loing rivers. Until the end of his life, the bulk of his artistic output derived from a narrow range of subjects, painted over and over, all from this particular area. In Saint-Mammès Sisley first gave shape to thorough, systematic series of works in which he explored given motifs, seen with audacity and intensity from different vantage points and with changes in light, time of day, seasonal effects, and activity. A proper scholarly survey of these most important paintings still remains to be conducted.

Sisley produced nearly fifty views of Saint-Mammès in 1884 and 1885. He used the village as a pretext to study, among other things, the constant flow of river traffic, as in the present painting. A range of boats is depicted in the Bloch Sisley, from the barge that glides along at the far right to the boat on the left carrying scaffolding. The picture focuses not just on the diversity of boats on the river but on the particular spot where boats slowed as they neared the lock at Saint-Mammès. The central motif, ironically, is almost invisible: the mechanism that contained and condensed the boat traffic upstream—the Saint-Mammès weir. This weir, like that painted by Pissarro near Bougival (cat. no. 6) more than ten years earlier, was constructed to manage growing shipping traffic as it approached Paris; a lock keeper raised and lowered the controlling mechanism, which was housed in the little red shed with a blue roof at the far left. The

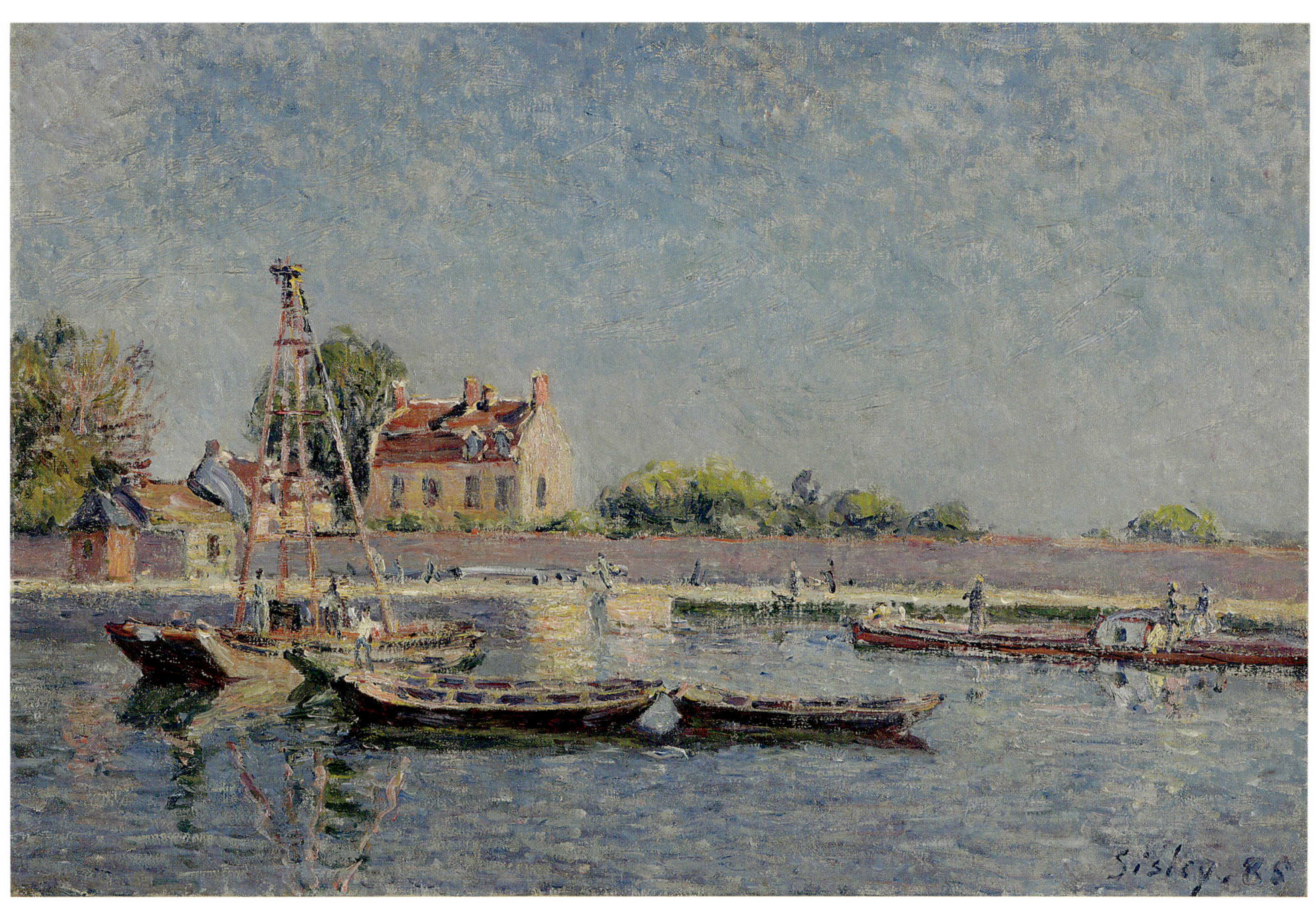
Sisley. 85

artist pushed to the margin the very element that regulated the passage of the river traffic, suggesting—as Matisse would soon do—that the center of the composition is everywhere, or that the center and the periphery of the composition hold equal significance.

The time of day seems to be late afternoon, when the energy and level of activity were still high, an intensity that is matched by the colors of Sisley's palette. The deep blues of the river Loing offset the varied quivering colors of the sky. Characteristic of Sisley's Saint-Mammès series, as here, the river and sky occupy a large part of the canvas. The noise, energy, and human labor conjured by the composition are in contrast to the serene calm of the surrounding natural setting. There is a regular, almost symmetrical ordering of the elements in three superimposed and parallel bands: the rectangle of sky that occupies more than half of the upper composition, the narrow stretch of land on which trees and houses stand, and the lower strip of deep blue water. These parallel bands anchor the composition, giving a solidity and stability to the various activities taking place.

The artist probably identified with the steady rhythm that pulses through this entire river landscape. The energy displayed in the sky and the water through the quick application of paint, the nervous and quivering accumulation of brushstrokes, the restless rhythm and agitation—all these seem to echo the buzz of human activity and, by extension, Sisley's restless representational urge. This is a painting of great depth that demonstrates Sisley's originality and his impact at this particular moment in the crisis of Impressionism. It also reveals, through the choice of an ordinary everyday scene and a semi-industrial subject, a profound humanity.

—JP

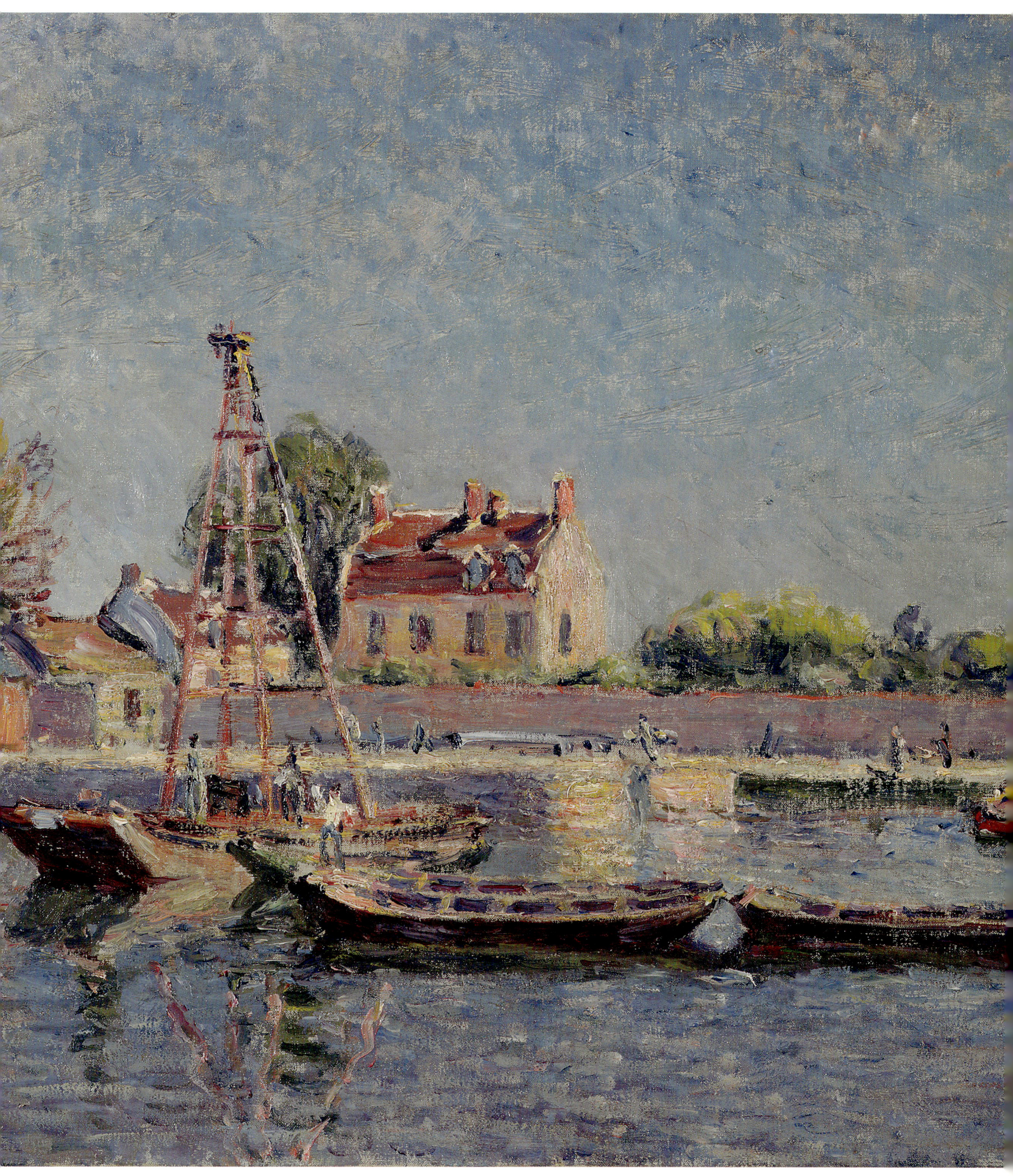

Jean-Baptiste-Armand Guillaumin

French, 1841–1927

12. *Landscape, Île de France (Paysage d'Île de France)*, c. 1876–77

Oil on canvas, 19⅜ × 25¾ in. (49.3 × 65.5 cm); signed lower left in red: *A Guillaumin*

Armand Guillaumin, a full-fledged member of the Impressionist group, has been paid remarkably little attention in academic or museum studies. Ironically, however, his art has never ceased to enjoy popularity on the auction market. Guillaumin was one of the founding members of the Impressionists and showed alongside them in the 1874 exhibition that gave the group its name. Like many of the other painters, he had little luck in being accepted at the Salon. Following Cézanne's path, Guillaumin never submitted to the official exhibition again after he was rejected in 1872. He resolved to exhibit outside the government channel and so joined with the Impressionists, most of whom he had known for several years. Pissarro and Cézanne were his closest friends and allies—he had met them both in the 1860s—and they hailed him as a cutting-edge member of the avant-garde. Both the style and the subject of the painting in the Bloch Collection testify to his close ties with Pissarro and Cézanne. Guillaumin worked with both artists in Pontoise in 1872, and, later that year, he collaborated with Cézanne on still lifes and a series of etchings which were produced at the house of a patron, the famous Paul Gachet, who happened to own a printing press.

The subject of this painting—the blunt, out-of-perspective juxtaposition of a factory and industrial smokestacks with a rural landscape—pays direct homage to works by Pissarro with which Guillaumin was familiar (fig. 27). Furthermore, the cropping of the walls in the foreground, the abbreviated brushstrokes in the foliage near the corner of the wall, the breaking of the pictorial space with oblique angles—all this is reminiscent of the paintings Cézanne showed in the Impressionist exhibitions of 1874 and 1877. The influence of Pissarro and Cézanne can also be found in the looser brushwork and strong color that characterize Guillaumin's work during the mid-1870s.

In the same way that the Bloch Caillebotte (cat. no. 13) juxtaposes factory and sailboat, industry and leisure, the Guillaumin represents the startling contrast between the rural landscape and the factories that came to inhabit it. The fields of Île de France were urbanized and industrialized in the late nineteenth century, and in Guillaumin's painting, the industrial development that was irreversibly transforming the countryside can be seen. Signs of the old ways are suggested by a horse and plowman in the upper left, horses pulling a hay cart along a road, or, closer to us, white horses in the foreground plowing a field. Strangely enough, in Guillaumin's artistic imagination, the two worlds, while coexisting, seem to ignore each other. Guillaumin

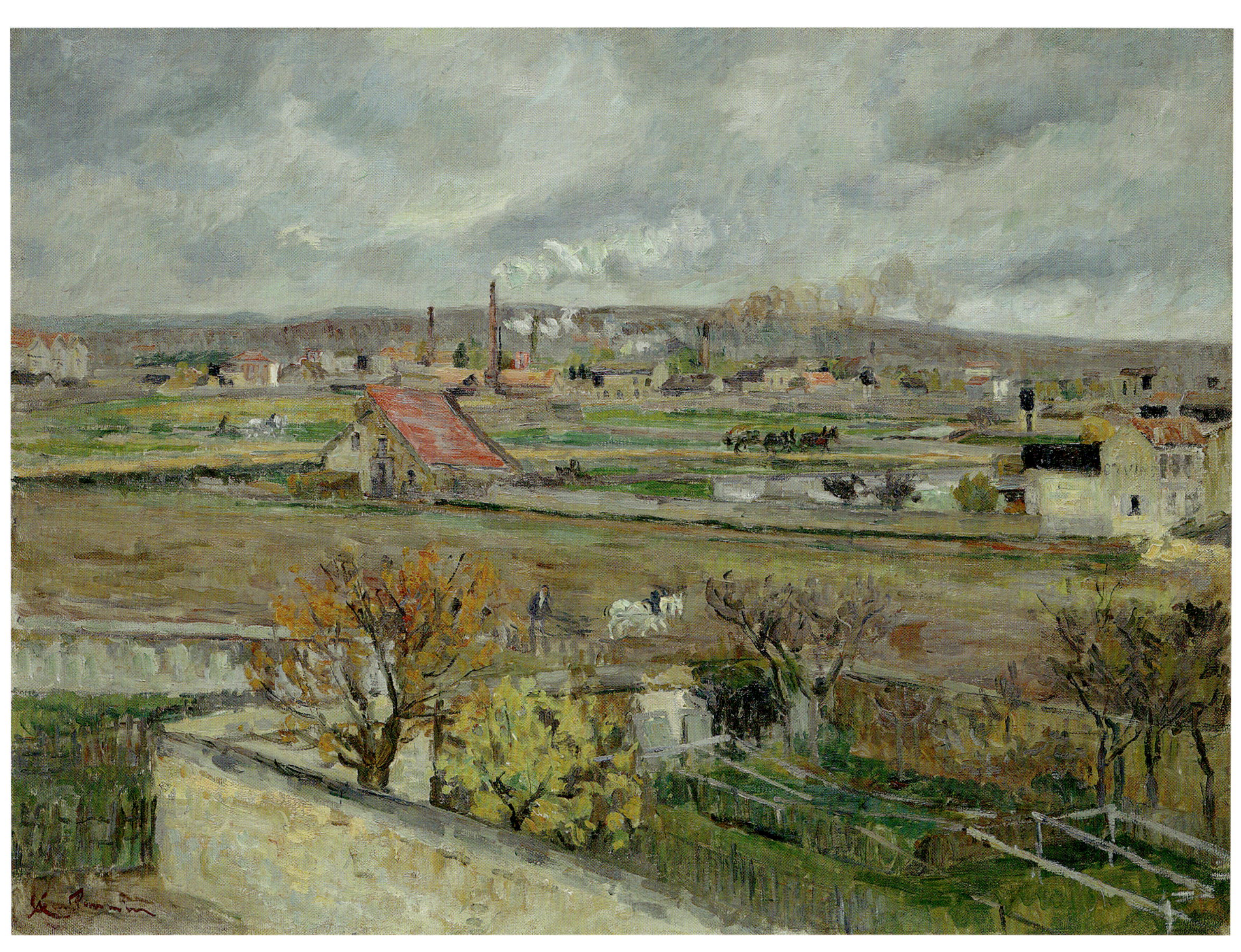

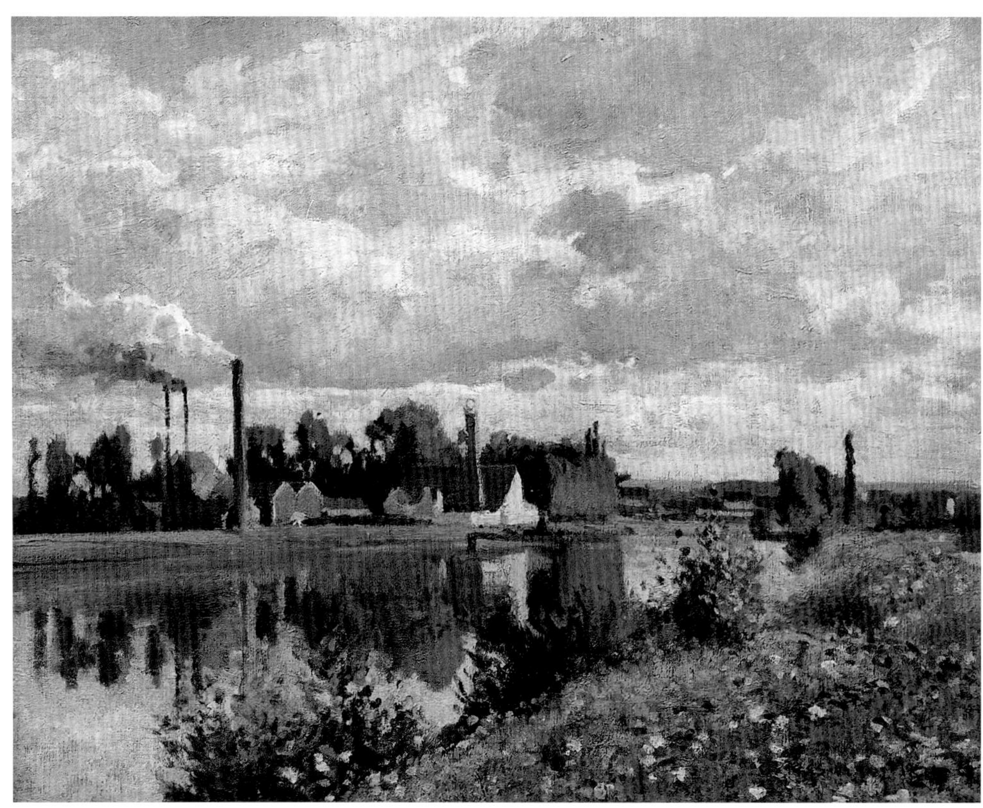

FIG. 27 Camille Pissarro, *The River Oise near Pontoise*, 1873, oil on canvas, 17⅞ × 21⅝ in. (45.3 × 55 cm). Sterling and Francine Clark Art Institute, Williamstown, Massachusetts

makes even fewer apologies than Caillebotte or Pissarro ever would for the stark contrast between the two facets of this new reality, neither of which he edited for the benefit of the other. One of these worlds seems bound to erase the other, although Guillaumin gives no clues as to how this dramatic confrontation between old and new will resolve. In Guillaumin's landscape, the work of the land is done horizontally, the movement of the horses naturally following the surface of the earth. Earth work is in visual opposition to industrial work, as symbolized by the smokestacks in the background, aggressively pointing to the skies. Standing vertically and churning out their thick white plumes of sulfur, these smokestacks are sure signs of the triumph of industry—for better or worse.

The juxtaposition of the two components—industrialization and an almost medieval rural society—produces a tough painting. Nothing in the way the painting itself was produced lessens the impact of this juxtaposition. The strange actuality of this work constitutes one of the very first ecological summations of what the modern world would hold in store for us more than a century later. As Guillaumin seems to announce, industry and nature can only live in mutual ignorance of each other: the antagonism generated by these two forces finds no point of harmonization other than that between a vertical and a horizontal.

Guillaumin's landscape can be linked to contemporaneous French concepts of nature. The great scientist and journalist Gustave Tissandier published the high-circulation illustrated journal *La nature* throughout the 1870s. Articles and illustrations in this publication documented current industrial advances in France, and it represented the exteriors and interiors of factories located in the fields surrounding French cities as frequently as it depicted more "natural" subjects such as birds, animals, vegetation, and geology. Surely these images were important for the later anarchist theorists of an agro-industrial paradise in which modern workers would leave congested, unhealthy cities to lead truly balanced lives by alternating field and factory labor. Guillaumin's landscape prefigures that sociopolitical ideal, which was to become so important for his friend, the anarchist Impressionist Pissarro.

—JP

Gustave Caillebotte

French, 1848–1894

13. *Boat Moored on the Seine at Argenteuil (Bateau au mouillage sur la Seine, à Argenteuil)*, c. 1884

Oil on canvas, 25¾ × 21⅜ in. (65.4 × 54.3 cm); indistinctly signed lower right: *Caillebotte*

Edgar Degas asked Gustave Caillebotte to submit to the second Impressionist exhibition in 1876. The young artist accepted and thereafter became a leading figure in the movement. Easily the wealthiest of the group, Caillebotte first became known as a preeminent collector of Impressionism. His gift of the works of his fellow artists to the French state at his death in 1894 constitutes the foundation of the Impressionist collections of the Musée d'Orsay in Paris. Yet, perhaps because of his primacy as a collector, his achievement as a painter was overshadowed until the 1960s, when American art museums and international private collectors began to buy his work. His full achievement was recognized in his first monographic exhibition, held in Brooklyn and Houston in 1976, and in the landmark *The New Painting, Impressionism, 1874–1886*, a 1986 show in which Caillebotte's greatest works were placed in context with those of his Impressionist colleagues.[1]

The Bloch painting, at first sight, falls readily within the group of industrial landscapes executed by the Impressionists—particularly Pissarro and Monet—in the 1870s and 1880s. Caillebotte offset the industrial motif by presenting it within a landscape dominated by a sailboat moored on the Seine. The complex organization of this picture results from an extraordinarily intricate interlocking of fragments of pictorial space. The artist collapsed space, presenting the distant factories and smokestack and the furled-up sail and mast within a single orthogonal frame. See also the rhyming verticals of the smokestack on the left, the upright boat mast, and the gnarled, thin tree trunk that goes from the bottom to the top of the picture at the far right. All this is clearly part of a formal program that unifies the pictorial space in a tightly ordered composition. The artist has us sweep our eye across the entire picture plane, from its upper left corner to its lower right. This is not the result of happenstance or an arbitrary decision of the artist. It was Caillebotte's conscious effort to create a unifying, visual rhythm and an overall sense of calm and ease.

At the same time, these formal devices reflect the larger oppositions within French society, as alluded to in the landscape by Guillaumin (cat. no. 12). The most obvious contrast sets industry, signified by the factory, against the leisure activities of society, exemplified by the sailboat. More subtle is the fact that the sailboat and the factory, both centers of potential activity, are still and silent, devoid of human presence. The boat is unused; no movement can be seen around the factory. Meanwhile, the curious association between factory and boat is the focus of an ongoing poetic contemplation that itself generates meaning.

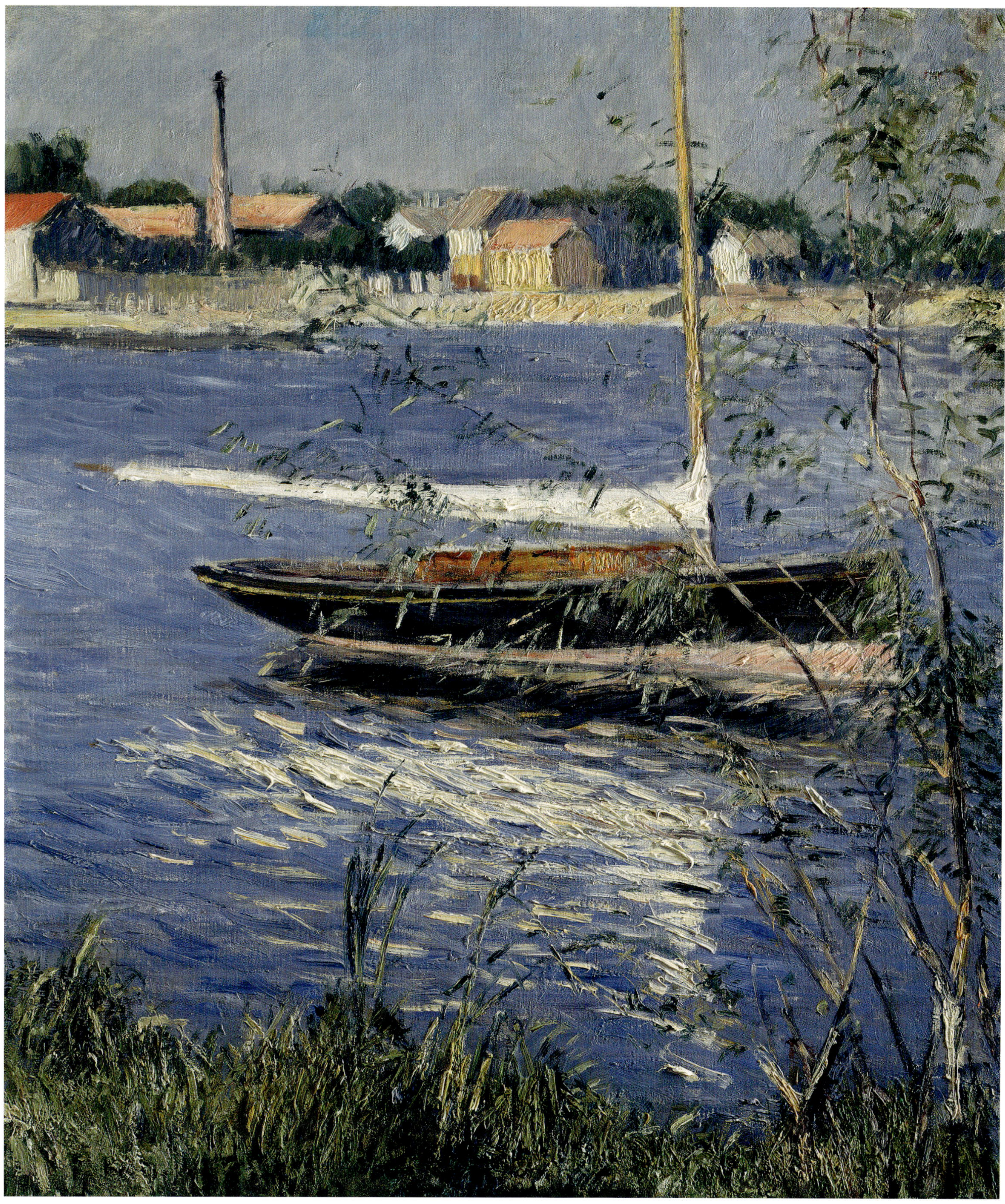

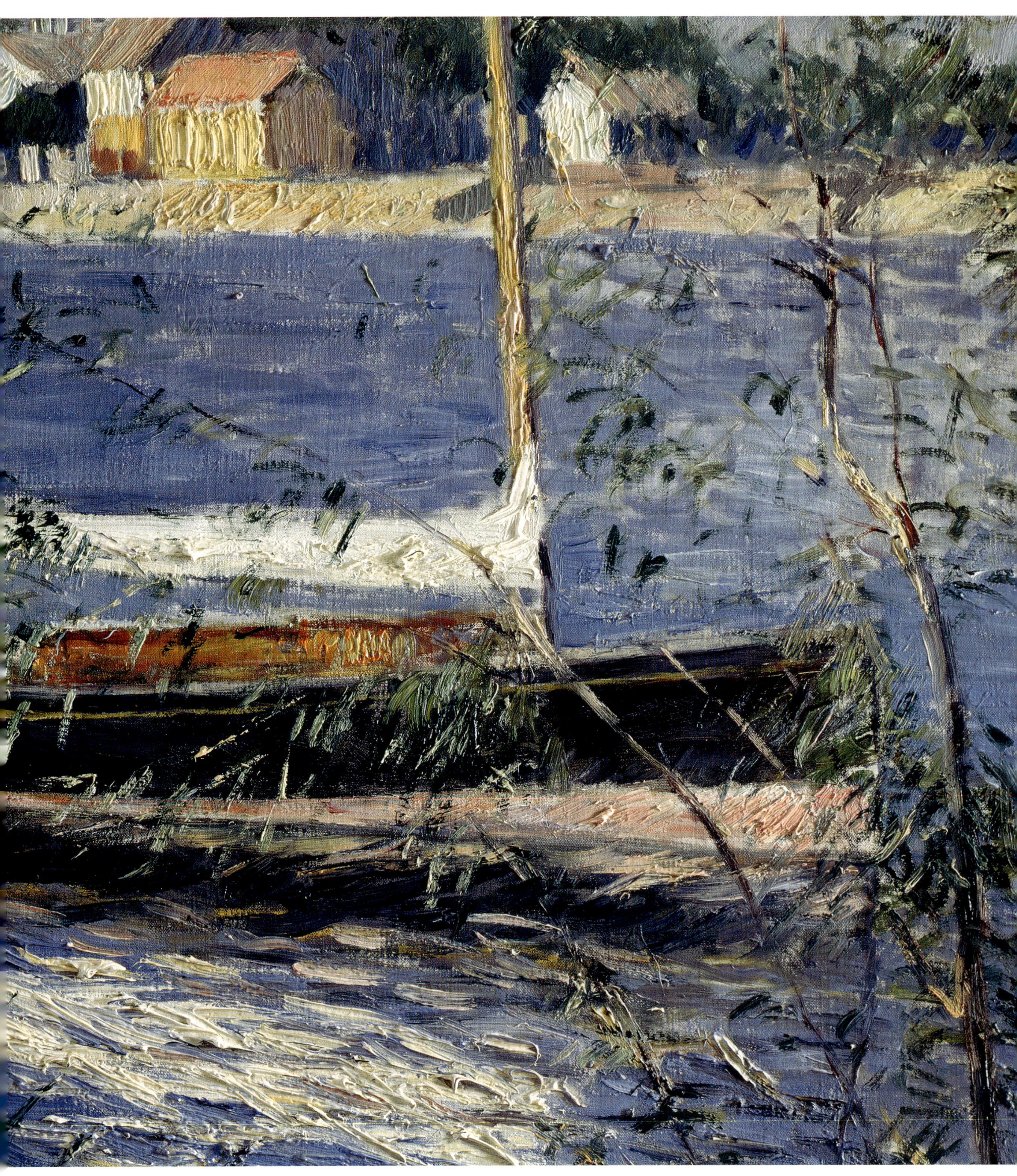

An underlying question about Caillebotte asks where he situated himself among the various aspects of this society. Was he on the side of the workers inside the factory? Or was he on the side of the people who sailed the boat? Clearly we know from Caillebotte's personal and social background that he was much more closely aligned with those who moored the boat, a boat that might very well have been his, than with the laborers in the factory on the riverbank. But this does not mean in any sense that the artist himself felt removed from the larger society. One thing is certain: it would have been far easier for him to edit out the factory; he would have thus produced a more "beautiful" (in the traditional and conservative sense), more bucolic, serene, and less troubled landscape. But this he did not do. Caillebotte, like many of his Impressionist colleagues, had no desire to cosmeticize society. What is interesting in the Impressionists' approach to reality is not that it favored industrialism over leisure, or vice versa, but that artists as varied as Caillebotte, Pissarro, Guillaumin, and Seurat presented both at the same time, in juxtaposition to each other, even as that juxtaposition was endlessly problematic.

Barnett Newman looked back at the Impressionists in a 1948 article that discussed art history from the Renaissance to modern times: "Michelangelo knew that the meaning of the Greek humanities for his time involved making Christ a man into Christ who is God. That his plastic problem was . . . to make a cathedral out of a man. In doing so he set a standard for sublimity that the painting of his time could not reach. Instead painting continued on its merry quest for a voluptuous art until in modern times the Impressionists, disgusted with its inadequacy, began the movement to destroy the established rhetoric of beauty by the Impressionists' insistence on a surface of ugly strokes."[2] The surface of "ugly strokes"—worth marveling about today—is a perfect description of how Caillebotte's picture was perceived during the 1880s. The artist insisted on these raw, quickly abbreviated, and coarsely intense brushstrokes (especially those visible in the reflection of the boom on the boat) to support the kind of reality he chose to depict. He made no effort to embellish anything. The thoughtful organization of the pictorial space clearly indicates that Caillebotte had come to this point of equilibrium and immediacy through a complex, calculated process. We can re-create this process mentally by going through the picture and identifying the manifold perceptions that are linked together in the interlocking elements of the composition. This complexity and organizational intelligence denote an important artist who has only recently been recognized for his significant contribution to Impressionism.

—JP

NOTES

1. J. Kirk T. Varnedoe et al., *Gustave Caillebotte: A Retrospective Exhibition* (Houston, 1976); Charles S. Moffett et al., *The New Painting, Impressionism, 1874–1886* (San Francisco, 1986).

2. Barnett Newman, "The Sublime Is Now," in *Selected Writings and Interviews*, ed. John P. O'Neill (Berkeley, 1992), p. 172.

Hilaire-Germain-Edgar Degas

French, 1834–1917

14. *Dancer Making Points (Danseuse faisant des pointes)*, 1879–80

Pastel and gouache on paper mounted on board, 19 × 14½ in. (48.2 × 36.8 cm); signed lower left: *Degas*

This is a remarkably beautiful work by Degas, an artist whose fascination with dancers defined his career and in part became his artistic signature. What distinguishes this particular work—besides its rich and varied media—is that the artist not only expressed a deep empathy for his model but also seems to have identified with her, not so much as a dancer but as someone who, like him, drew forms in space. There is a parallel between the artist and the performer he represented—both can be described as artists who put their minds or bodies through practiced rituals in order to express form. Just as his dancers are constantly seen stretching and exercising their limbs, Degas himself never ceased honing his skills as a draftsman. He was his own most severe critic, forcing himself to do the same thing, to produce the same figure, hundreds of times until he got it right.

For Degas, the foot of the dancer, as the title indicates, was "making points"—drawing figures or forms. The foot was to the dancer what the pastel crayon was to Degas; both artists created forms with their respective tools. There is, therefore, a much deeper empathy than one might think between artist and dancer. While many have stressed Degas's voyeuristic interest in dancers or have linked him with the Parisian leisured society to which he belonged, it would be reductive to imagine that the entire meaning of this work lies in the artist's gender and position in society.

Degas was a far more complex, demanding, and tenacious individual than simple categories can imply. Precisely because of its complexity, this particular work gives us a sense of Degas's visual curiosity. His treatment of space is especially moving. Degas represented the stage as a wide expanse of floorboards, almost like a minimalist surface extending in front of our eyes. This open space, a space of potential, almost fills the lower half of the composition and is animated only by the dancer. Thus the stage is for the dancer to conquer; as she is claiming that very space, the artist helps her along by charting her progress along the lines of the floorboards that fly away toward the right. For Degas, the dancer herself activated the stage. The chromatic sobriety of the stage floor creates a curious contrast with the effusion of background colors. The reserve and economy of the lower half of the composition are offset by the rich and explosive variety of brush marks in the upper part; greens versus light yellows, oranges, exuberant splashes of colors—in an almost abstract manner—bring the painted flats of the stage behind the dancer to life.

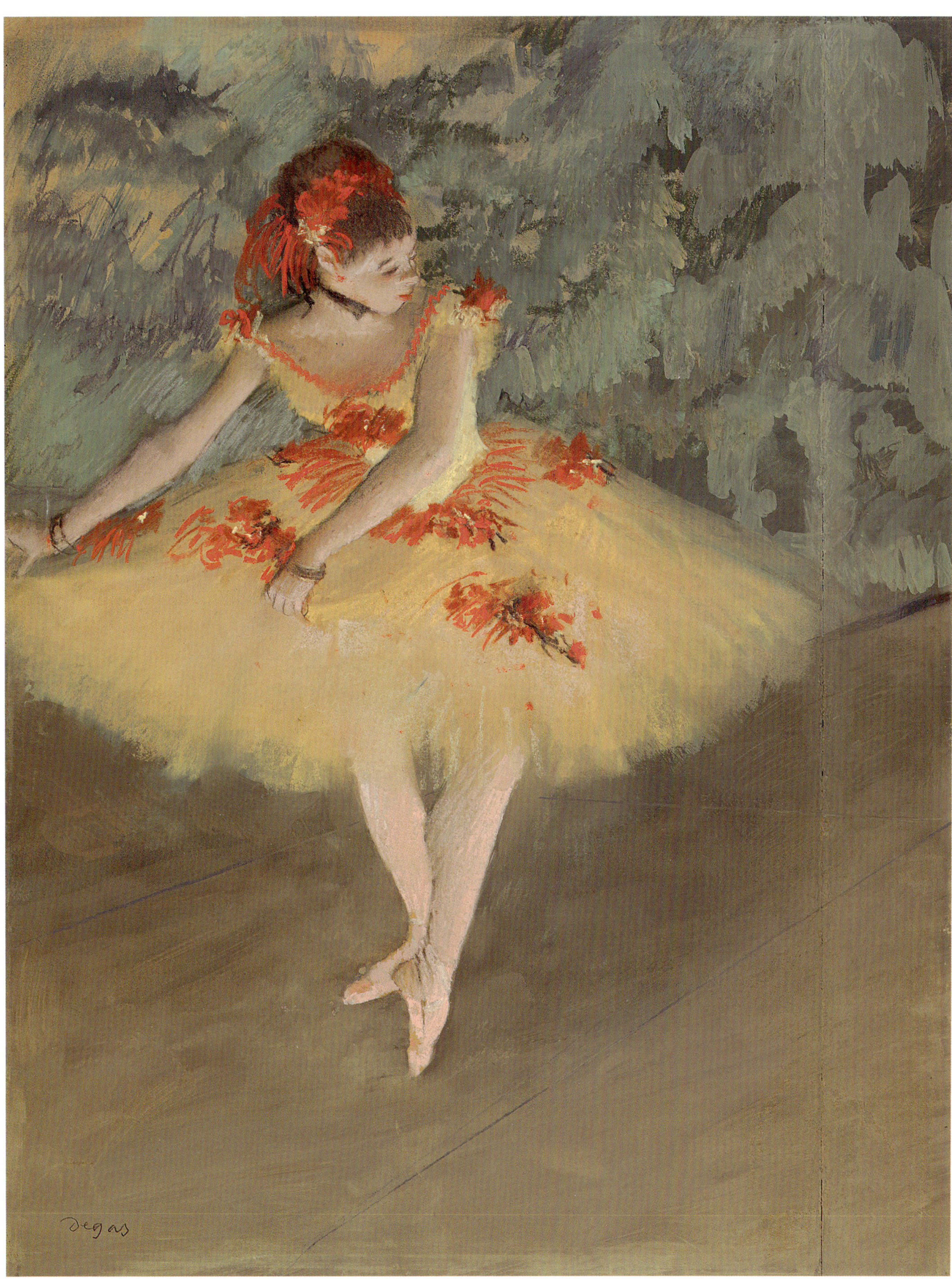

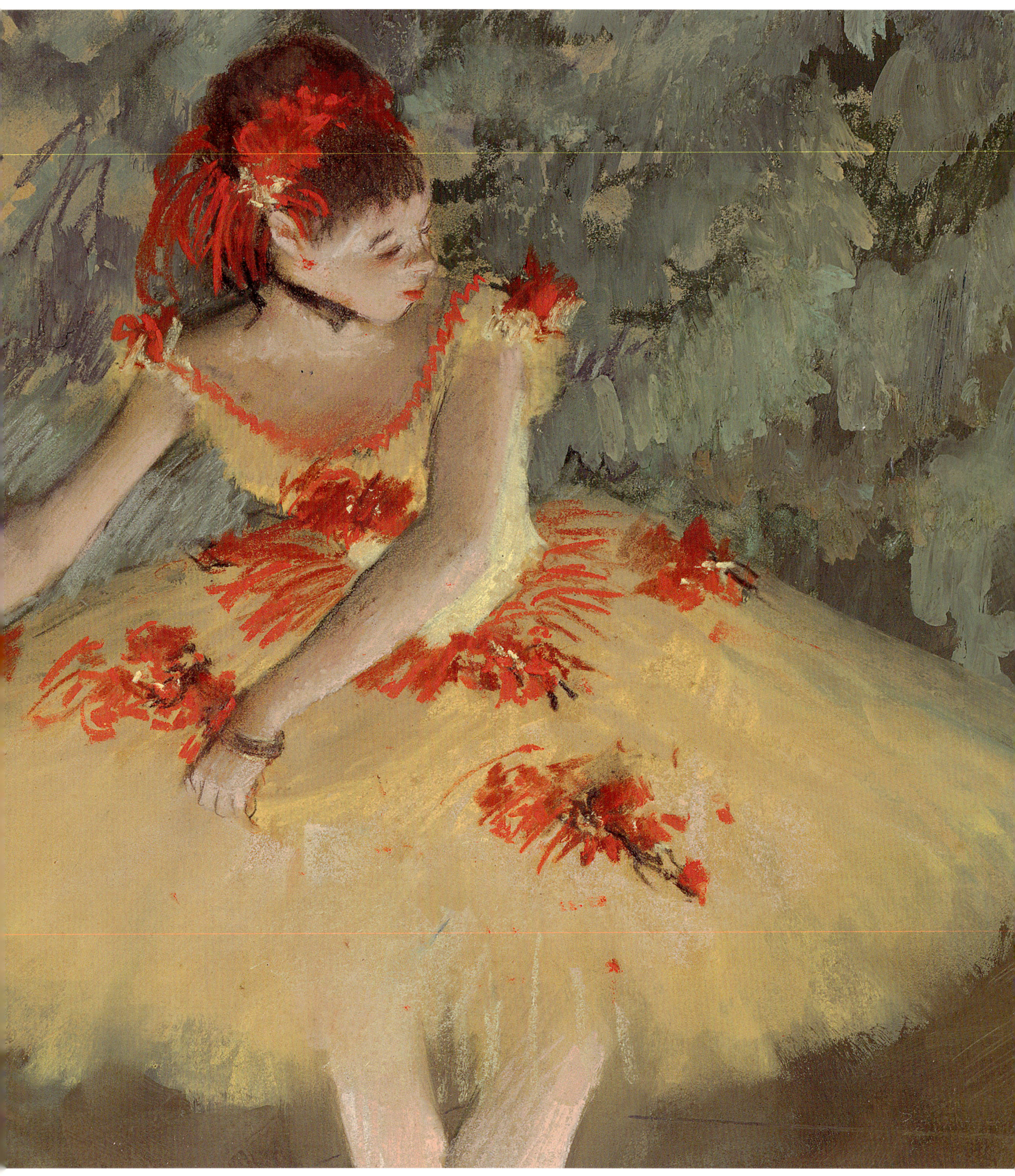

Everything about this work is stunning. The light molds the volumes of the arms and legs, highlighting the flesh seen through the stockings on those legs and drawing our attention to its light salmon pink. At the same time, the extraordinary diaphanous texture of the tutu absorbs and filters that very light, creating a paradoxical volume of void and tulle. The exquisite marks of the silk flowers on the tutu as well as the chain of tiny orange daubs that runs around the neckline give the work an almost spectral dimension. What, we might ask, is this painting all about, if not to give us a sense of the spectacle of a dance performance on a theater stage? As viewers we need only focus on the general glow that reverberates throughout the work, those marks of blazing orange, those pastel traces picked up by the artist, here and there, sending waves or echoes throughout the picture. They rhyme with other marks of the same color, as in the lips of the dancer and the tip of her ear and the red ribbon holding her hair. The color of her flesh is offset by the choker around her neck and by the pair of bracelets on her arms, which serve to both highlight and contrast the qualities of the light that engulfs her figure.

—JP

HILAIRE-GERMAIN-EDGAR DEGAS

French, 1834–1917

15. *Grande Arabesque, Third Time (Grande arabesque, troisième temps)*

Bronze, dark brown patina, 17⅞ × 22 × 10⅜ in. (45.5 × 56 × 26.5 cm); original wax model, c. 1882–95, cast, 1919–21; inscribed: *Degas*; stamped: *60/M* and *Cire Perdue A. A. Hébrard*

Degas exhibited only one sculpture in his long working life as an artist, *The Little Dancer of Fourteen Years*, which made its only public appearance in the Impressionist exhibition of 1881. The words "mixed media" can easily be applied to this masterpiece, which was made from various waxes on a metal armature fixed to a wooden base with the addition of linen, tulle, human hair, dancer's shoes, and a silk ribbon to bring the little dancer to life. Smaller than life-size but large enough to be commanding, she looked as much like a scientific model or wax effigy as a work of art. Most early viewers found her ugly and even hideously vulgar. Whether Degas was affected by the negative criticism, we will never know definitively. But he never again exhibited sculpture. Yet he made nearly two hundred three-dimensional works, all with wax on wire armatures mounted in wood. He kept these pieces at home, where few people saw them, and those who did spoke of them as having been stored (rather than displayed) on shelves in large glass vitrines. Scholars have conclusively shown that the artist actually used individual sculptures as models for figures or horses in now famous pastels, drawings, and oil paintings, actually preferring the silence and stability of a wax sculpture to the variability on all counts of a live model.[1] It is also clear from the sculptures themselves that, in certain cases, Degas actually heated the wax, bent the armature, and re-formed the horse or figure to adapt it to different pictorial needs. Hence Degas's sculptures can be described not only as models but also as works in progress.

Others, principally the great dealer Paul Durand-Ruel, tried to convince Degas to have his sculptures cast in bronze, a medium the artist had never used. But it was not until 1919, two years after his death, that seventy-three wax sculptures were cast in bronze. An enormous amount has been written about this process, from the creation of an entire set of bronze *modèles*, to be used as the basis for subsequent casting (now in the collection of the Norton Simon Museum, Pasadena, California), to the making of editioned casts, which are now scattered in public and private collections throughout the world. The Parisian bronze-casting firm of A. A. Hébrard carried out the entire project, stamping the individual bronzes in each edition with a letter from A to T. None of the bronzes from the original waxes was cast or even supervised by Degas, so we can only speculate about his intentions for their use, patination, or exhibition.

Because the original Degas waxes were so fragile, Hébrard cast a single bronze *modèle* from each that could sustain editioned casting, and this was chased and worked to be as close to the

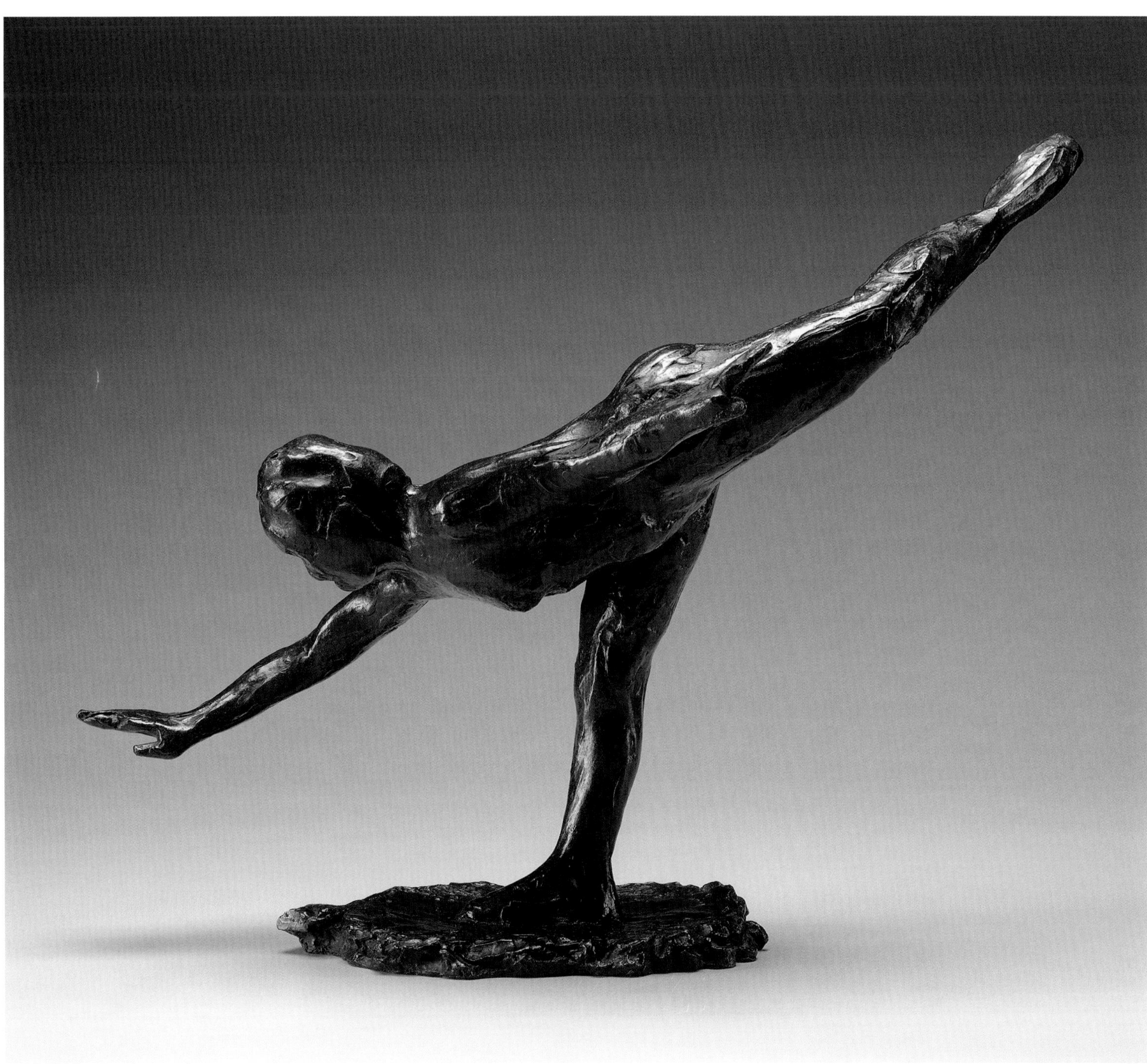

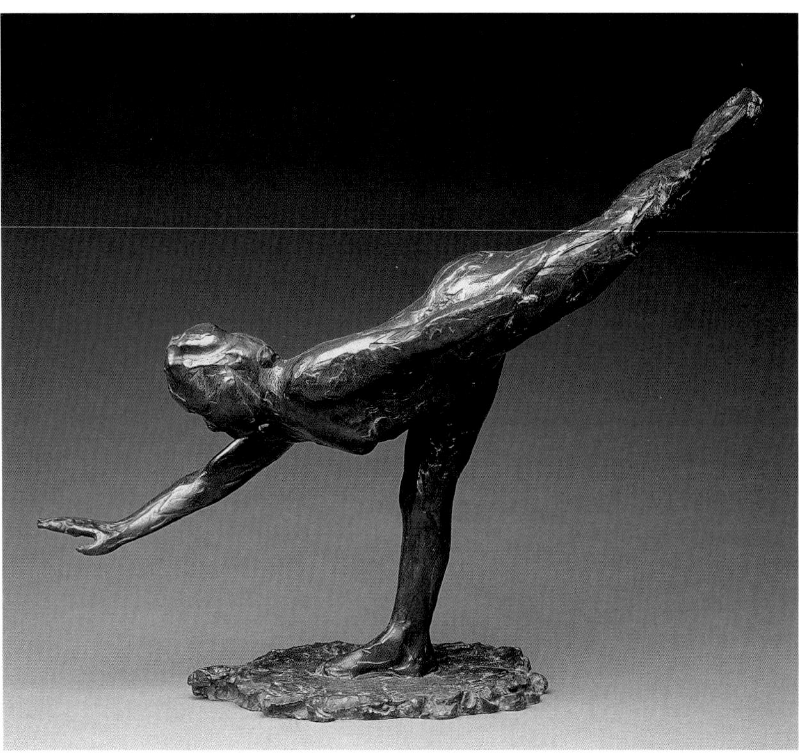

FIG. 28 Edgar Degas, *Dancer, Grande Arabesque, Third Time* (first study), wood and wax, 18⅜ × 20¾ × 10⅛ in. (46.5 × 52.7 × 25.5 cm), Musée du Louvre, Paris

wax original as possible. Hence each editioned bronze was checked for accuracy not against the wax but the more durable *modèle*. Complete sets of the editioned bronzes can be found at the Metropolitan Museum of Art (the Havemeyer family helped to finance the project and received a complete set), the Musée d'Orsay in Paris, and the Museu de Artes de São Paulo, Brazil. The Bloch bronze, stamped with the letter M, was made indirectly from a wax now in the Musée du Louvre (fig. 28) and directly from the appropriate *modèle* (fig. 29).

The figure in the Bloch bronze is performing what is known in ballet as a "grand arabesque." Degas himself studied the pose in several media before making the sculpture, which scholars have dated broadly from 1882 to 1885. Like most ballet positions, this one is to be held long enough to be admired by the audience as a test of the strength and balance of the individual dancer. Degas preferred the close study of these stable poses to the quick movements—the leaps and jetés—often associated with performance and with the Impressionists' interest in the representation of motion. The generic quality of the body suggests that Degas made the wax original not from a real ballerina hired as a model but from drawings and memories of the numerous performances and rehearsals he had witnessed. This remove from life allowed Degas to treat the entire body rather than to imagine the forms beneath the large tulle skirts worn by dancers onstage. In life as in his own art, it was the process, and not the product or result, that interested him.

The various positions of the dancer while performing an arabesque fascinated Degas, who made seven different waxes representing the position. In his catalogue of the bronzes, John Rewald grouped and numbered these "Rewald 36–42."[2] These waxes, perplexingly, are given different dates, from 1880 to 1890, without any real evidence. Degas's arabesque studies include two works in which the upper body is raised above the arm; two in which the line of the sculpture traces the body and left leg, but not the right arm; and three in which the upper body bends beneath the raised leg. Each is of a somewhat noticeably different scale, suggesting that they were made one by one and not as an ensemble. No two are alike in pose, and this proves that Degas ultimately was interested in balance and technique more than sequential motion.

There are cracks in the wax original along the buttocks and raised leg of the figure, suggesting that Degas probably broke, reheated, and re-formed this figure until the contours and physical balance were correct for his new purpose. He may even have changed the position more completely, but we do not know this. What he wanted to achieve in wax was the long, continuous diagonal line through the body, running from the right hand to the left foot of the dancer. Once the line was in place, he could observe its effect on the rest of the body, and Degas often represented ballet figures from unconventional angles so as to emphasize the sheer effort and strength needed in the proper execution of the dancer's art. Degas was the first in a long line of painter-sculptors in modern art—Matisse, Picasso, Miró, Newman—and his works play equally important roles in the histories of modern painting and of modern sculpture.

—RB

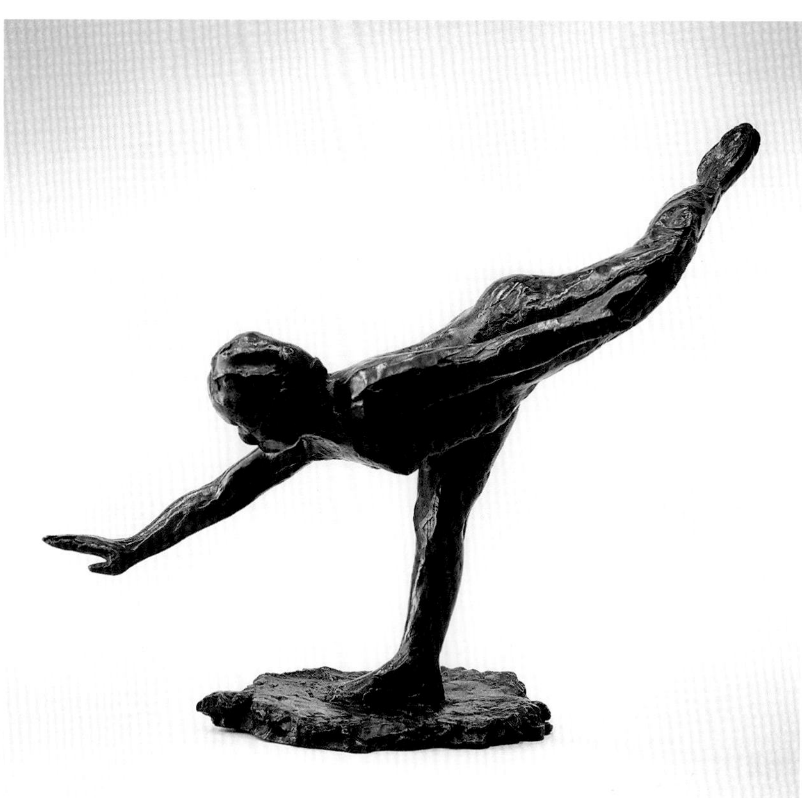

FIG. 29 Edgar Degas, *Grande Arabesque, Third Time*, 1882–95, bronze, 17⅝ × 25⅛ × 9⅞ in. (44.8 × 63.8 × 25 cm). Norton Simon Art Foundation

NOTES

1. So many scholars have discussed the interplay of Degas's "sculptured models" and his pictorial work that their findings are difficult to summarize. Richard Kendall has been the most persistent of these students; see his *Degas and the Little Dancer* (New Haven, 1998) and his essay "The Role of Sculpture," in *Degas beyond Impressionism* (New Haven, 1996), pp. 254–75. Richard Thomson has also dealt seriously with these relationships in *Degas: The Nudes* (London, 1988), pp. 119–224. The most succinct early discussion of the interplay between sculpture and painting can be found in George T. M. Shackleford's "A Way of Seeing Form," in *Degas: The Dancers* (Washington, D.C., 1985), pp. 64–83.

2. More than fifty years after its appearance, the most persuasive book on Degas's sculpture is John Rewald's *Degas, Works in Sculpture: A Complete Catalogue* (New York, 1956). Museum publications for the three best remaining "complete sets" of the bronzes can also be consulted at the Musée d'Orsay, Paris; the Museu de Artes de São Paulo, Brazil; and the Metropolitan Museum of Art, New York.

Pierre-Auguste Renoir

French, 1841–1919

16. *Woman Leaning on Her Elbows (Femme accoudée)*, 1875–85

Oil on canvas, 5½ × 9 in. (15 × 24 cm); signed lower left: *Renoir*

At the time of his death in 1919, Pierre-Auguste Renoir had been considered the greatest living French painter for more than a decade. His rival as an Impressionist figure painter, Edgar Degas, had all but stopped painting by 1900, and Renoir's close friend, Paul Cézanne, died in 1906. Although Claude Monet outlived Renoir by seven years, the fact that he was essentially a pure landscape painter kept him out of the pantheon of true greatness in art, which, since the Renaissance, had been reserved for painters of the human form. Like many artists with extravagant reputations in their lifetimes—one thinks immediately of Andrea del Sarto, Peter Paul Rubens, and Jean-Honoré Fragonard—the status of Renoir fell sharply after his death, and, by the time of World War II, his paintings, though popular with collectors, were considered saccharine and morally empty by art historians and professional art critics. Yet, as with all such declines, a correction was due, and, with the scholarship of Barbara Ehrlich White, John House, Anne Distel, and Christopher Riopelle, Renoir's star is beginning once more to rise.

This painting—a small oil study on canvas—occupies an important place in the larger study of Renoir's art because it was made from life of an unposed figure. Renoir seems to have begun the practice of informal figure study in the mid-1870s, when he had a studio and apartment with a small garden in Montmartre where friends would drop by. While chatting with the painter and each other, they became the subjects of small-scale oil sketches, which were, for Renoir, a form of pictorial practice. Renoir did not paint them as studies for particular figures in already conceived compositions but, instead, as exercises in rapid figural transcription. In this he demonstrated his opposition to a centuries-old studio practice in which artists "studied" carefully posed models, who maintained their positions for hours on end. For Renoir, it was important that the modern painter transcribe the modern figure literally from life, not from an artificial pose. Indeed, in the mid-1870s, Renoir painted scores of such paintings as he began to conceive his first truly informal group figure painting, *Le Moulin de la Galette* (Musée d'Orsay, Paris), which appeared in the third group exhibition of the Impressionists in 1877. In a lengthy essay, the young critic Georges Rivière characterized Renoir as an artist who made even large-scale paintings "from life," and he actually claimed that Renoir painted the large and complex *Le Moulin de la Galette* directly in the beer garden itself rather than in his nearby studio.[1]

Many small Renoir paintings from the mid-1870s survive, but there is little doubt that the artist destroyed or threw away many more. His quest for an informal immediacy was so intense

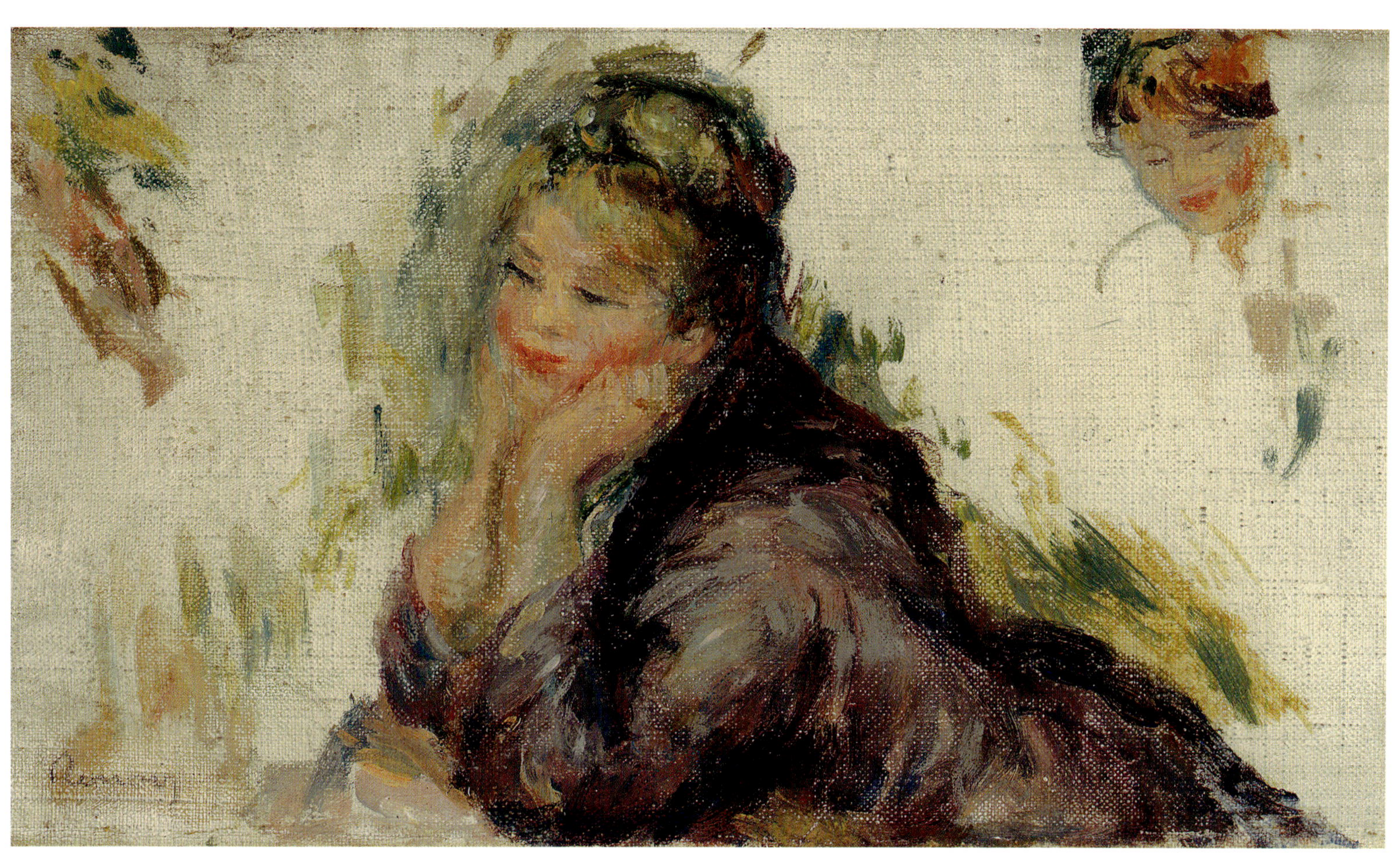

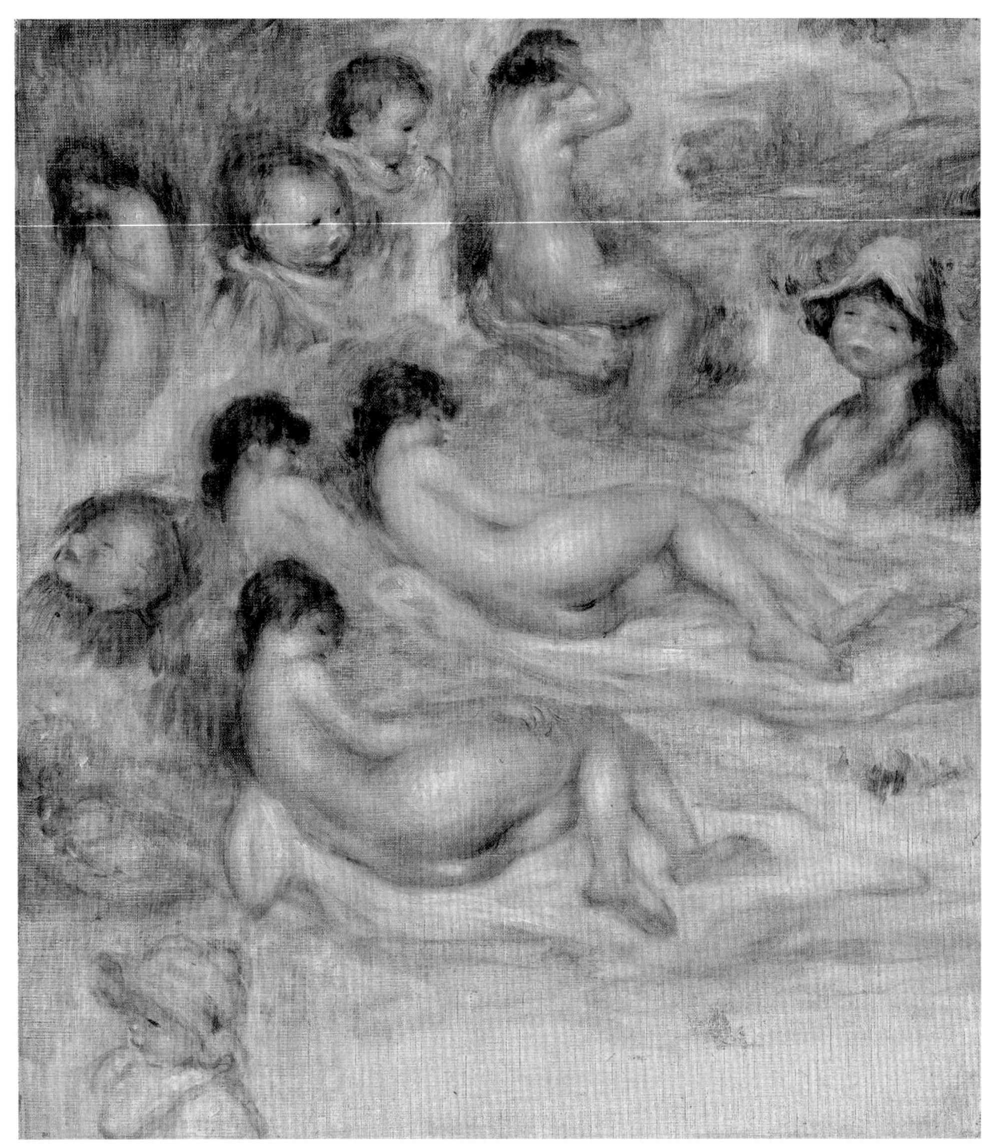

FIG. 30 Pierre-Auguste Renoir, *Studies of Pierre Renoir; His Mother, Aline Charigot; Nudes; and Landscape*, 1885–86, oil on canvas, 18⅛ × 15½ in. (46.1 × 39.2 cm). The Art Institute of Chicago, restricted gift of The Phillips Family Collection

during those years that he worked with increasing ardor to capture unposed figures rapidly in oil. Indeed, his art of that time can be contrasted sharply with that of the other major Impressionist figure painter, Edgar Degas (cat. no. 14), who was so calculated in his pictorial decisions. Renoir represented his figures naturally as they sat, walked, chatted, danced, or ate, dressed in their ordinary clothes, and placed seemingly without being "composed" on the pictorial surface. His figural art was more thoroughly impressionistic than that of his colleagues Degas and Caillebotte, who each specialized in highly contrived compositions of modern figures.

It is difficult to place the Bloch painting securely in time because of its sheer informality. Its strokes of paint are larger than is the norm for the surviving small-scale paintings of the mid-1870s, and it lacks the suave elegance of the figure studies from the 1880s, such as an extraordinary set of separate studies on a single canvas now in Chicago (fig. 30). We know that

Renoir made many small figure paintings in the 1890s, but the blocky strokes of paint in the Bloch picture are not at all in accord with the mellifluous, contour-hugging smooth surfaces of those canvases. And there is no real affinity with the numerous small works of the first decade of the twentieth century, when Renoir painted various subjects on long continuous rolls of canvas, the most successful of which he cut out for his dealer to stretch separately. The quivering facture of the arthritic elderly artist is not at all evident in the confident strokes of the Bloch painting.

The largest single collection of paintings by Renoir in the world, at the Barnes Foundation in Merion, Pennsylvania, contains numerous small-scale figural studies, many of which remain unpublished to this day. This, and the fact that Renoir remains the only great Impressionist painter without a catalogue raisonné—or even an illustrated list of his complete works—means that it is not possible to date this painting conclusively in relation to other documented works. Perhaps when the Wildenstein Institute, Paris, completes this monumental task a decade from now, the Bloch Renoir will find its rightful place in the oeuvre of one of the greatest French painters in history.

—RB

NOTE

1. Georges Rivière, in *L'impressioniste* (1877), reprinted in Ruth Berson, ed., *The New Painting: Impressionism, 1874–1886: Documentation* (San Francisco, 1996), vol. 1, pp. 179–87.

Pierre-Auguste Renoir

French, 1841–1919

17. *The Flowered Hat (Le chapeau épinglé)*, 1890–95

Pastel on paper, 25⅝ × 20⅛ in. (65 × 51 cm); signed lower right: *Renoir*

For most members of the art public, the pastel medium and Edgar Degas are virtually synonymous. Yet, although that great artist made the most important and experimental contributions to the medium, other avant-garde artists also practiced it with enthusiasm, and a well-selected exhibition of Impressionist pastels would feature major works by Pissarro, Monet, Sisley, Renoir, Jean-François Raffaëlli, Jean-Louis Forain, and Boudin as well as Degas. If one were to add the brilliant pastels of their mentor, Édouard Manet, the exhibition would prove the real renaissance in a medium that had last been important in French art of the eighteenth century. Pastel seems to have arrived in France from Italy in the eighteenth century and was so enthusiastically received that most of the greatest French artists of that century used the colored crayons. Yet by the late eighteenth century and the ascendancy of Jacques-Louis David, the medium all but died as a vehicle for serious artists, and, as a consequence, very few pastels survive by French artists from David through Delacroix. The pastel revival of the last third of the nineteenth century took place largely through the example of Jean-François Millet as well as through the efforts of Eugène Boudin (cat. no. 3). The writings of the two great critics Jules and Edmond de Goncourt, whose essays on eighteenth-century French art in the 1860s discussed the medium fervently, also led to a reassessment of its qualities by the most important artists of their time.

Renoir was, perhaps, the Impressionist most often—and most persuasively—linked to the eighteenth-century masters François Boucher and Jean-Honoré Fragonard. Like them, he used the human figure as a carrier of emotion, and, also like them, he preferred the sunnier side of life to the socially and sexually ambiguous urban realms of Manet and Degas. Of all the Impressionists, his contribution to the pastel medium is the least well documented. No scholar or amateur has compiled a catalogue raisonné of Renoir's drawings, leaving a significant gap in the history of art.[1] Without the benefit of the full context in which individual works of art were made, Renoir's entire oeuvre cannot be intelligently assessed—unlike virtually any other major figure of his generation.

This important signed pastel by Renoir is thus impossible to place or date with precision. Renoir himself preferred not to date his works, frustrating those pedants among us who are obsessed with chronology. Fortunately, the Bloch pastel belongs to a family of works in various media that represent the same composition of two young women, and these have been assigned

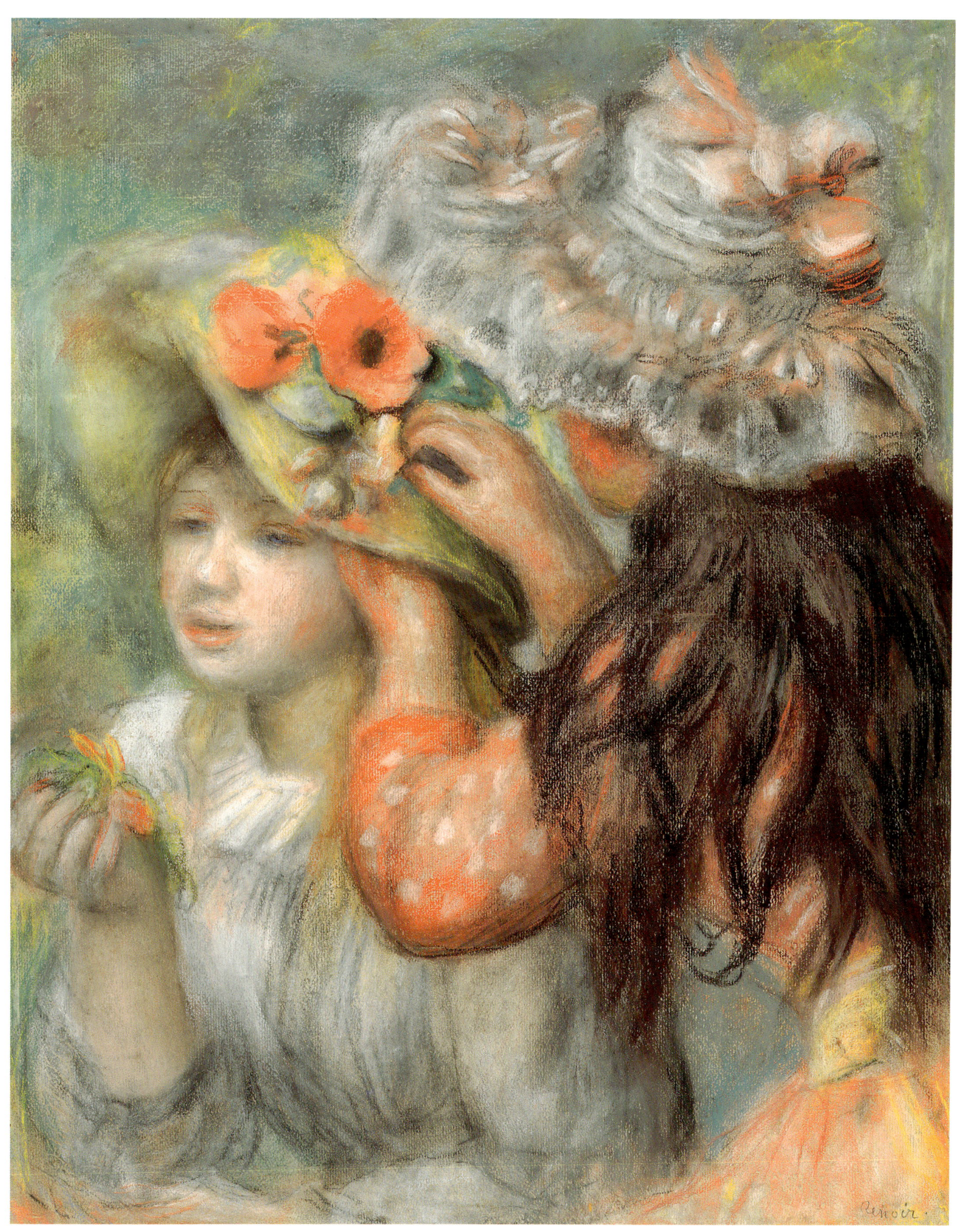
Renoir.

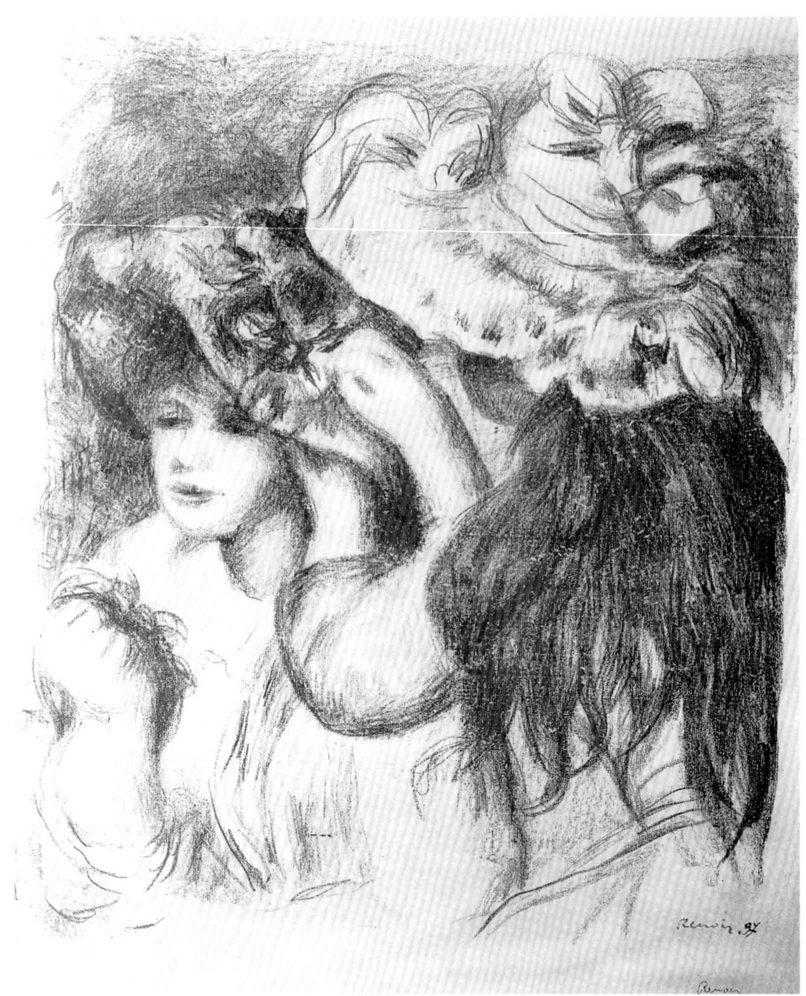

FIG. 31 Pierre-Auguste Renoir, *The Hat Pin (Le chapeau épingle)*, 1897, lithograph (Delteil 29), 24½ × 19½ in. (62 × 49.3 cm). National Gallery of Art, Washington, Rosenwald Collection

dates. The series of prints of the composition—three etchings and a lithograph—are compellingly catalogued by Joseph G. Stella.[2] He dates the etchings to circa 1894, because one of them appeared in Gustave Geoffroy's *La vie artistique*, published in 1894 in Paris; this etching and another of the same composition appeared again in publications in 1910, 1914, and even after Renoir's death in 1921. Renoir actually dated the lithograph on the stone to 1897, showing the comparatively long life the composition had for him (fig. 31). The very ubiquity of the composition across several media proves that, along with the famous image of young girls at the piano, found in both paint and print (there are painted versions in the Metropolitan Museum of Art, the Musée d'Orsay, and the Hermitage), it was a signature motif for the painter.

The subject Renoir chose has deep roots both in his art and in that of his fellow Impressionist Degas. Both artists were fascinated by women's hats—Degas by their production in the picturesque milliners' shops of Paris (the Nelson-Atkins owns a superb pastel by Degas on this motif; fig. 32) and Renoir by their informal decoration by women who bought simple hats and then personalized them with ribbons and flowers. For Degas, the hat was the thoroughly

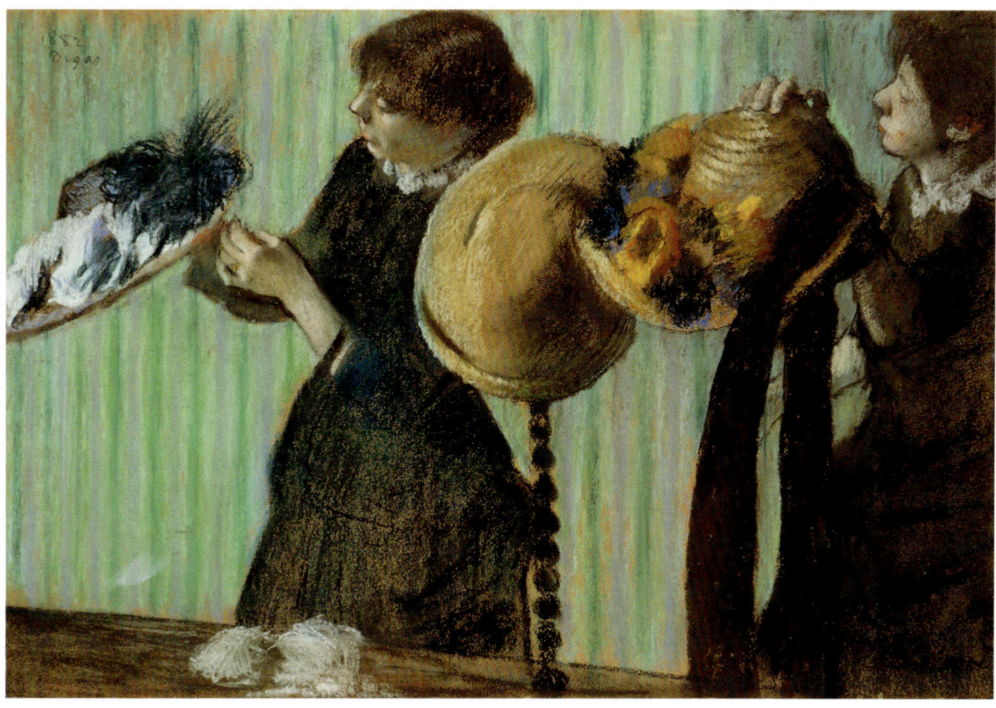

FIG. 32 Edgar Degas, *Little Milliners*, 1882, pastel on paper, 19¼ × 28¼ in. (48.9 × 71.8 cm). The Nelson-Atkins Museum of Art, Kansas City

professional achievement of a practiced artist, and there is even evidence that he identified with his milliners—as Joachim Pissarro has shown he did with his dancers (see cat. no. 14)—in their mutual attempts to create beauty from simple means.

Renoir's easy sensuality was evident from the very earliest moments of his career as a painter of pastoral scenes on porcelain, and for him, a hat that a woman adorned with fresh or silk flowers was more beautiful and personal than an expensive store-bought one. Renoir's writings on the decorative arts clearly show that the artist was an enemy of anything made by machine and valued, above all else, personal expression in handwork.[3] In the early 1880s Renoir painted his now-famous *Two Sisters* (fig. 33), which he exhibited in the penultimate Impressionist exhibition of 1882. Here the silk flowers on the hats are compared both to fresh flowers and to brilliantly colored yarns in a basket proffered to the viewer by the younger sister. The visual implication is that color can be found both in nature and in art, and even untrained girls can create colored realms with material from a garden or a nearby sewing shop.

The Bloch pastel represents two young girls, perhaps in late adolescence, one of whom adjusts the trimmings on the hat of her companion. The girls are a study in contrast, one with flowing brunette hair, and the other with reddish hair, which makes it possible to identify the latter as Julie Manet, the daughter of the Impressionist painter Berthe Morisot and her husband, Eugène Manet, the famous artist's younger brother. The same figures have been identified in the etchings, and the dark-haired girl is said to be a cousin of Julie Manet.[4] Renoir loved to contrast hair colors and made almost a fetish of painting the long, flowing tresses of blond, brunette, and

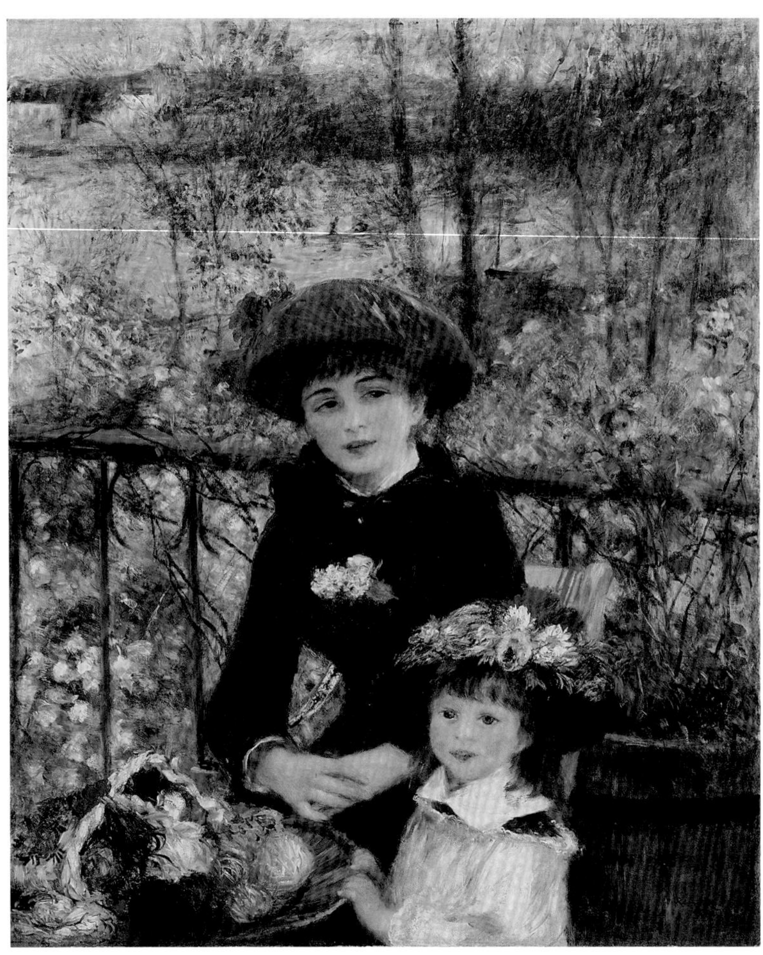

FIG. 33 Pierre-Auguste Renoir, *Two Sisters (On the Terrace)*, 1881, oil on canvas, 39⅝ × 31⅞ in. (100.5 × 81 cm). The Art Institute of Chicago, Mr. and Mrs. Lewis Larned Coburn Memorial Collection

auburn-haired models. Morisot herself often painted Julie's red hair, derived from the Manet side of the family (see the wonderful late painting in the Bloch Collection, cat. no. 18). Renoir was close to the entire Manet family. An intimate friend of both parents, he painted both Julie and her mother. After Morisot died in 1895, he served as executor of her estate, and he was Julie's legal guardian following the death of Eugène Manet. It is perhaps for that reason that Renoir made repeated use of an earlier composition featuring Julie Manet in the year of her mother's death, when the first of the three etchings of this composition was published.

Technically, the Bloch pastel is fascinating. Conservators have noted that it must at one time have been mounted on canvas and stretched, and the remains of puckering from the stretcher can be seen in all four corners of the composition. Yet it seems to have been removed from the canvas and remounted at an early point in its life, perhaps even by Renoir or a studio helper, because the top and bottom edges of the paper have been unfolded and mounted directly on a piece of cardboard. This suggests a complex physical history for the pastel—more so than is usual for Renoir. Perhaps the explanation can be found in the powdery, faint surface of the pastel itself. Because Renoir reversed the composition in the etchings, and then reversed it again in the lithograph, one can speculate that this pastel either might have been a counterproof of another pastel or was itself the basis for a counterproof (a reverse impression made by passing a print or drawing through a press with a sheet of dampened paper).[5] Although there is no documentary proof that Renoir employed this practice, there is plenty of evidence in the pastels of Degas, Pissarro, and Gauguin that his contemporaries did. Peter Segers of the Art Institute of Chicago, who has studied this technique more than anyone, has demonstrated that it is possible to make as many as three counterproofs from a single pastel armature, whereby an artist can effectively create four "originals" from one work, with perhaps a bit of touch-up on the final impression or two.[6] For a composition particularly appealing to collectors, this technique would have been both convenient and efficient. Until other impressions related directly to the Bloch pastel can be found, we can only surmise from the similarities between its surface and that of other known counterproofs that Renoir adopted the practice.

The sultry innocence of this work makes it appealing to all viewers. The fact that the girls have been identified as cousins—and as family friends of the painter—allows us to gaze at it without a hint of prurience. Yet Renoir's visual obsession with the sense of touch is surely communicated to the viewer, who yearns to caress the lustrous hair of Julie's cousin, to touch the youthful flesh of their innocent arms, to place a finger gently on the soft cheek of young Julie Manet. Renoir communicated this sensuous tactility in every medium he used for this glorious composition—through the multiple etched lines, through the soft side of a lithographic crayon, through the fine hairs of a brush in oil paint, and through the crumbling powder of pastel. If, as we have deduced from physical and circumstantial evidence, this pastel itself was printed (or printed from), Renoir himself touched it lovingly as he sought to replicate the work for the pleasure of others.

—RB

NOTES

1. The great Impressionist scholar John Rewald wrote a well-illustrated monograph on Renoir's drawings just as he did for Gauguin, but it includes only a tiny fraction of works on paper by the master.
2. Joseph G. Stella, *The Graphic Work of Renoir* (Bradford and London, n.d.), nos. 6–8, 29–30.
3. Robert L. Herbert, *Nature's Workshop: Renoir's Writings on the Decorative Arts* (New Haven, 2000).
4. Stella, *The Graphic Work of Renoir*, no. 6.
5. Conservators have noted that the paper originally was stretched, as can be seen from raised indentations 1.5 cm from the top and bottom edges.
6. See Richard R. Brettell et al., *The Art of Paul Gauguin* (Chicago, 1988), esp. pp. 297–378.

Berthe Morisot

French, 1841–1895

18. *Under the Orange Tree (Sous l'oranger)*, 1889

Oil on canvas, 21½ × 25⅞ in. (54.6 × 65.7 cm); estate stamp lower right: *Berthe Morisot*

The Impressionists were the earliest professional association of artists to admit women and men equally. Their first group exhibition, which opened in Paris on April 15, 1874, featured the work of Berthe Morisot, and she was joined as the years went on by other women, the most prominent of whom was the American Mary Cassatt. Morisot continued with the Impressionists through thick and thin, exhibiting in seven of the eight exhibitions they organized between 1874 and 1886, taking one year off in 1879 after the birth of her daughter and only child, Julie Manet. The great painter Édouard Manet had befriended Morisot in the late 1860s and, rather than treating her simply as a muse, spurred her to adopt an ambitious independent career as a painter. Édouard was already married when the two met, and both Manet and Morisot were of sufficient social and economic standing that they did not accept a physical relationship. It was Manet's sensitive and intelligent brother, Eugène, who married Morisot and provided the stability and the family connections she sought.

Morisot's work was well known during her lifetime and appreciated by many upper-class French collectors and by the painters Manet and Renoir. Few of the early American and British collectors of Impressionist pictures purchased her works, and her large oeuvre became part of the extensive art holdings of her daughter and son-in-law following her death in 1895. For that reason, Morisot's work was not effectively rediscovered until the late twentieth century, when catalogues and exhibitions have allowed us to become better acquainted with this essential member of the Impressionist group.

Like many of her colleagues, Morisot underwent a kind of pictorial crisis in the mid-1880s, when the group began to disintegrate. Her work before that date had been very freely painted and, to some eyes, almost messy in its brushwork. Her figures merged into their backgrounds, and her landscapes were alive with quivering touches of paint. Yet, by the mid-1880s, Morisot began almost to draw with paint, caressing the figures and forms with enveloping lines so that they attain a physical fullness lacking in her earlier work. Morisot was among the first to see Renoir's *Large Bathers* (Philadelphia Museum of Art) on a visit to the artist's studio in January 1886, and the very sight of this masterpiece made her realize that her painting would have to respond to the new solidity and almost classical grandeur he sought to reinject into French painting.

Unlike her male counterparts, who painted a good deal of the public realm, Morisot, as a wealthy bourgeois woman, was unable to walk through Paris alone, to visit cafés and restaurants

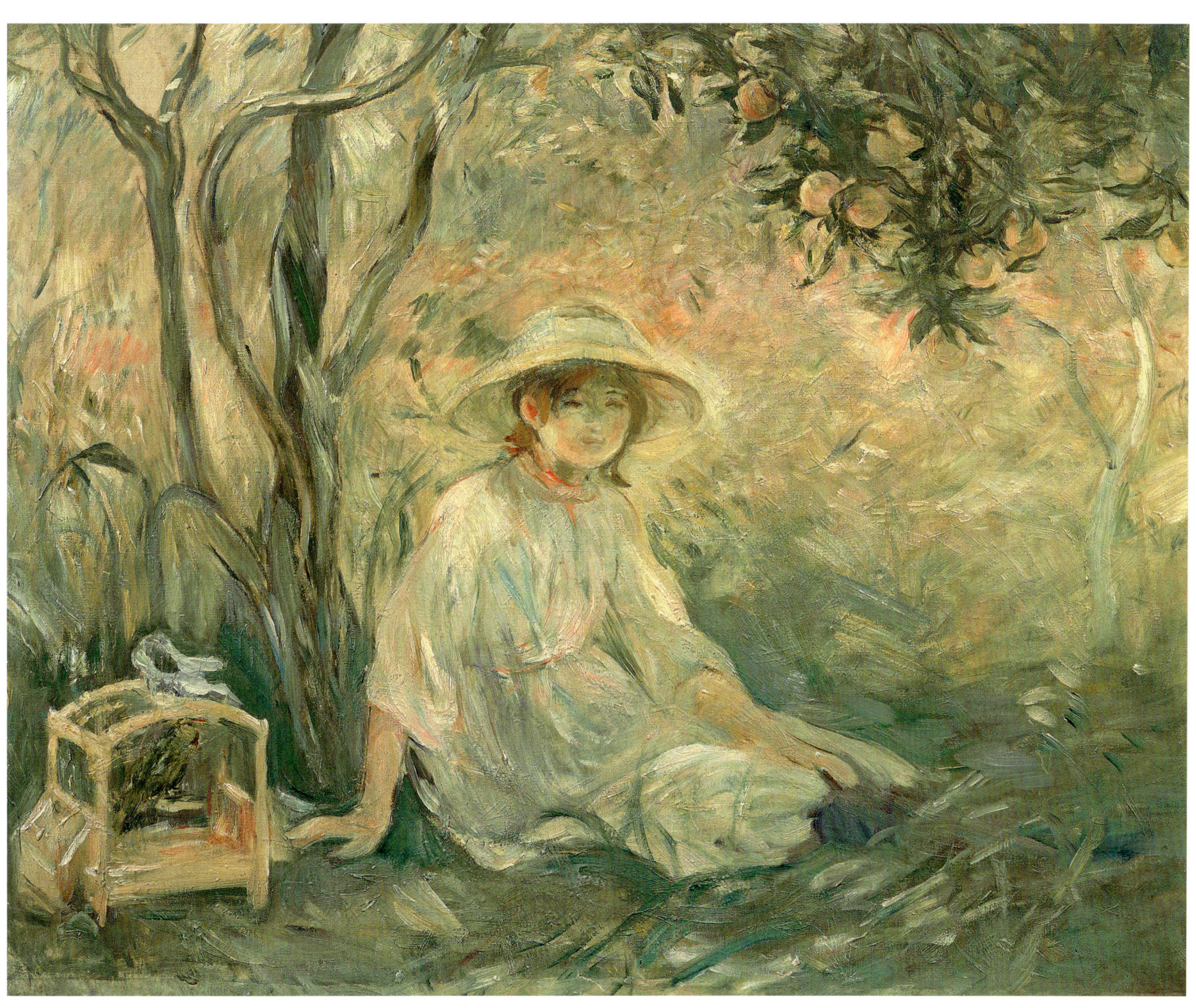

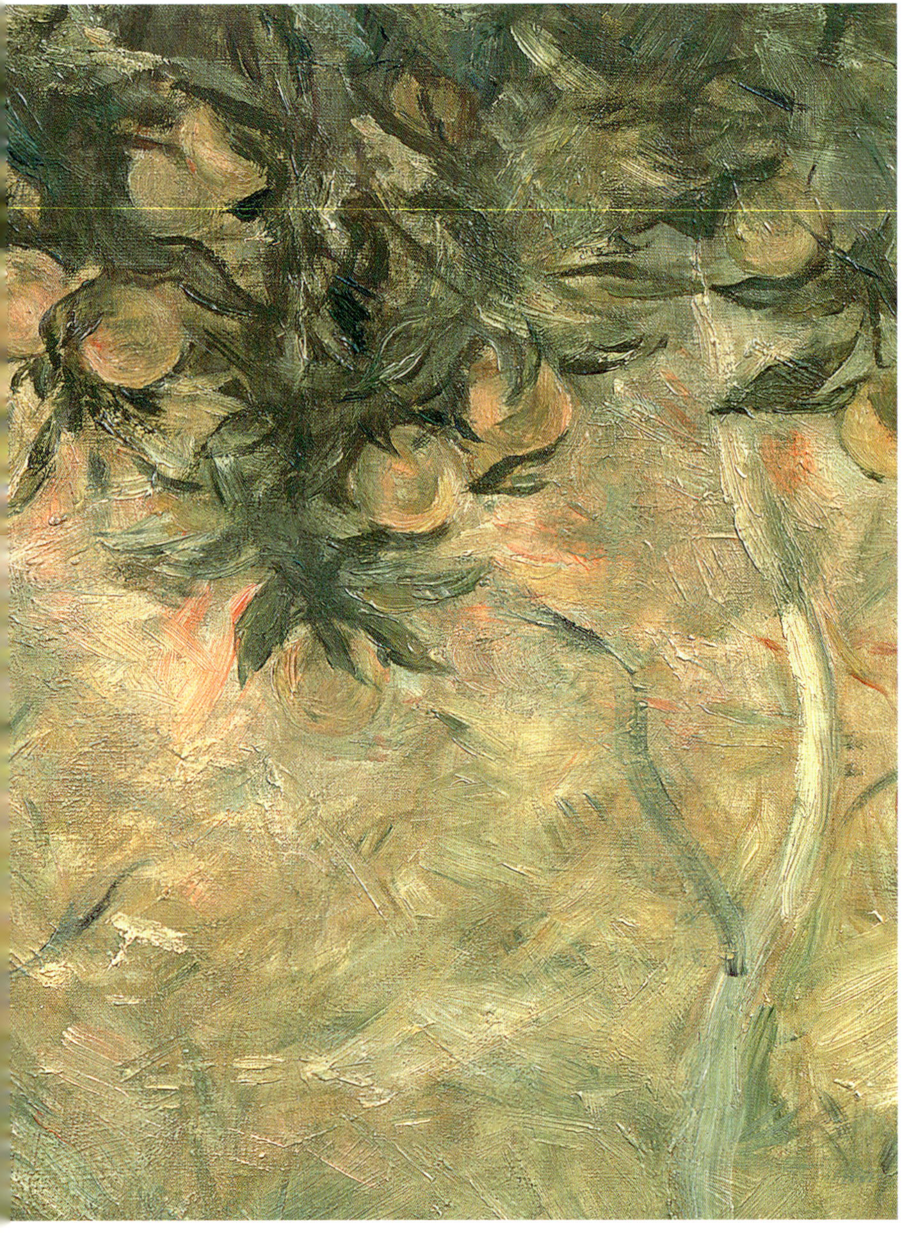

without an escort, or to attend cabarets or other public entertainments. Her art represents a confined and utterly feminine world—in which women, children, and female servants moved without constraint but with clear boundaries beyond which they could not go. Her favorite subject throughout the last two decades of her life was her only child, Julie, whose entire life was at once recorded and celebrated by her mother. As we have seen from Renoir's pastel (cat. no. 17), Julie had inherited the wonderful red hair of the Manet family, and, as she grew, her mother painted her playing, running, smelling flowers, arranging her clothing, sitting in the garden, boating, petting dogs, walking on the beach, eating meals, sewing, and at other mundane tasks. Never are these representations critical or emotionally complex. We do not see her crying, yelling, or even sleeping, and, when her pictorial life is taken in its totality, it is charmed, if somewhat dull.

The Bloch Morisot represents Julie seated beneath an orange tree in the garden of a rented winter home called the Villa Ratti in Cimiez, near Nice in the south of France. Julie had celebrated her tenth birthday on November 14, 1888, in this large villa with its spacious garden and views of the Mediterranean. Morisot and her daughter remained there through April 1889, and Morisot worked on an ambitious series of garden paintings, mostly centered on the orange trees that seemed so exotic to Parisians. She was not often alone; her friends the painters Monet and Pierre Puvis de Chavannes, as well as the great poet Stéphane Mallarmé, visited her; Renoir was invited but was unable to come. She even considered the creation of a series of prints for a book, perhaps with poetic texts by Mallarmé, but this never came off. Instead, she remained in her garden and worked on a series of paintings.

In the Bloch painting, Julie is alone, seated passively but apparently contentedly in the shade of the orange tree. She wears a protective smock over her simple dress, and her face is shielded from the sun by a straw hat. All the girlish roundness of Julie is accentuated by her mother, who rhymed her face with the circles and ovals of the hat. Charles Stuckey, in the longest and most intelligent essay ever written about Morisot, tells us that Renoir particularly admired this painting, and we can see why.[1] Neither portrait nor genre scene, the painting straddles artistic conventions, all the while dealing forthrightly with two pictorial tropes often associated with women in art. To Julie's left, Morisot placed a small portable birdcage with her daughter's green parrot inside. On top, she summarily painted a blue bird, which, being wild, is free to fly beyond the garden in which the painting is set. In the upper right, diagonally opposite the birdcage, Morisot painted the pendant, fruit-laden branches of the orange tree, raising questions of temptation and mortality. Oranges and parrots, fruits and flight, seem to provide the ten-year-old Julie—and her viewer—with ample material for contemplation.

The fruit and its pictorial potential provided Morisot with a good deal of stimulus. Surviving from the 1888–89 campaign are two paintings of servant girls gathering oranges. The most gorgeous of all is a pastel study (Musée d'Art et d'Histoire, Grasse, inv. no. 43) for one of the paintings, *The Orange Gatherer*, which, with the Bloch painting, tells us all we need to know about temptation, freedom, and confinement for French women in the nineteenth century.

—RB

NOTE

1. Charles F. Stuckey et al., *Berthe Morisot, Impressionist* (New York, 1987), pp. 15–177, particularly pp. 136–42.

Georges-Pierre Seurat

French, 1859–1891

19. *The Channel at Gravelines, Petit-Fort-Philippe (Le chenal de Gravelines, Petit-Fort-Philippe)*, 1890

Oil on panel, 6¼ × 9⅞ in. (15.9 × 25.1 cm)

Georges Seurat transformed the course of European and American painting in the nineteenth century. He was, with Cézanne, Gauguin, and Van Gogh, part of the group of artists that critic Roger Fry referred to as the "Post-Impressionists." The fact that the Bloch Collection holds major works by each of these four pioneering artists makes this ensemble a major Post-Impressionist collection.

Seurat's impact on nineteenth-century painting is usually restricted to his introduction of the means of scientific investigation to the language of painting. As a leader of the Neo-Impressionist group, Seurat formalized the need felt by artists at the time to analyze and then break down perception into many individual, fragmentary units. But to reduce Seurat's role to that of a scientist/artist is too simplistic. As Robert Herbert has pointed out, one of Seurat's rich and complex contributions was to ally this positivist science-oriented approach to reality with a definite interest in poetry, emotional expression, and even dreams.[1] The paradoxical rich tensions that are active within Seurat's career are epitomized in *The Channel at Gravelines, Petit-Fort-Philippe*. Seurat executed this work—a small oil painting on panel—on the northern coast of France at the meeting point of the English Channel and the North Sea, between Calais in France and the Belgian border. Seurat painted four canvases of this tiny coastal harbor in the summer of 1890. He also produced four smaller oil studies for the larger paintings and eight drawings. This group of sixteen works was executed during Seurat's last summer; he would meet a cruelly premature death in March 1891, only months after his thirty-first birthday.

The four large paintings that form this ensemble are *The Channel at Gravelines, Grand-Fort-Philippe*, in the National Gallery, London; *The Channel at Gravelines, Evening*, at the Museum of Modern Art, New York; *Toward the Sea, Gravelines*, in the Kröller-Müller Museum, Otterlo; and *The Channel at Gravelines, Petit-Fort-Philippe* (fig. 34), at the Indianapolis Museum of Art. The present oil panel is a chromatic and compositional study for the Indianapolis painting, and comparing the two offers a wonderful example of the dialectics of Seurat's late oeuvre. The painting of the Bloch picture is direct, quasi-instinctive, and almost visceral in contrast to the more studied, carefully crafted, and meticulously ordered layout of the larger Indianapolis canvas. There are also significant compositional changes in the final work. In the Bloch study, for example, a two-masted boat alongside the quay dominates the composition. Seurat removed this boat from the final canvas and added a bollard, which divides the picture in

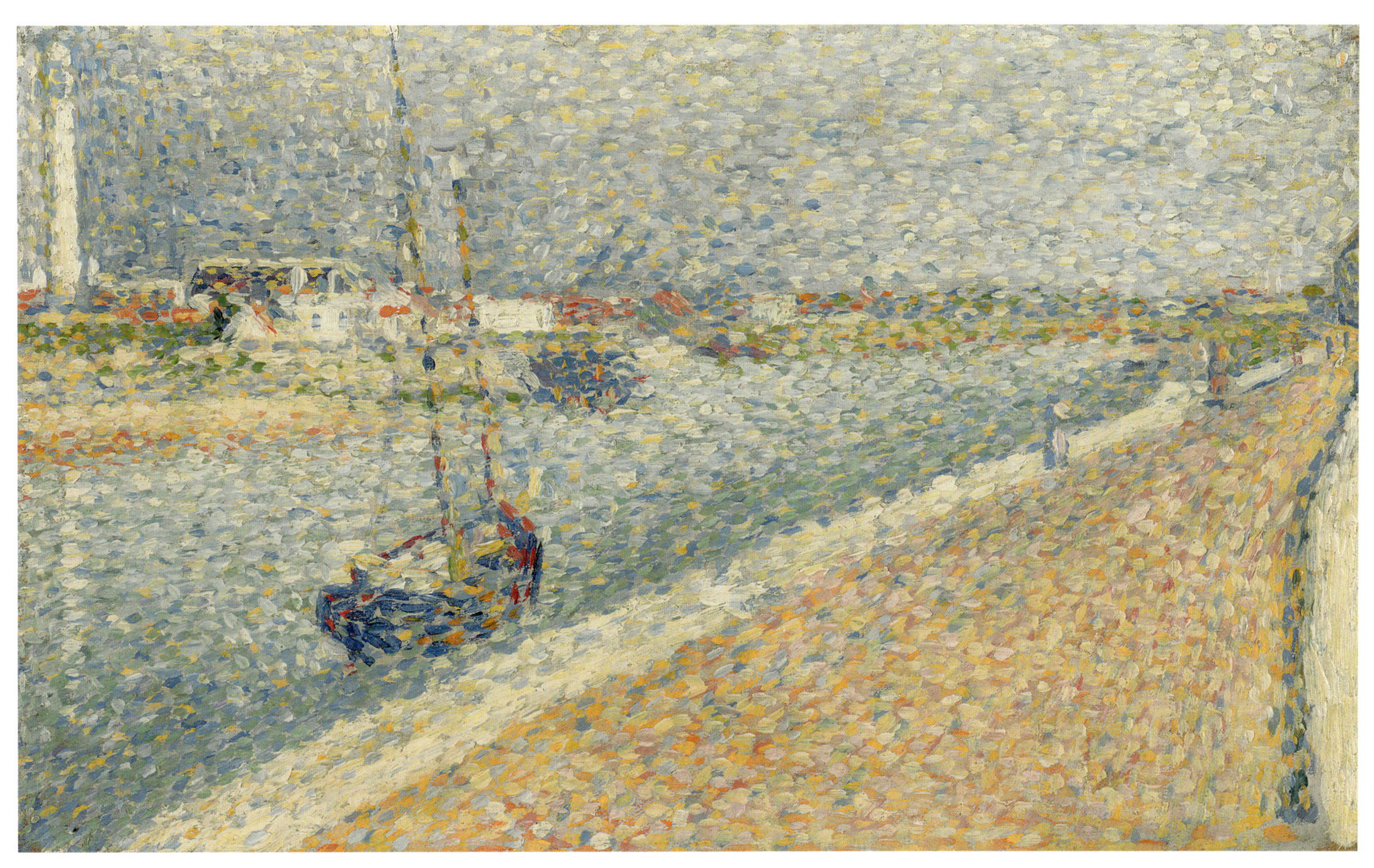

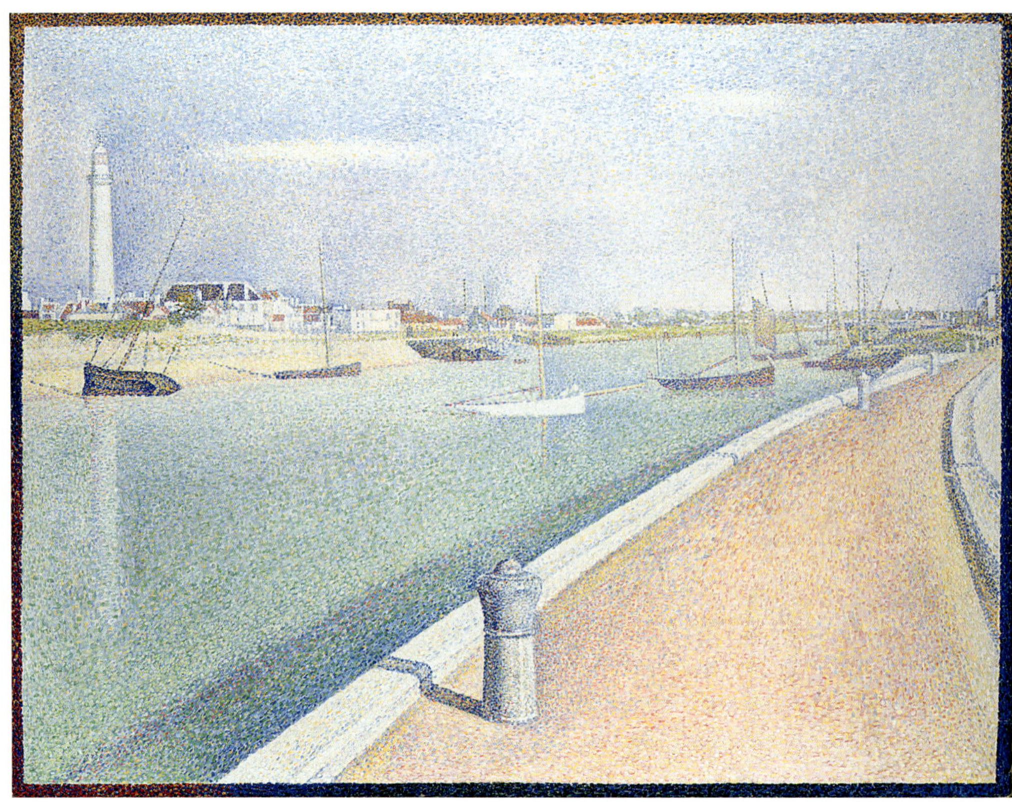

FIG. 34 Georges Seurat, *The Channel at Gravelines, Petit-Fort-Philippe*, 1890, oil on canvas, 29 × 36⅝ in. (73.7 × 58.6 cm). Indianapolis Museum of Art, gift of Mrs. James W. Fesler in memory of Daniel W. and Elizabeth C. Marmon

half and provides a focal point for its lower part. Seurat also adapted the tonality of the composition, changing the warm tones of the Bloch study to a cooler chromatic range in the Indianapolis work.

In the Bloch painting, the masts of the boat are made up of color fragments: lines of blue, yellow, and even vermilion. This is an exercise in chromatic construction and variation, and yet the identity of these upright elements as masts is unmistakable. Likewise, the depiction of the lighthouse in the upper left of the panel and its subtly broken-down reflection in the waters of the channel offer a fascinating example of the dialectical relationship between abstract strokes of paint and their representational content. The reflection is divided into a countable number of horizontal, superimposed strokes of white or beige paint. To an inattentive eye, they almost seem to blend into the pale light reflections of the water, whereas if one stands back from the painting, the vertical prolongation of the light is suddenly obvious.

We know that Seurat, like other Neo-Impressionists, read a great deal of current scientific literature on the capacity of the eye to separate and recombine the various colors contained within the light spectrum. One should be careful, however, when applying the content of Seurat's readings to his canvases, as it is easy to let it overdetermine his works. "Reading" Seurat's paintings as a sort of artistic illustration of an optical hypothesis would be very distorting. One could say—with no pun intended—that there is far more to Seurat's art than meets the eye.

One concept, however, does carry a cogent relevance to the Bloch and Indianapolis paintings: the principle of dynamogeny put forward by the pivotal color theoretician Charles Henry (1859–1926). This term, which Henry used in his *Introduction à une esthétique scientifique* (Paris, 1885) and perfected in an article of 1889,[2] designates forms that move upward and to the right as pleasurable, as opposed to forms that move downward and to the left, which Henry designated inhibitory. The concept of dynamogeny applies fittingly to this painting. Here the lines that begin along the left edge and even the lower edge of the canvas all seem to meet and converge at the same point on the horizon toward the upper right corner of the panel.

While this analysis appears to fit with what we know of Seurat's readings, the organization of the present work allowed for a certain amount of improvisation and spontaneity as Seurat applied the tiny brushstrokes of paint to the panel. In fact, this painting brings a powerful qualification to the definition of Seurat as the prototypical follower of a true, scientific, orthodox Neo-Impressionist method. It demonstrates the obvious degree of liberty the artist allowed himself. As we look at this small painting, the definition of Seurat's role in modern art becomes all the more complex and elusive. Seurat: a prophet of abstraction? Seurat: an introducer of scientific method within the practice of painting? Seurat: a forerunner of the Italian Divisionists? Seurat: an illustrator of Charles Henry's methods and grammar of the arts? There is some truth to all these labels, but none begins to do justice to what the author of this small, powerful picture achieved.

—JP

NOTES

1. Robert L. Herbert, *Georges Seurat* (New York, 1991), pp. 3–10.
2. Charles Henry, *Éléments d'une théorie générale de la dynamogénie autrement dit du contraste, du rythme et de la mesure avec applications spéciales aux sensations visuelle et auditive* (Paris, 1889).

Paul Signac

French, 1863–1935

20. *Portrieux, The Bathing Cabins, Opus 185 (Beach of the Countess) (Portrieux, Les cabines, Opus 185 [Plage de la comtesse])*, 1888

Oil on canvas, 13⅛ × 18¼ in. (33.3 × 46.4 cm); signed and dated lower left: *P. Signac 88*; inscribed lower right: *Op 185*

Paul Signac was the most energetic and important follower of Georges Seurat and can be counted, after that great painter, as the second artist—and primary theorist—of Neo-Impressionism. Signac made his debut as a member of the new movement at the last of the eight Impressionist exhibitions, held in Paris in the spring of 1886. There his first major pointillist (dotted) painting of urban seamstresses at work (Bührle Foundation Collection, Zurich) hung next to Seurat's *A Sunday on the Grande Jatte* (Art Institute of Chicago), the most important painting of the movement. Across from Seurat's painting hung Camille Pissarro's large-scale *Apple Harvest* (Kurashiki Museum, Japan)—also his most ambitious pointillist effort. Thus two generations of artists, the late-middle-aged Pissarro and the young Seurat and Signac, declared themselves leaders of this new kind of painting within the context of Impressionism itself. These three large paintings were effectively a visual manifesto of "scientific Impressionism," and their artists derived a newly regularized technique less from past art practice than from the thoroughly modern scientific study of light, the human eye, color, and proportion. Hence, their art emerged from the ideas of the Impressionists, to which they applied a scientific rigor that the older artists, save for Pissarro, actually repudiated. Indeed, both Monet and Renoir refused to exhibit with Signac, Seurat, and Pissarro in 1886.

The Bloch Signac looks as if it came directly from the artist's easel. Neither lined nor varnished, it preserves perfectly the subtle facture of dots and daubs of pure color the twenty-four-year-old artist placed, one by one, on the surface. Although it has been related to a larger painting of the same beach (Kröller-Müller Museum, Otterlo), this latter scene is composed so differently that the Bloch Signac should instead be interpreted as an independent work derived from a small painting on panel still in a private French collection (fig. 35), which Signac painted relatively quickly in two or three short sessions. It has a completely different palette and light effect, suggesting that Signac probably conceived it first, using it as a compositional model for the larger Bloch work, which he painted outdoors to capture the different light effects he sought.

The Bloch painting was first exhibited at the Société des Artistes Indépendants in Paris during the spring of 1890. In the catalogue for that large exhibition it appeared as number 741, with a title that is both fascinating and different from that used today: *La mer—de Portrieux (Côtes du Nord), juin, juillet, aout, septembre 1888* (The Sea—Portrieux [North Coast], June, July, August,

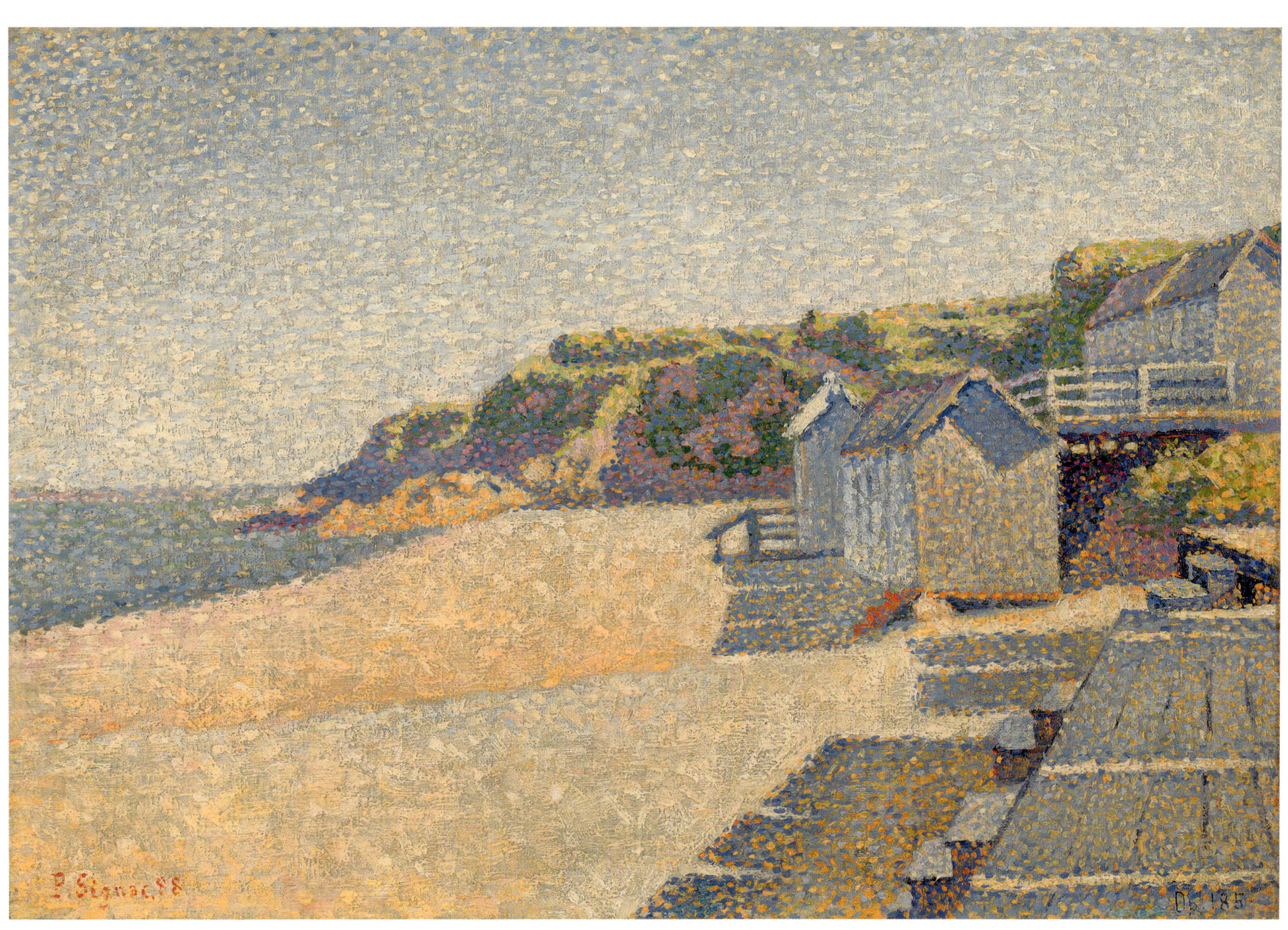
P. Signac 88
Op. 185

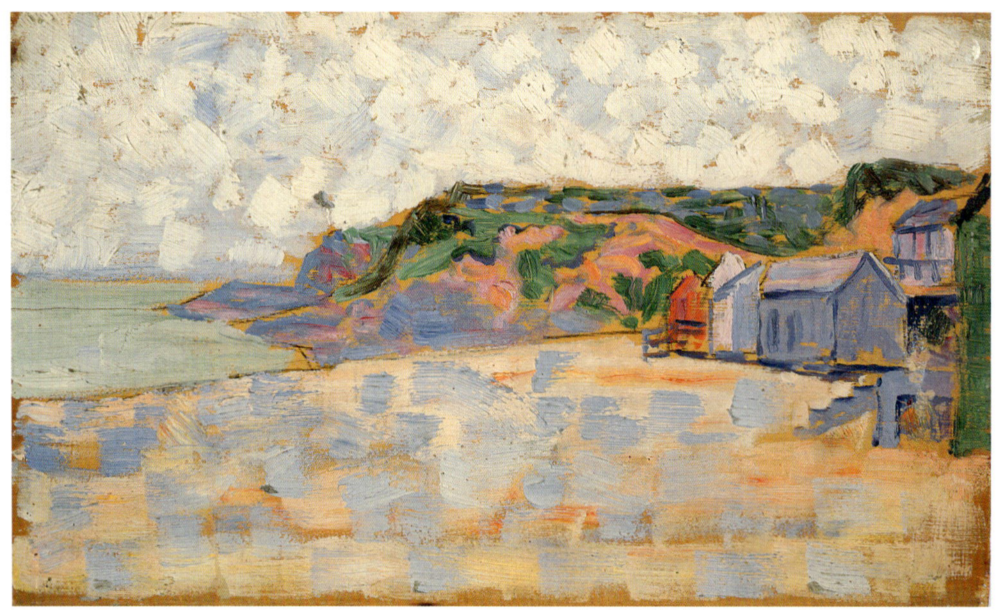

FIG. 35 Paul Signac, *Portrieux, La Comtesse* (study), 1888, oil on panel, 6⅛ × 9¾ in. (15.5 × 24.8 cm). Private collection

September 1888). Signac liked to indicate the precise duration of his work on a particular painting in its title. The Otterlo painting was first exhibited with "June to September 1888" in the title in Brussels, and again at the Indépendants, with the Bloch painting. The titles of the paintings listed four successive months individually, as if to form a pictorial litany of patient work. (Interestingly, Signac's journal indicates that he arrived in Portrieux not in June, as the titles suggest, but on July 7. Perhaps he had forgotten this when he titled the paintings almost two years later.)

Neither painting has a human figure. Signac clearly wanted to make a permanent record of recurring diurnal light rather than to record, as Boudin and Monet had before him, the social life of a bustling beach resort during its busiest months. Signac spent the entire summer of 1888 in Portrieux and valued his pictorial production there to such an extent that he wrote an article discussing the group of nine paintings he completed that season for the periodical *Art et critique*, ostensibly as a review of the exhibition of Les XX in Brussels in which the most finished of them first appeared.[1] This 1890 article and the summer issue of *Les hommes d'aujourd'hui*, devoted to Signac and written by the dealer-critic Félix Fénéon, prepared the way for a larger group of Portrieux paintings that included the Bloch canvas.[2]

The almost eerie silence and emptiness of Signac's small masterpiece make it very different from the two Boudin beach scenes also in the Bloch Collection (cat. nos. 3, 4). For Boudin, the beach was a social space, inhabited temporarily by visiting Parisians, who strolled, swam, basked, chatted, and gathered along its vast sandy spaces. Boudin, like Signac, loved the small bathing cabins of the beaches but used them less as forms in their own right than as temporary place markers in the "humanscape" of his pictorial world. Signac is everywhere the opposite. Indeed, the lengthy shadows from the east in his representation of the Beach of the Countess in Portrieux suggest that Signac must have habitually gotten up at dawn, rushed to the beach, and painted the early morning effects of light well before the lazy vacationers had left their beds. The contrast between this landscape of leisure with the patient work of its transcription fascinates us today as much as it did Signac in 1888. If Boudin was a kind of pictorial equivalent of Trollope or Balzac in his creation of a messy, noisy human realm, Signac was a set designer who organized the place of human action without the slightest interest in its narrative consequences. As a result, his emptiness seems almost akin to the silence and ennui found in the plays of Strindberg or Ibsen, which were to take Paris by storm in the 1890s.

Much has been made of Signac's somewhat affected use of "opus" numbers on his paintings. German publishers had introduced opus numbers to identify groups of musical works as early as the sixteenth century, and generally composers themselves did not employ them. Although Signac was avidly interested in classical music, he adapted the system of ordering musical compositions in a way that suggests he failed to understand it completely. Had a musicologist been ordering Signac's paintings from the summer of 1888, he would have given all of them the same opus number, followed by a sequential listing of individual works by number (e.g., opus 35, no. 1, 2, 3, etc.). But Signac gave each individual work a different opus number, often in defiance of the actual order in which he had produced them. For example, the large and complex Otterlo painting has a lower opus number than the smaller Bloch canvas, and their numbers are lower than that of the small panel in a private collection which surely preceded them all.

Whatever their opus number, there is little doubt that Signac was at the very top of his pictorial game in the summer of 1888. Not a single work from that period slips to a lower level of quality, and each has a pictorial integrity and rigor that he was not always able to sustain throughout his working life. He made each painting with the idea that he would show it to Pissarro and Seurat when he returned to Paris from his painting holiday. While Signac was in Portrieux, Seurat worked nearby in Port-en-Bessin, where he painted an inspired group of landscapes of the sea, the port itself, and the quays of the town. These latter works are much better known than those of Signac but scarcely more important in the history of French avant-garde painting.

—RB

NOTES

1. See Paul Signac [S.P., pseudo.], "Catalogue de l'exposition des XX à Bruxelles," *Art et critique* 2, no. 36 (February 1, 1890), pp. 76–78.

2. Félix Fénéon, "Signac," *Les hommes d'aujourd'hui*, no. 373 (1890), reprinted in Félix Fénéon, *Oeuvres plus que complétes*, ed. Joan U. Halperin (Geneva, 1970), vol. 1, pp. 174–79.

Vincent van Gogh

Dutch, 1853–1890

21. *Restaurant Rispal at Asnières (Le restaurant Rispal à Asnières)*, 1887

Oil on canvas, 28⅞ × 23⅝ in. (73.3 × 60 cm), wax lined

In 1886 Van Gogh moved from Holland to Paris and lived with his brother, the art dealer Theo van Gogh, on rue Lepic (fig. 36). This Parisian period, from 1886 to 1888, transformed the artist's career. He immersed himself in academic practices, becoming a pupil in Cormon's studio (where Toulouse-Lautrec had already studied) and refining his drawing skills in life classes. At the same time, he was exposed to the explosion of currents and trends that defined the Parisian avant-garde as the Impressionists broke apart. Van Gogh was insatiably curious about everything—from the most academic constructs to the most adventurous and cutting-edge avant-gardism. His artistic appetite and personality were such that he thrived among these conflicting currents. He met the Impressionists and the next generation of artists, the so-called Neo-Impressionists—Georges Seurat, Paul Signac, Charles Angrand—who would become especially important to him. He saw their works in exhibitions such as the 1887 Salon des Indépendants and during visits to the studio of his good friend Signac. Van Gogh also turned his attention to Japanese art, beginning to form a collection of prints that he purchased from the famous dealer Siegfried Bing.

A major event on the Parisian art scene in 1886–87 was the sudden success of the Neo-Impressionists. As can be seen in *Restaurant Rispal at Asnières*, Van Gogh characteristically absorbed certain aspects of the new technique while keeping his distance from it. For instance, in the Bloch painting, the foliage of the trees is made of fractured brushwork and loose marks that resemble Seurat's famous "dots"—the ultimate Neo-Impressionist signature—whereas the application of paint in the rest of the composition is entirely different. Overall the work is almost a painted drawing, as Van Gogh intentionally blurred the line between the two media. This important painting anticipates the famous works the artist would produce in Provence only a few months later in which his color and thickly impastoed textures pushed his experiments with pictorial freedom even farther.

For his motif Van Gogh chose one of the least glamorous and most prosaic aspects of suburban Paris. The cafés and working-class social environments of Provence would later attract him in much the same way. He and his friends Émile Bernard, Paul Signac, and Georges Seurat were equally drawn to lowly Parisian districts, and all three painted the industrial suburbs of Asnières, a short hour away from the center of Paris, where they found an authentic vernacular culture.

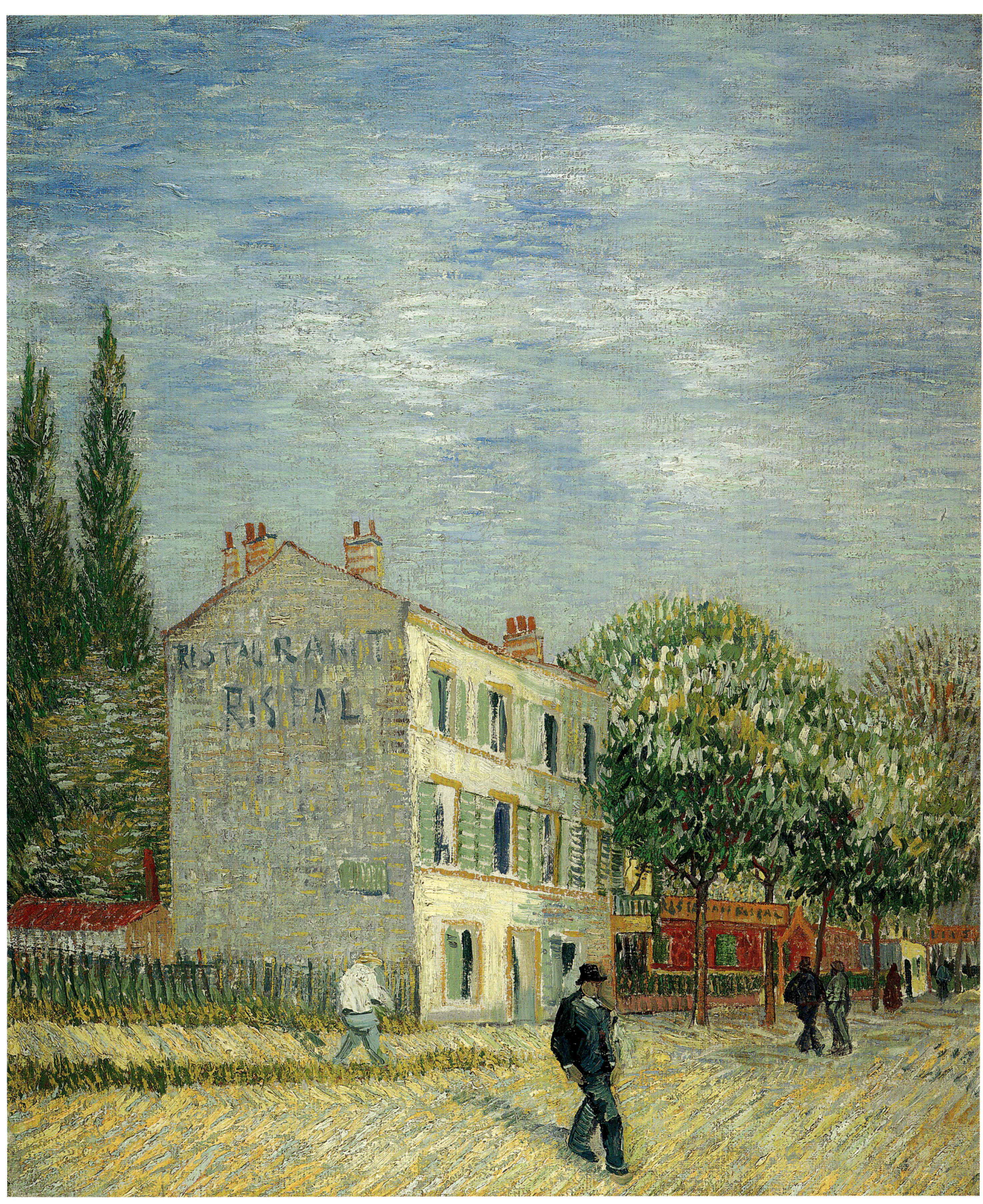
RESTAURANT
RISPAL

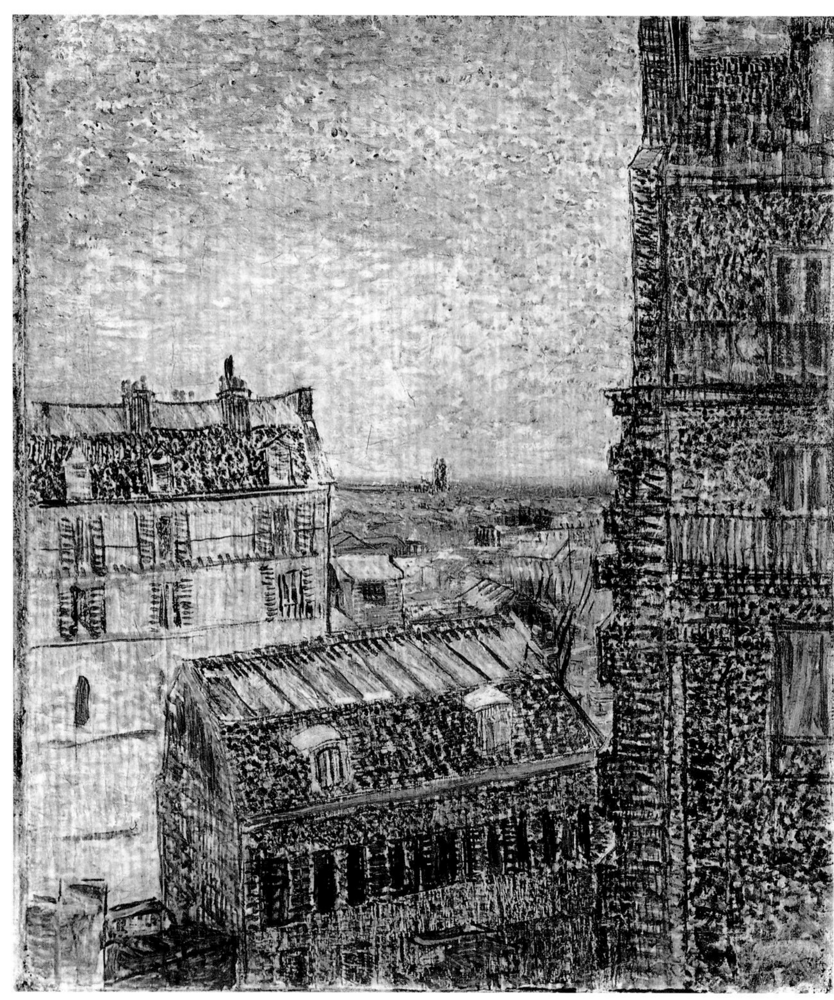

FIG. 36 Vincent van Gogh, *View of Paris from the Bedroom of Vincent, Rue Lepic*, 1887, oil on canvas, 18⅛ × 14⅞ in. (46 × 38 cm). Van Gogh Museum, Amsterdam (Vincent van Gogh Foundation)

When looking at the Bloch painting, one cannot help but be impressed by its astonishing dynamism and restlessness. The painting represents ordinary people crossing the street in front of the restaurant that gives the painting its title, a working-class eatery in which a basic meal cost only a few centimes. Thick capital letters on the side wall of the building identify the three-story structure, and one wonders if it is also a hotel or even a brothel. Judging from the lopsided figure crossing the street in the foreground, the restaurant fulfilled its chief function of serving quantities of cheap alcohol.

Were it not for Van Gogh, this ordinary restaurant certainly would have fallen into oblivion. Its banality is offset by the way it was painted. A principal opposition structures the theme. A triangular, complementary link among three colors holds the building together: purplish blues, yellows (light to lemon), and green. They are enlivened by thin lines of vermilion red, which delineate the roofline of the building and the chimneys—four of them—that adorn the roof and echo these few marks of red. An added complementary exchange makes the construction even more interesting. In the bluish purple facade, odd yellow marks are interwoven within cooler

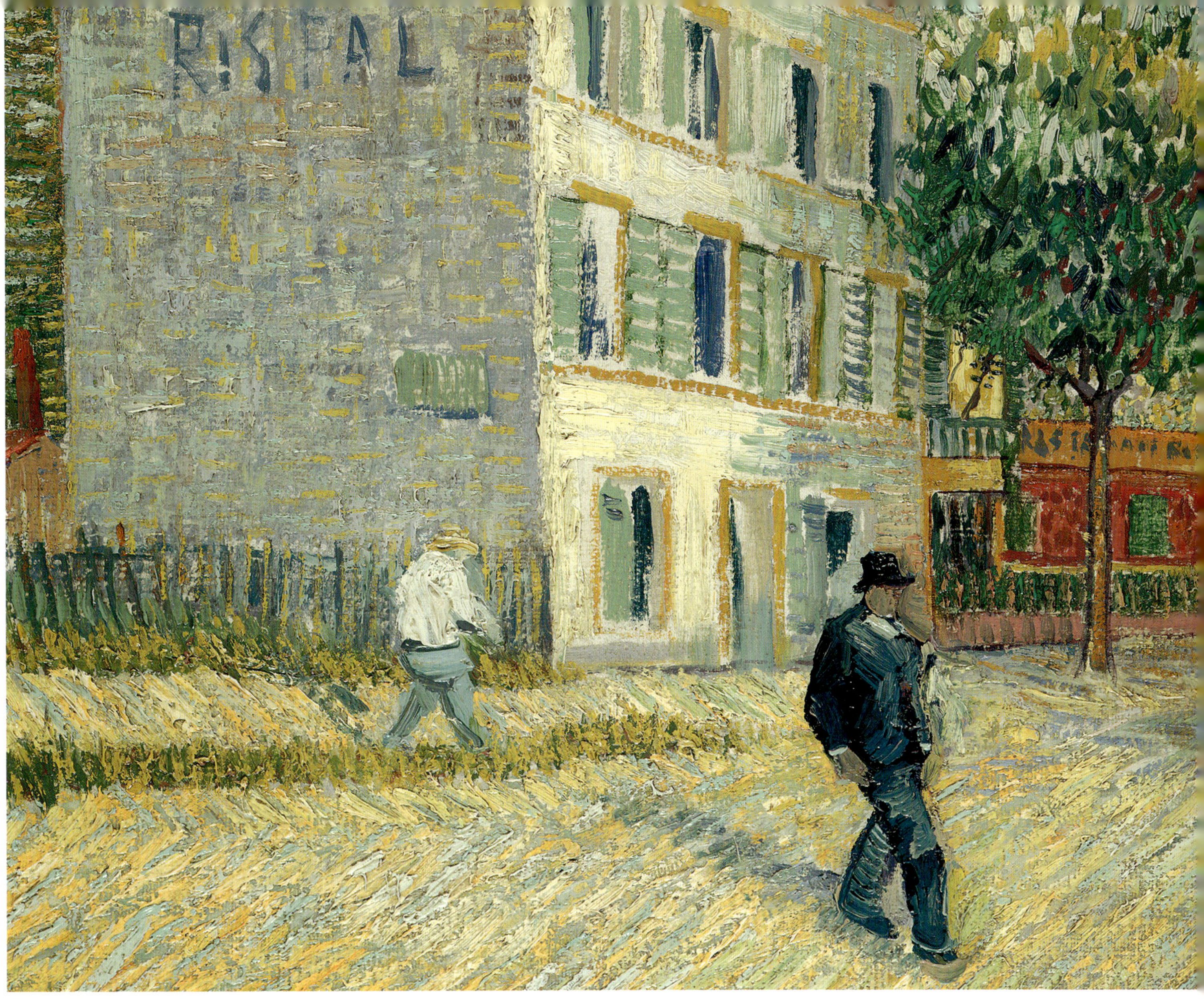

shades of color. Exactly the same kind of opposition can be observed in the light-struck facade: inside the windows, marks or slabs of blue or purple indicate the darkness—and the coolness—of the interior rooms.

Everything about this painting breathes intensity, vivacity, and audacity. The color scheme is striking, with colors broken down into slabs of paint. But this work is far more than an exercise in chromatic virtuosity; it essentially tells us about the ethos of modern art and society. Van Gogh chose to produce a vivid representation of this inconspicuous building—the center of activity of the lives, gatherings, and entertainments of the local working-class population, many of whom were Van Gogh's friends. Thus Van Gogh also contributed a new sense, and a new center of gravity, to the activity of art making.

—JP

Paul Gauguin

French, 1848–1903

22. *The Willow Tree (Le saule)*, 1889

Oil on canvas, 36¼ × 28⅞ in. (92 × 73.5 cm), unlined; signed and dated lower right: *P. Gauguin '8_*

Paul Gauguin is the only celebrated member of the Impressionist group who was not formally trained as an artist. A stalwart businessman who worked in the Paris stock market, he was encouraged by his guardian, the great collector Gustave Arosa, to acquire paintings, and Gauguin joined the Impressionist movement more as a collector than as an artist. He was, in the truest sense of the word, an "amateur," or lover of art, who in the evenings and on weekends perfected his skills as a painter, sculptor, ceramicist, and printmaker. Fortunately for us, he chose only the most powerful avant-garde mentors. He is known to have painted with Pissarro, Degas, Guillaumin, and Cézanne in the late 1870s before striking out on his own as a professional artist in 1883, at the age of thirty-five.

The years 1888 and 1889 were the most productive of Gauguin's three-decade artistic career. Always a careful, even deliberate, painter, he tended to work obsessively on his canvases until he achieved the correct effects, and, for that reason, he completed fewer works per year than his friend Van Gogh or his Impressionist friends. Yet in 1888 and 1889 he finished seventy-two and seventy-one paintings respectively, more than one painting per week.[1] When compared to the forty paintings of 1886, twenty-three of 1887, and twenty-five of 1890, the extent of Gauguin's productivity in these two years becomes clear. Gauguin truly became himself as an artist in this period, casting off the false starts and doubts that had characterized his career until this point. The list of principal masterpieces he created during 1888–89 demonstrates his sheer mastery: *The Vision of the Sermon* (National Gallery of Scotland, Edinburgh); *Yellow Christ* (Albright-Knox Gallery, Buffalo); *Self-Portrait with Portrait of Bernard* (Van Gogh Museum, Amsterdam); *The Young Wrestlers* (private collection); *Van Gogh Painting Sunflowers* (Van Gogh Museum, Amsterdam); *Old Women of Arles* (Art Institute of Chicago); *Misères Humaines* (Ordrupgaard, Copenhagen); *The Blue Trees* (Ordrupgaard, Copenhagen); *The Schuffenecker Family* (Musée d'Orsay, Paris); *La Belle Angèle* (Musée d'Orsay, Paris); *Bonjour M. Gauguin* (Narodni Gallery, Prague); *Self-Portrait* (National Gallery of Art, Washington); *Christ in the Garden of Olives* (Norton Museum of Art, West Palm Beach); *The Green Christ* (*Breton Calvary*; Musées Royaux des Beaux-Arts, Brussels); *Ondine* (Cleveland Museum of Art); *The Flageolet Player on a Cliff* (Indianapolis Museum of Art); *Still-life with a Fan* (Musée d'Orsay, Paris); and *The Ham* (Phillips Collection, Washington).

The Bloch picture, from 1889, is a type of painting that Gauguin made with some regularity. Buying canvases and stretchers of standard sizes, Gauguin in 1888 began to work more regularly

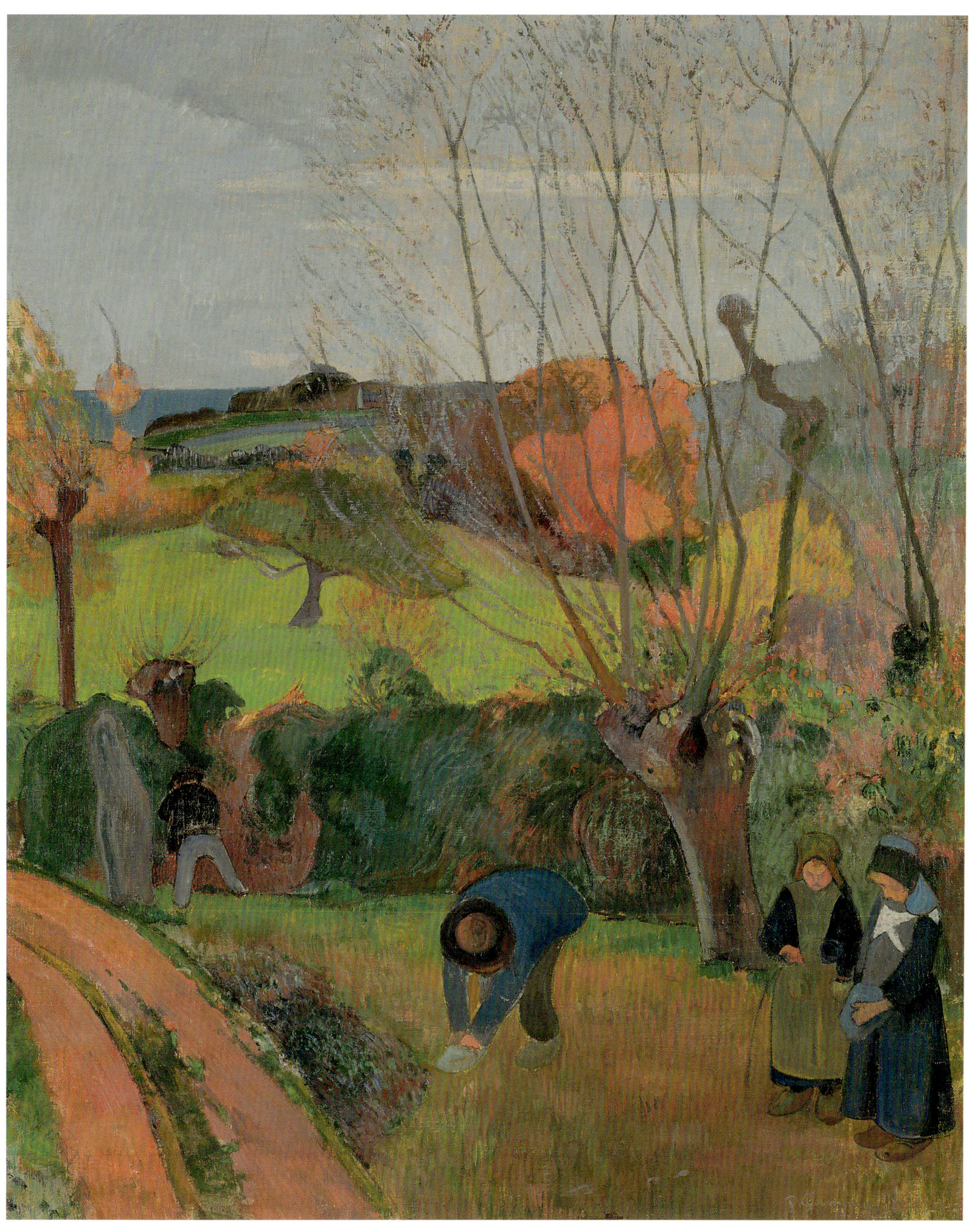

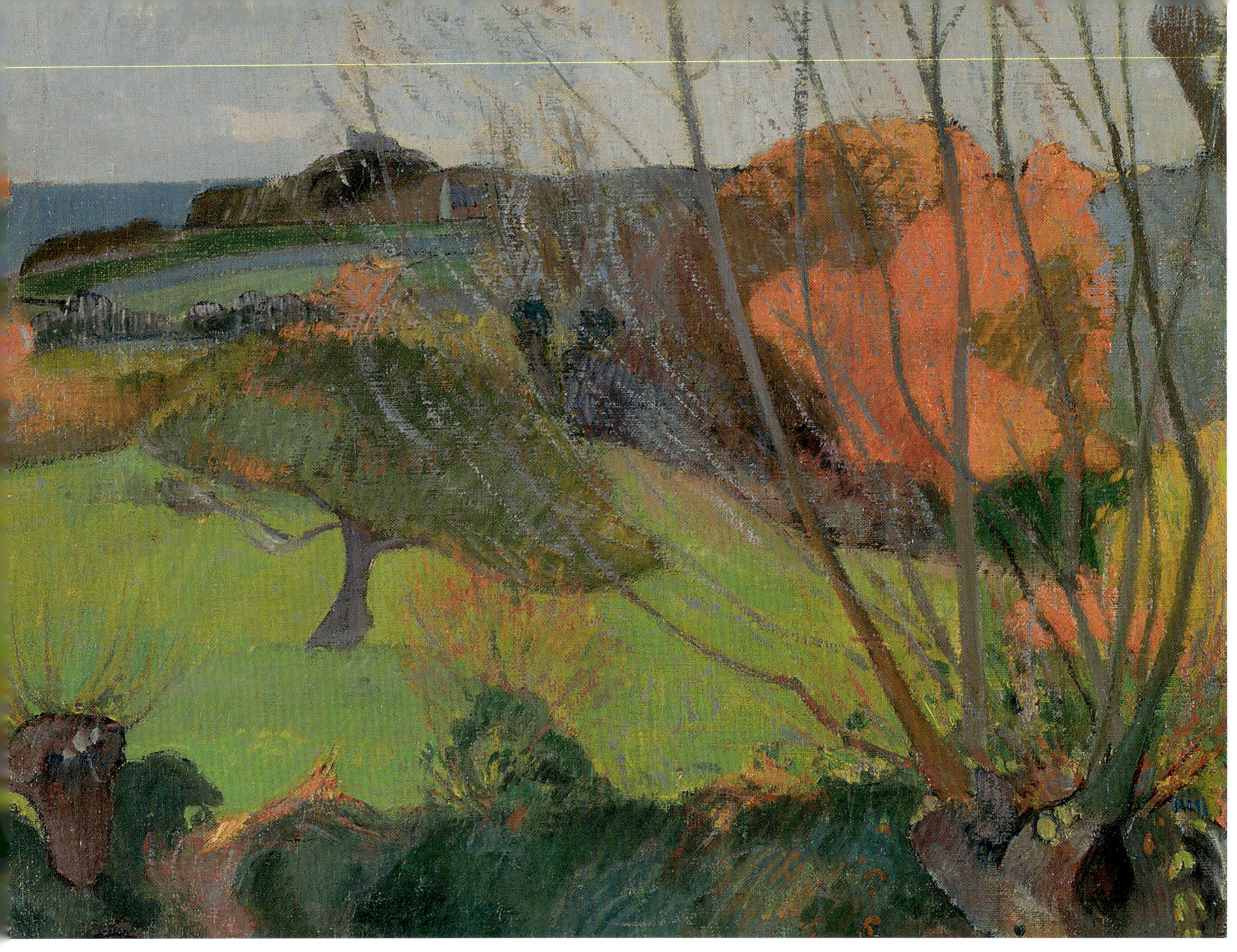

on a larger scale than he had before, and paintings of the size of the Bloch canvas are common from that time. From 1888, ten vertical landscapes and two vertical figure paintings of the same size survive, and from 1889 there are eight vertical figure paintings and ten vertical landscapes of the same size. When one adds the twenty-eight horizontal paintings of the same commanding size, Gauguin's sheer pictorial ambition in the last two years of the 1880s is apparent. One could easily mount a major exhibition of Gauguin's paintings just from those years, as the two selected here for generic comparison make clear.

This pictorial confidence was well rewarded by a steady increase in Gauguin's reputation. He already was becoming the leader among a large group of younger painters that included Charles Laval, Émile Bernard, Paul Sérusier, Jacob Meyer de Haan, and others in Brittany as well as Édouard Vuillard, Pierre Bonnard, and Maurice Denis in Paris. His participation in a group exhibition at the Café Volpini, in association with the Universal Exposition of 1889, and in the vanguard exhibitions of the Belgian group Les XX launched him as a major force in European painting. Thus he had come to think of himself as a leader in the white-hot world of the Parisian avant-garde, and, although this success was not monetary, it did impel him to greater pictorial heights.

Yet with the exception of the repeated showing of a small group of masterpieces from these years, Gauguin exhibitions have not come to terms with this peak in his career, and the most neglected paintings of this group are the vertical landscapes, of which the Bloch Gauguin is a principal masterpiece. The vast majority of landscape paintings in the history of art are horizontal, the sheer reach of the format stressing the spaciousness of the motif. Vertical landscapes are comparatively rare, except as panels in decorative schemes, and, perhaps for that reason alone, Gauguin, the persistent contrarian, actually preferred them. He had begun to favor this vertical format for landscapes as early as 1883, when he first left Paris to paint in the suburbs of Rouen, and in the summer of 1885, he painted a triptych of large vertical landscapes that leads directly to the Bloch painting.[2] Indeed, Gauguin chose a size and format more associated with portraiture in deciding to paint the twenty vertical landscapes on 36-by-27-inch canvases in 1888–89.

The Bloch painting is perfectly preserved, its fine canvas unlined and on its original wooden stretcher, without any modification. Oddly, the signature and date in the lower right, painted in a pale warm gray shot with pink and blue, are abraded and hence almost invisible, which, for Gauguin, who made the act of signing almost a fetish in the late 1880s, is highly unusual. One can, with effort and good light, read "P. Gauguin '8_," but there is no trace of the second digit whatsoever. The presence of the deep blue sea and the distant cliffs indicates that the painting was made near the coastal town of Le Pouldu, where Gauguin stayed briefly in 1888 and for a longer period in 1889. The style of the painting and its clear relationship to other signed and dated works painted in Le Pouldu in 1889 suggest that it was made in the later year, when he worked in that landscape with the Dutch artist Meyer de Haan from October 2, 1889, until early February 1890.

The Bloch picture represents an almost completely decorative landscape in the chromatically charged season of autumn. The flame reds and brilliant oranges of the deciduous foliage combine with the brilliant greens of winter grasses to spark the painting with a kind of chromatic electricity. When these strong colors are joined with an almost infinitely subtle array of pale blues, violets, whites, creams, apricots, pinks, and variously colored dark hues, the canvas becomes nothing less than a symphony of color. Gauguin had already written about the emotional and pictorial importance of color in his "Notes Synthetiques" of 1885, but he did not put these notions into pictorial form with confidence until the late 1880s. And his writings about color did not reach a mature level until the second half of the 1890s, when he wrote eloquently in the pages of his unpublished manuscript of 1894–95, laconically entitled "Diverses choses" (Diverse Things). Here, he linked color to sound—painting to music—in complex ways, evoking sounds as diverse as Tibetan mountain horns, oriental chants, and Beethoven symphonies. In a letter to his friend André Fontainas of March 1899, ten years after the Bloch painting, Gauguin spoke of "color, which is vibration as well as music, attaining what is more general and, hence, more vague in nature, its interior force."[3]

The Bloch painting has a kind of waxy surface, and certain areas in the left-hand portion of the sky seem suffused with wax. The reverse of the canvas too shows traces of wax, which

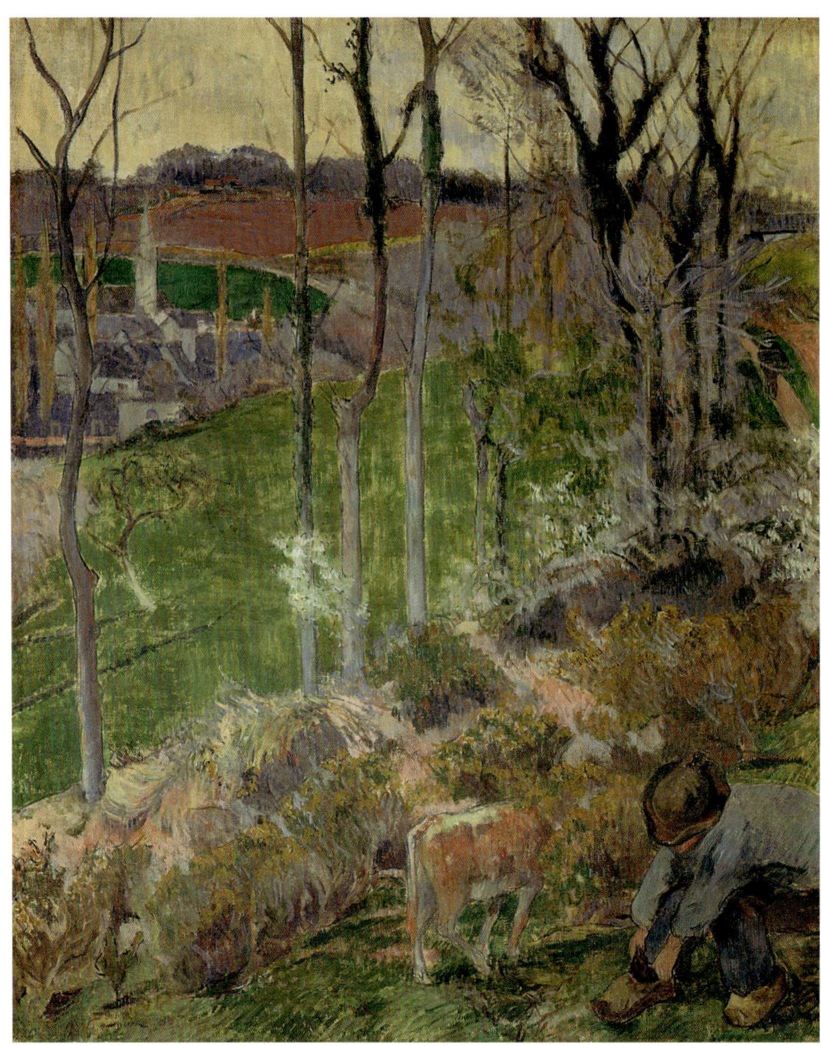

FIG. 37 Paul Gauguin, *Winter, A Young Breton Adjusts His Clogs*, 1888, oil on canvas, 35⅝ × 28 in. (90.5 × 71 cm). Ny Carlsberg Glyptotek, Copenhagen

Gauguin was beginning to use in pictorial experiments during these years. Earlier he had joined Pissarro and Monet in refusing to varnish his canvases in order to avoid the effects of yellowing and surface glare. He may have actually liked the dull sheen of wax when mixed with pigment. Yet he never entirely gave way to encaustic, always using it in combination with conventional oil paint.

The peasant figures that populate the foregrounds of many of these vertical landscapes (fig. 37) exist here in pairs. Two women stand protectively and passively together in the lower right, while two male figures actively engage and interact with the landscape. The men are painted much more summarily than the women, whose figures relate to other pairs of young Breton peasants painted by Gauguin in 1888–90, particularly an identically sized figure painting of the same year in a private Swiss collection (*Fillettes au Pouldu*; Wildenstein 345). Hence none of the figures was invented for the painting but, instead, migrated into it from sketchbooks or other works, as if rehearsed for an appearance here. The title of the painting, which is not

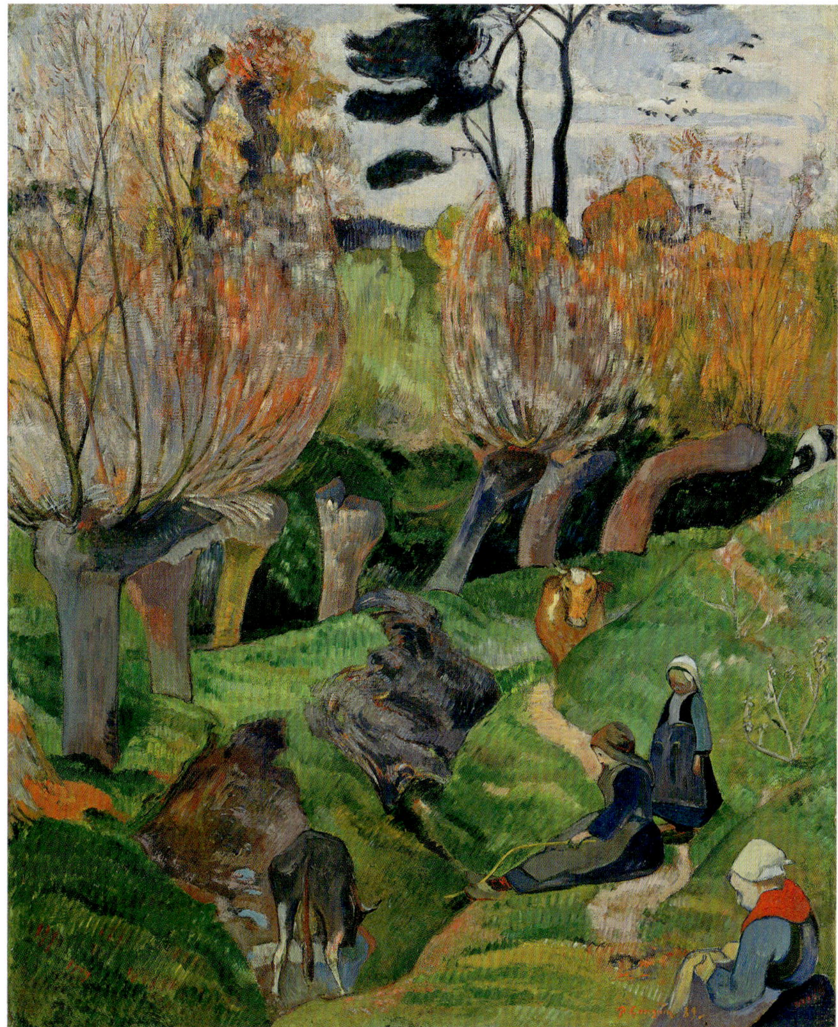

FIG. 38 Paul Gauguin, *The Willows (Les saules)*, 1889, oil on canvas, 36¼ × 28¾ in. (92 × 73 cm). National Museum of Art, Architecture, and Design, Oslo

original, refers us to the pollarded willows that spring from the hedge dividing the foreground from the background. Gauguin had been fascinated by such trees for many years. He had included paintings of willows in the Impressionist exhibition of 1886 and painted the trees again and again throughout the late 1880s (fig. 38). The contrast between the bulbous and deformed stumps of the trees' trunks and the lengthy, lithe young sprouts harvested to make baskets and brooms gave Gauguin a charmingly diverse pictorial material.

—RB

NOTES

1. Georges Wildenstein, *Gauguin* (Paris, 1964).
2. See Richard R. Brettell and Anne-Brigitte Fonsmark, *Gauguin and Impressionism* (New Haven, 2005), pp. 266–69.
3. Maurice Malinque, *Lettres de Gauguin à sa femme et à ses amis*, rev. ed. (Paris, 1949), p. CLXX.

Paul Cézanne

French, 1839–1906

23. *Quarry at Bibémus (Carrière de Bibémus)*, 1895–1900

Oil on canvas, 25¾ × 21½ in. (65.5 × 54.5 cm)

Bridging the gap between Impressionism and Cubism with real élan, the oeuvre of Paul Cézanne was little known to the French public until November 1895, when the dealer Ambroise Vollard mounted a large exhibition in the painter's fifty-seventh year. Nothing by Cézanne had been seen publicly in Paris since the Impressionist exhibition of 1877. It was, perhaps, this very delayed entrance into the febrile Parisian art world that made Cézanne instantly famous, and, when he died in 1906, he was acclaimed as the greatest French artist of his generation. All students of Cézanne have considered him to be fundamentally "Provençal"—a painter of his native Provence in the south of France—and, in keeping with this anti-Parisian aura, both of the Bloch Cézannes represent Provençal subjects.

Cézanne spent a good deal of his life shuttling between Paris, where his wife and son lived, and Provence, the home of his parents and sisters. After the death of his father in 1886, his wife came more often to Provence for holidays, but she disliked the south, and the painter remained essentially a loner in the landscape of his birth, searching it for motifs that would symbolize its history and endurance. His Provençal work is a good deal easier to discuss and analyze than his Parisian work, but the two existed in a kind of aesthetic dialogue until the early years of the twentieth century, when he stopped going to Paris for good, remaining in his native landscape until his death. The sheer iconic power of Cézanne's later Provençal landscapes has few precedents in French painting. Whether centered on the great Mont Sainte-Victoire, the abandoned quarry at Bibémus, a single ancient tree in the landscape, or the abandoned buildings of the so-called Château Noir (Black Chateau), each painting seems to embody the mythic struggle between man and nature in a landscape that was older than the Romans. No trains, factory chimneys, railroad bridges, or modern aqueducts, which Cézanne had allowed into his landscapes of the 1870s and 1880s, mar the timeless Provençal scenes of his old age.

The Bibémus quarry east of Aix-en-Provence was far enough from Cézanne's last studio, at Les Lauves, that he rented a small stone hut (*cabanon*) at the site in 1895 (fig. 39). There he stored a portable easel or two, paint supplies, and stretched canvases so that he did not have to lug them back and forth from the quarry. It is not known how long Cézanne continued this practice, but he did produce at least ten canvases of the quarry that can be dated on stylistic grounds between 1895 and 1902. Although these have never been brought together for study,

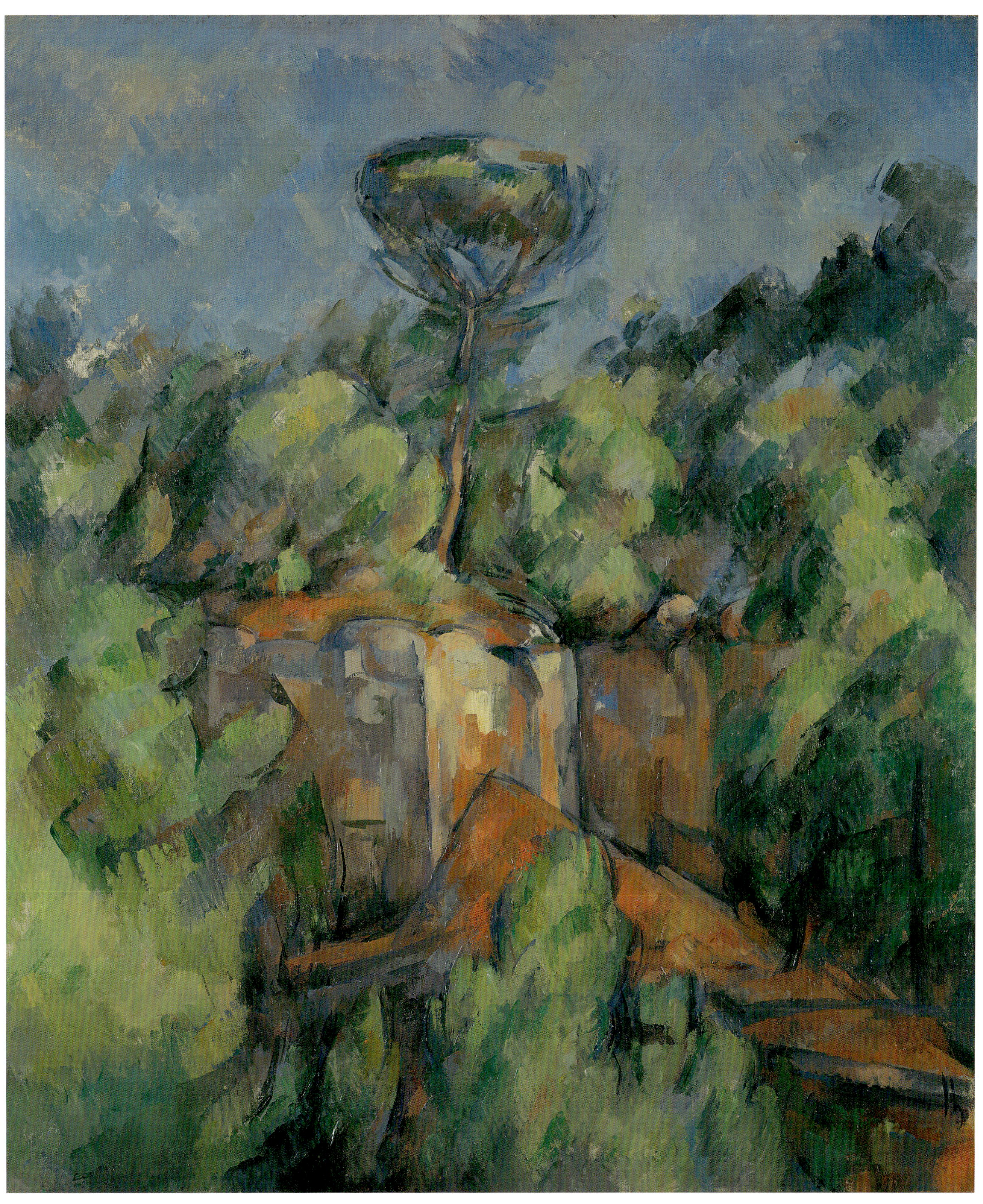

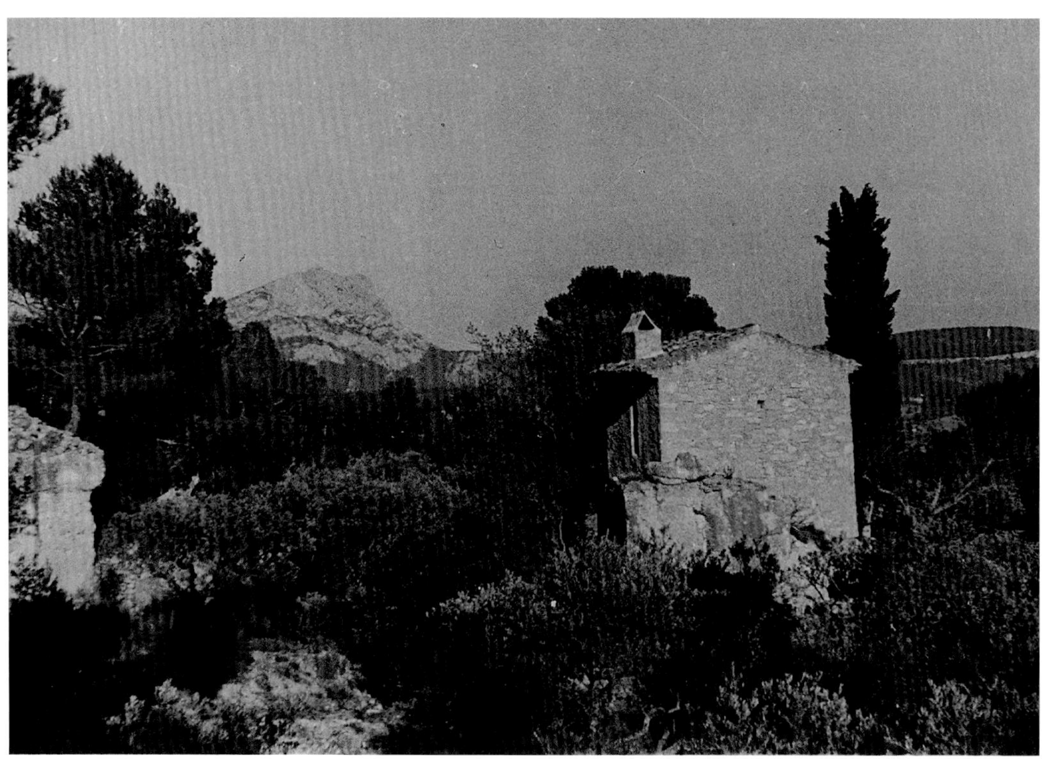

FIG. 39 Cézanne's *cabanon* at the Bibémus quarry, c. 1933–35. John Rewald Archive, Department of Image Collections, National Gallery of Art Library, Washington

John Rewald, the most persistent student of Cézanne, has divided them into two groups. The earlier of these he dates to 1894–95 (Rewald 795–799), while the second group, in which the Bloch painting fits (Rewald 836–839), ranges from 1895 to 1900.[1] And a single later picture that surely represents the quarry (Rewald 888) is dated 1900 by Rewald and as late as 1902 by others. Since Cézanne failed to sign or date any of these pictures and none is known to have been exhibited in his lifetime, it is not possible to document any sequence. Yet surely, if Cézanne did rent a hut for his supplies, he kept all the Bibémus canvases there, most likely working on them over the entire duration of the rental, bringing certain of them to completion sooner than others. The stylistic links among certain of the works, including the Bloch painting, to the documented canvases of the late 1890s suggest that he kept the cabin for at least five years, and it is likely that all the Bibémus paintings remained there until the end of Cézanne's life.

Cézanne, like French landscape painters of the previous Barbizon generation, was obsessed by the interplay of large rocks and trees. Whether he found them in the forest of Fontainebleau (as had Théodore Rousseau, Jean-Baptiste-Camille Corot, and others), in the overgrown environs of the Château Noir, or at Bibémus, these rocks engaged in an interplay with foliage that for Cézanne surely symbolized the contrast between the profoundly deep time of geology and the relatively brief seasonality of arboreal growth. This almost Wordsworthian idea of natural time beyond man is central to Cézanne's landscape aesthetic, whether in Provence or northern France. Indeed, the persistent idea of what the French themselves call *la France*

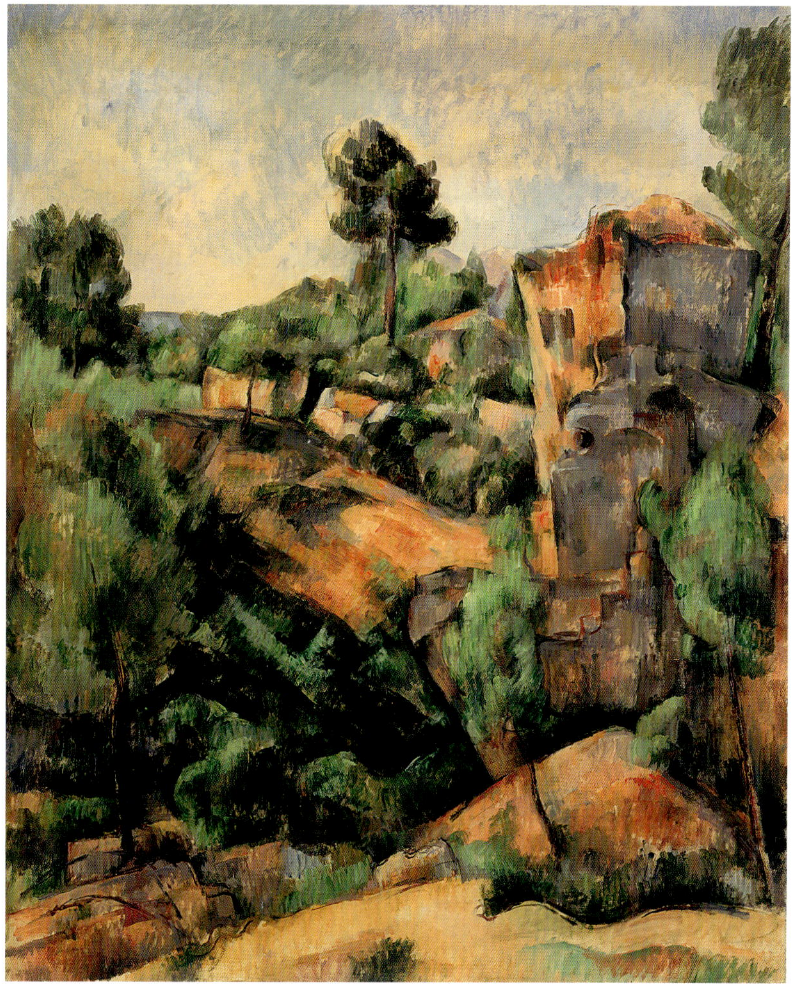

FIG. 40 Paul Cézanne, *Bibémus Quarry (Carrière de Bibémus)*, 1898, oil on canvas, 36¼ × 28⅝ in. (92 × 72.8 cm). The Barnes Foundation, Merion, Pennsylvania

profonde (or lasting, "profound" France) seems to lie behind Cézanne's entire career, making this most direct of painters a pictorial recorder of persistence rather than change.

Nina Kallmyer has written persuasively about what she calls the geological past of Provence and Cézanne's own knowledge of the literature around this branch of the natural sciences.[2] Kallmyer has linked the Bibémus quarry to Roman times and documents its active operation by private owners until the 1830s. By the time Cézanne came to it in 1895, the quarry had been closed for nearly sixty years, and it had almost returned to a natural state with large pine trees growing near the variegated quarry pits. Cézanne painted five vertical canvases—half the total number—on this site, of which the Bloch canvas is among the best preserved. The largest of these are in the Musée de l'Orangerie, Paris, and the Barnes Foundation, Merion, Pennsylvania (fig. 40). Albert Barnes, in his time the most important single collector of Cézanne paintings in the world, owned another of the Bibémus canvases.

The Bloch Cézanne is one of two identically sized vertical compositions that occupied the artist from 1895 to 1900; the other is in a private collection (fig. 41). The similarities of size,

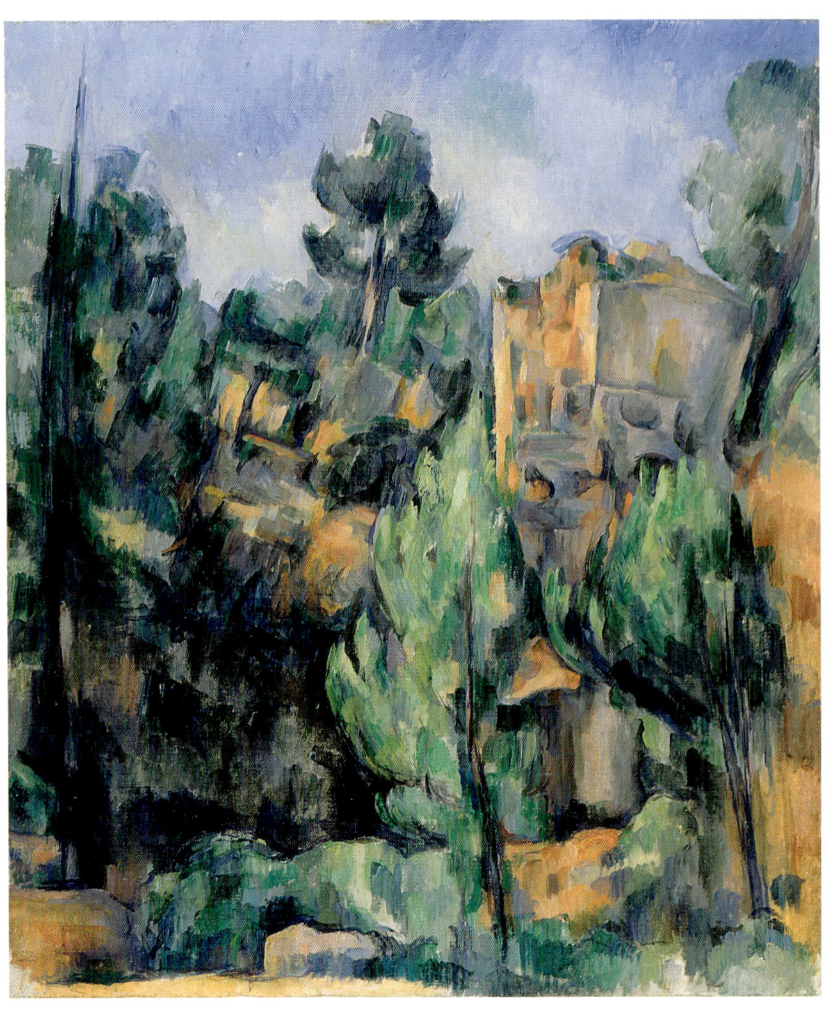

FIG. 41 Paul Cézanne, *Bibémus Quarry (Carrière de Bibémus)*, 1896–97, oil on canvas, 25⅝ × 21¼ in. (65 × 54 cm). Private collection

composition, and point of view between the canvases almost suggest that Cézanne worked on them simultaneously in a form of pictorial competition. The two possibly represent views from a high point in the quarry toward somewhat different motifs. Each is centered on a large tree that rises in lone splendor from the rocky landscape, almost like a single flower on a stem. Cézanne divided the Black composition into distinct halves that seem to struggle for dominance beneath the great tree. By contrast, the Bloch painting is arranged around a centrally located rectangular rock that anchors the tree, which bursts forth into the deep blue sky. The Black painting is dominated by the brilliant orange of the stone, while the Bloch view restricts the rocky portion to the lower center of the canvas, which is dominated by greens and blues.

The Bloch painting is perfectly preserved on a preprimed canvas, which survives unlined. Cézanne seems to have used a small brush and dark blue paint to draw the major outlines of the forms onto the priming. He then worked with larger brushes and colors to fill in areas of rock, foliage, and sky with thick, parallel strokes of paint. The priming itself shows through in many scattered areas throughout the composition, suggesting that Cézanne worked in an all-over manner at every stage, allowing bare areas to remain wherever a stroke of paint was not required for the structural integrity of the painting. At the end, he again took up the small brush and, with darker purplish blue paint, added drawn lines to certain portions of the painting, thereby bringing the pictorial process full circle: drawing to painting to drawing.

—RB

NOTES

1. John Rewald with Walter Feilchenfeldt and Jayne Warman, *The Paintings of Paul Cézanne: A Catalogue Raisonné* (New York, 1996), vol. 1, pp. 500–503, and vol. 2, pp. 292–93.

2. Nina Maria Athanassoglou-Kallmyer, *Cézanne and Provence: The Painter in His Culture* (Chicago, 2003), pp. 163–73.

Paul Cézanne

French, 1839–1906

24. *Man with a Pipe (L'homme à la pipe)*, 1890–92

Oil on canvas, 17 × 13½ in. (43.2 × 34.3 cm)

M*an with a Pipe* belongs to a group of Cézanne oil studies of standing male figures that project, despite their relatively small formats, a definite monumentality. They all relate to a group of paintings representing card players, one of the most important pictorial projects Cézanne undertook. In these works a few men play cards in a café, sometimes with and other times without witnesses. In painting this subject, Cézanne made a conscious contribution to a theme important in the history of European painting largely as a pictorial investigation of luck, predetermination, intelligence, and subtlety. Card players must disguise their true intentions to win a game, and for that reason, great artists, including Caravaggio, Georges De la Tour, Valentin de Boulogne, and Hendrick ter Brugghen, have represented them as pictorial metaphors for players in the larger game of life.

The figure in the Bloch painting appears as a spectator in two versions of the *Card Players*: the monumental painting (fig. 42) at the Barnes Foundation and the smaller but equally finished version in the Metropolitan Museum of Art (fig. 43). In these larger works, three men are seated around a square table. The front of the table has a drawer and on it lies a pipe pointing toward the viewer. At the back, facing the viewer, a man stands, his arms crossed, smoking a pipe and wearing a hat, and most likely watching the game but possibly momentarily lost in thought. The Bloch painting offers the first fully resolved oil study for this particular figure.

There is a major difference, however, between the Bloch figure and those in the Barnes and Metropolitan paintings. Seen on its own in the Bloch study, the figure plays no clear narrative role. If we did not know that this standing man relates to Cézanne's *Card Players*, we would interpret his representation differently. In the larger paintings Cézanne seems to have been uncertain as to how to connect him to the rest of the group. Is he a neutral observer? Is he a player who has just completed a game? Is he waiting for his turn, once the present game is over? Is he just standing there—lost in his own world? In the larger figural scenes he does not actively participate, but he is important as an observer. One can imagine him as a kind of umpire, a controller who enforces the rules and makes certain the game evolves as it should, but none of this is definite in the Barnes and Metropolitan paintings. In the Bloch painting, with the context of the café and the card players omitted, we must deal with the figure on his own terms—and those set up by the artist. The general facial features of the Bloch figure appear less menacing, less drawn out and intense, than the features of the corresponding figure in the two larger paintings.

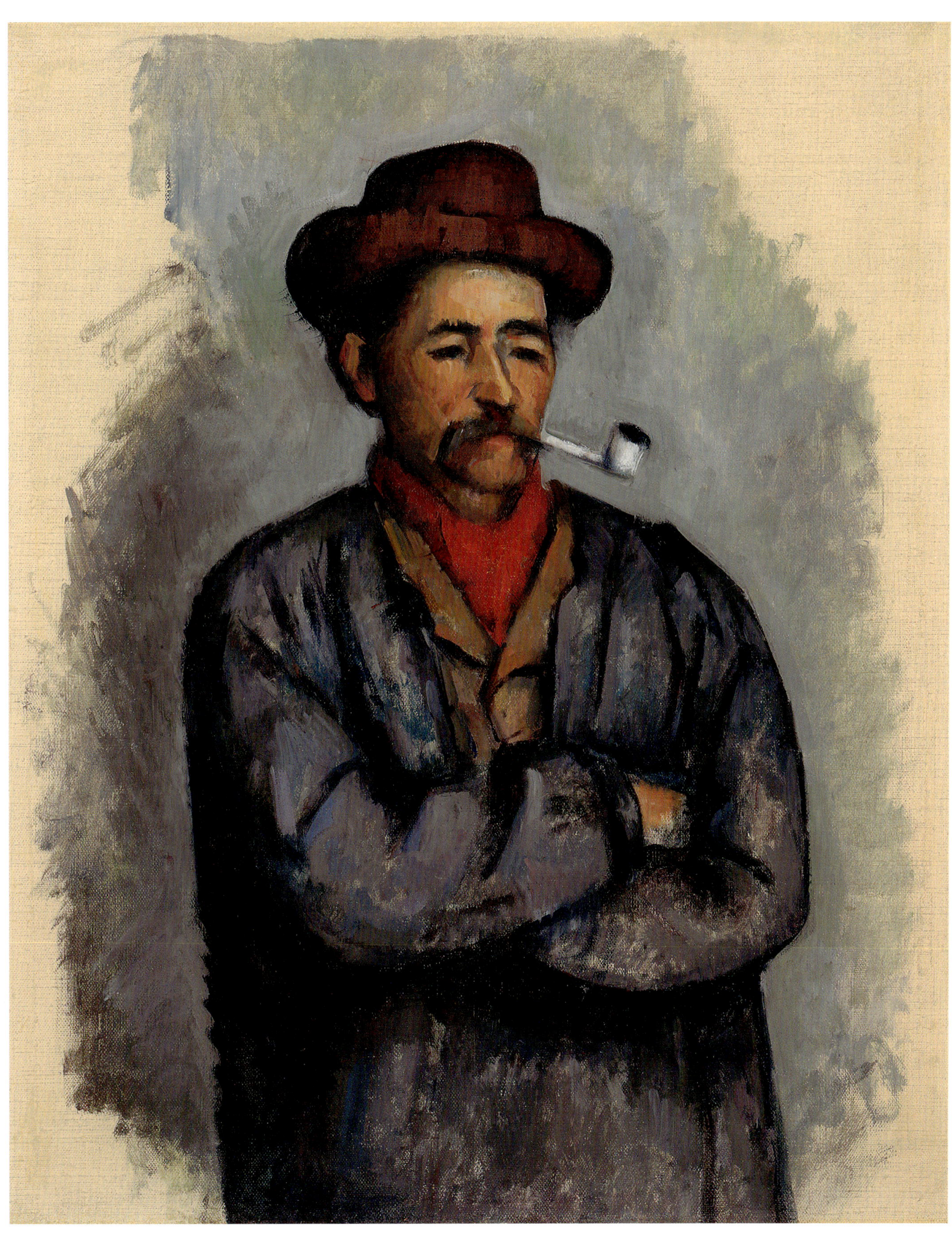

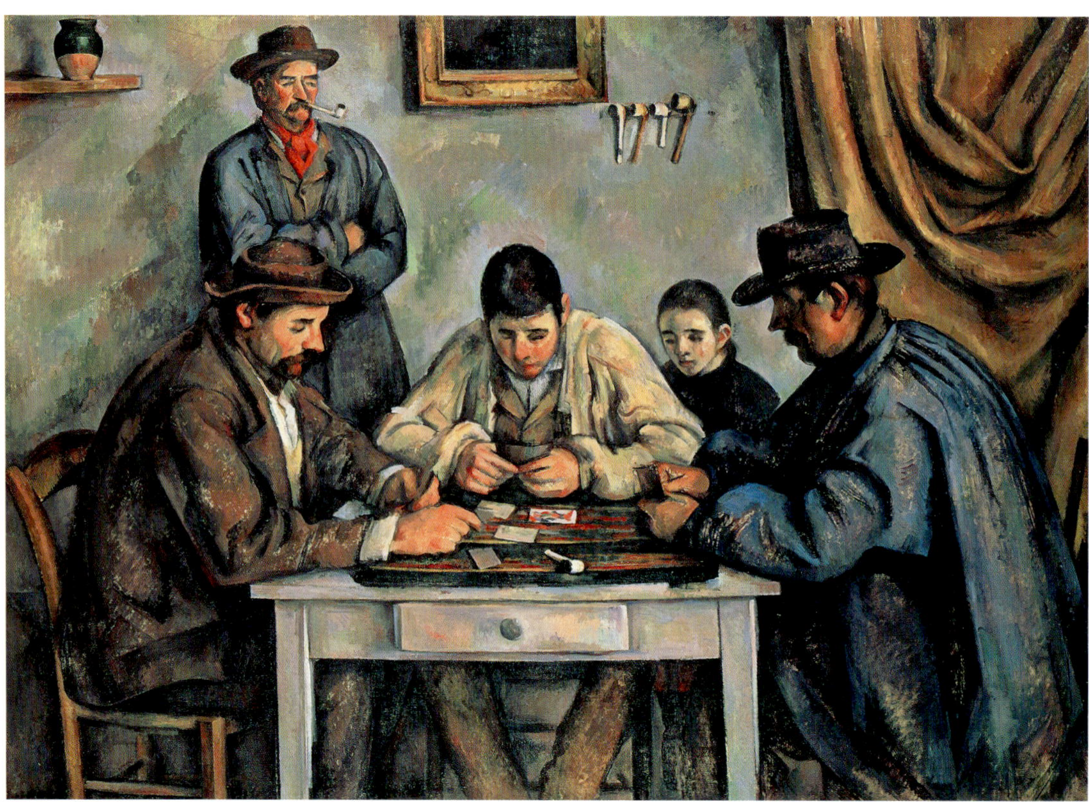

FIG. 42 Paul Cézanne, *The Card Players (Les joueurs de cartes)*, 1890–92, oil on canvas, 53¼ × 71⅝ in. (135.3 × 181.9 cm). The Barnes Foundation, Merion, Pennsylvania

The Bloch painting relates to several other small studies of the individual players in differing poses.[1] Cézanne clearly saw the *Card Players* as a complex project in which each constituent part had to be studied independently. Yet each single figure painting stands on its own, and, as a result, the Bloch painting cannot be interpreted simply as a study for the multifigure composition. It is not even necessary to take into account the role of the figure in the two larger paintings in order to understand it, and, similarly, the standing figure at the back of the two larger paintings tells us little we need to know about the Bloch painting. This painting stands on its own because of the astonishing force the artist displayed in applying touches to the canvas, creating folds, masses, and volumes from nothing but paint. The various details of relief, the angles, and the different segments of the garment are all painted with an audacity and intensity that give this work its own raison d'être, its own uniqueness.

The slate blue coat the man wears appears to have been almost sculpted with paint. The effort and energy unleashed by Cézanne to produce this result is what is at stake in this picture—not the narrative function of a male figure. The same is true for the treatment of the shirt and the incredibly intense red scarf. These volumes appear as if they were carved with color, producing an impressive relief, like a geological structure that holds together the head and pipe of the figure as they emerge from a block. The head itself is strangely detached, serene, meditative; likewise, the eyes, almost closed, seem to express no need, no desire, no intention. The scene of

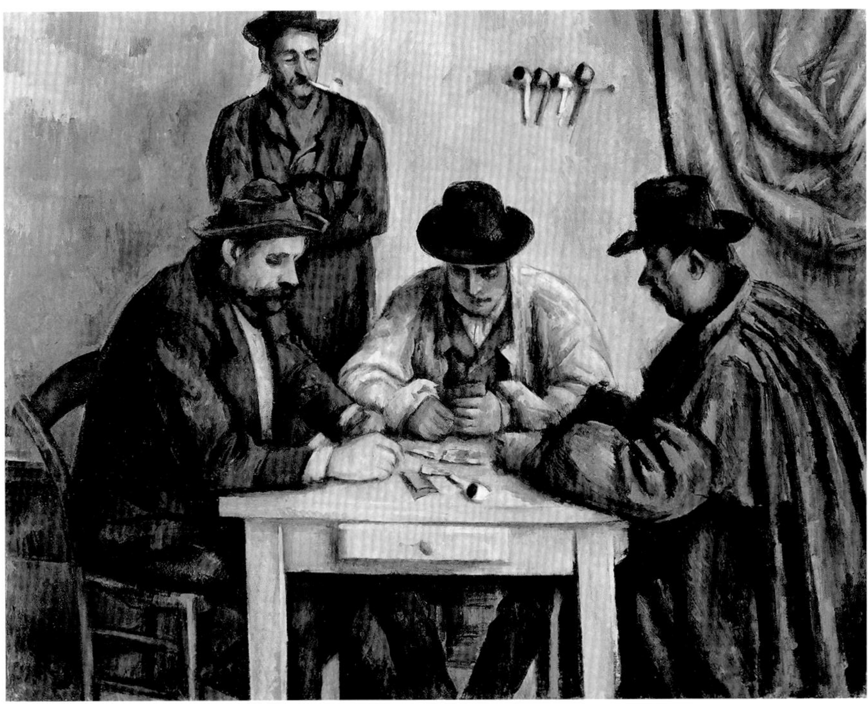

FIG. 43 Paul Cézanne, *The Card Players (Les joueurs de cartes)*, 1890–92, oil on canvas, 25¾ × 32¼ in. (65.4 × 81.9 cm). The Metropolitan Museum of Art, New York, bequest of Stephen C. Clark, 1960

the card players, out there in the two large paintings, is not necessary here. In a protomodernist fashion, this standing figure invites us to meditate on the fact that what we see is simply that—what we see—something made by the artist.

—JP

NOTE

1. See, for example, nos. 708 (Worcester Art Museum), 709 (Musée d'Orsay, Paris), 711 (National Gallery of Art, Washington), and 712 (Courtauld Institute, London) in John Rewald with Walter Feilchenfeldt and Jayne Warman, *The Paintings of Paul Cézanne: A Catalogue Raisonné* (New York, 1996).

Henri de Toulouse-Lautrec

French, 1864–1901

25. *General Séré de Rivières (Le Général Séré de Rivières)*, 1881–82

Watercolor over pencil on paper, 10 × 7 in. (25.4 × 17.8 cm);
signed with monogram and inscribed lower right: *FROM A PHOTO*

The famously gifted Toulouse-Lautrec perfected the techniques of drawing, watercolor, and oil painting while still in his teens, largely under the influence of the Salon painter and family friend René Princeteau (1843–1914). A well-known painter of horses in both racing and hunting contexts, Princeteau was much sought after by the French aristocracy as well as its nemesis, the haute-bourgeoisie. By the early 1880s Princeteau had already submitted large equestrian portraits of Toulouse-Lautrec's parents to the Salon and would have spent a good deal of time with the family precisely when the Bloch watercolor was made. Toulouse-Lautrec's membership in the highest levels of the waning French aristocracy is essential to an understanding of his career and his later repudiation of the privileged class as a proper subject for art. But early in his artistic life (he was seventeen or eighteen when he painted this skillful watercolor, and his earliest known works were made in his fourteenth year), Toulouse-Lautrec confined his art to the world of aristocrats and their servants.

General Séré de Rivières was the scion of a French noble family associated with the highest levels of the military since Napoleonic times (to the ancient Toulouse-Lautrec family, he was simply an arriviste). He wears the formal or parade uniform of the French army and sits astride a horse, which appears to stand at attention on the direction of the general. A crude graphite inscription in the lower right corner reads "from a photo." And, although it is most certainly not from the hand of the artist himself (he would not have written in English), it is surely correct. Indeed, the composition is so like that of many photographic equestrian portraits that it undoubtedly was derived not from life but from a photograph of about the same size as the watercolor itself. The horse stands still not because it was pictorially effective but in order to be in focus for the relatively long exposure time of 1880s photography. The photograph made it easier for the young artist to work patiently through the problems of modeling and summary description than if he had sketched from life as the general sat on his horse. Furthermore, a man of the general's standing would never have posed for a teenage artist, even such a well-born one as Henri de Toulouse-Lautrec. The traditional date of 1881–82 given to the watercolor is utterly plausible.

—RB

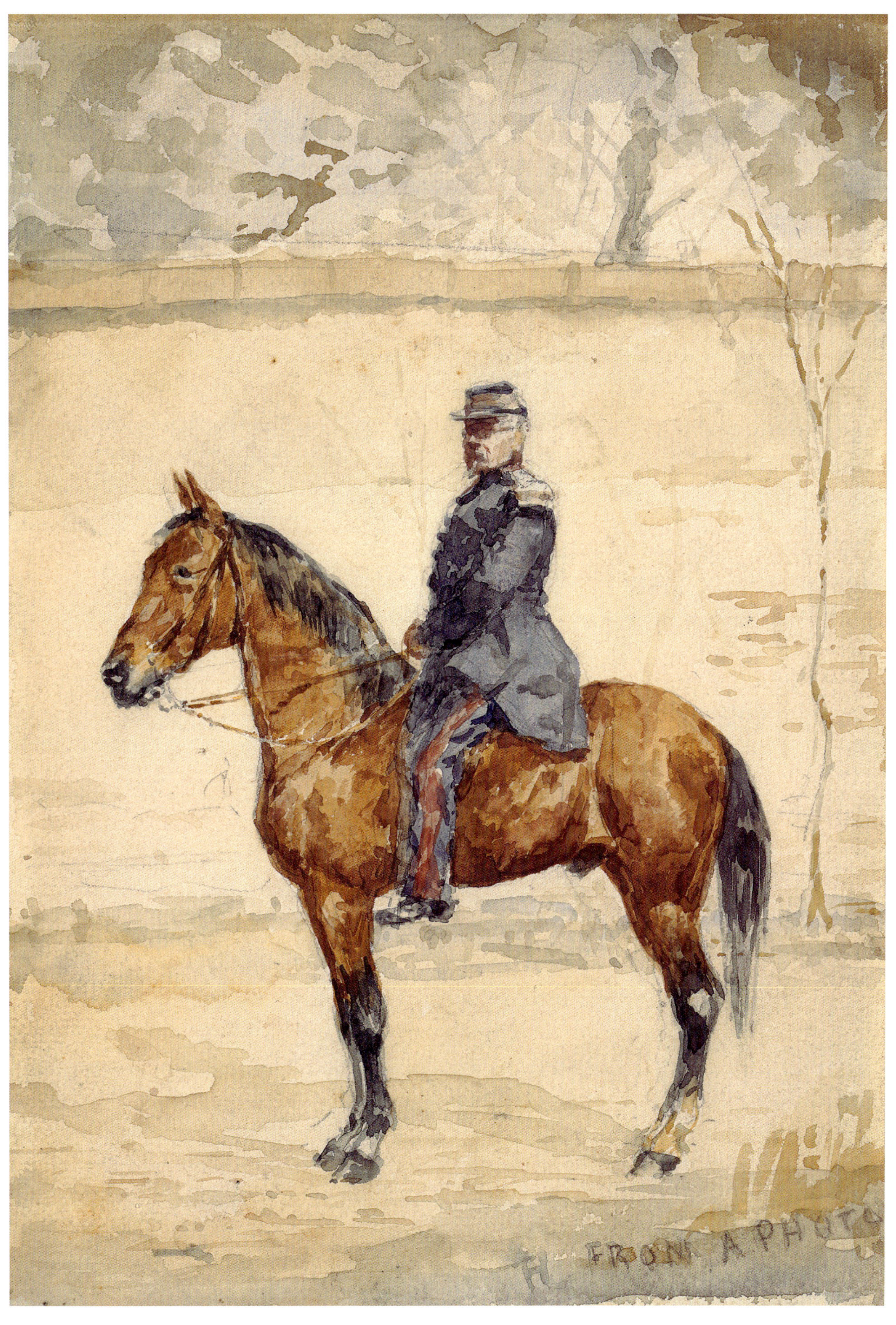
FROM A PHOT

Henri de Toulouse-Lautrec

French, 1864–1901

26. *Jane Avril Looking at a Proof (Jane Avril regardant une épreuve)*, 1893

Oil and crayon on paper, 20¼ × 12¾ in. (51.3 × 32.3 cm)

This personal and vivid artwork hangs on a visual dialogue between two worlds, one exemplified by Jane Avril (1868–1943), a great star of popular entertainment at the turn of the nineteenth century, and the other by the print she holds. Is the print by Toulouse-Lautrec, and does it represent her? Does the dancer confront an image of herself, thus juxtaposing art and life? Following in the footsteps of Degas, Toulouse-Lautrec focused most of his imagery on the demimonde, the cabaret, and the brothel. Suffering from a congenital disease that stunted his growth, he was permanently handicapped, but in the world of brothels and dance halls he found a hospitable shelter where his condition was neither questioned nor questionable. Though an aristocrat, he lived on the margins of society, and he made its rejects the center of his pictorial world.

Toulouse-Lautrec went farther than his mentor Degas in blurring the distinctions between himself and those he portrayed. He represented prostitutes and stars of popular culture not as society's outcasts but as his closest allies and friends. Nowhere was this truer than in the relationship Toulouse-Lautrec developed with the dancer and singer Jane Avril, whom he regarded as a colleague and equal. Indeed, to a large extent he projected his own personality onto the actresses, dancers, and prostitutes who moved with an ease he himself could never manage.

The daughter of a prostitute, Jane Avril is popularly said to have spent part of her youth in a mental institution and even to have cured her psychological malady by dancing. The numerous portraits of her are among the best of Toulouse-Lautrec's oeuvre and testify to their friendship and mutual respect. Avril's own art of dancing could even be described in kinetic terms as another form of graphic activity. She was well known for choreographing her dance routines and quasi-acrobatic poses, which mesmerized her largely male audiences. Toulouse-Lautrec's admiration for Avril's dancing as an art form lies behind the Bloch sketch, a mirror of their relationship. Though it is mere conjecture, Jane Avril becomes her own audience if the proof does indeed represent her (perhaps dancing, as in a lithograph of her produced by Toulouse-Lautrec in 1893 [fig. 44]). For Toulouse-Lautrec, the performer becomes the admirer and critic of his work as she absorbs and interprets his performance, the representation of her performing. Avril here engages with the work and establishes a dialogue with the artist on equal terms.

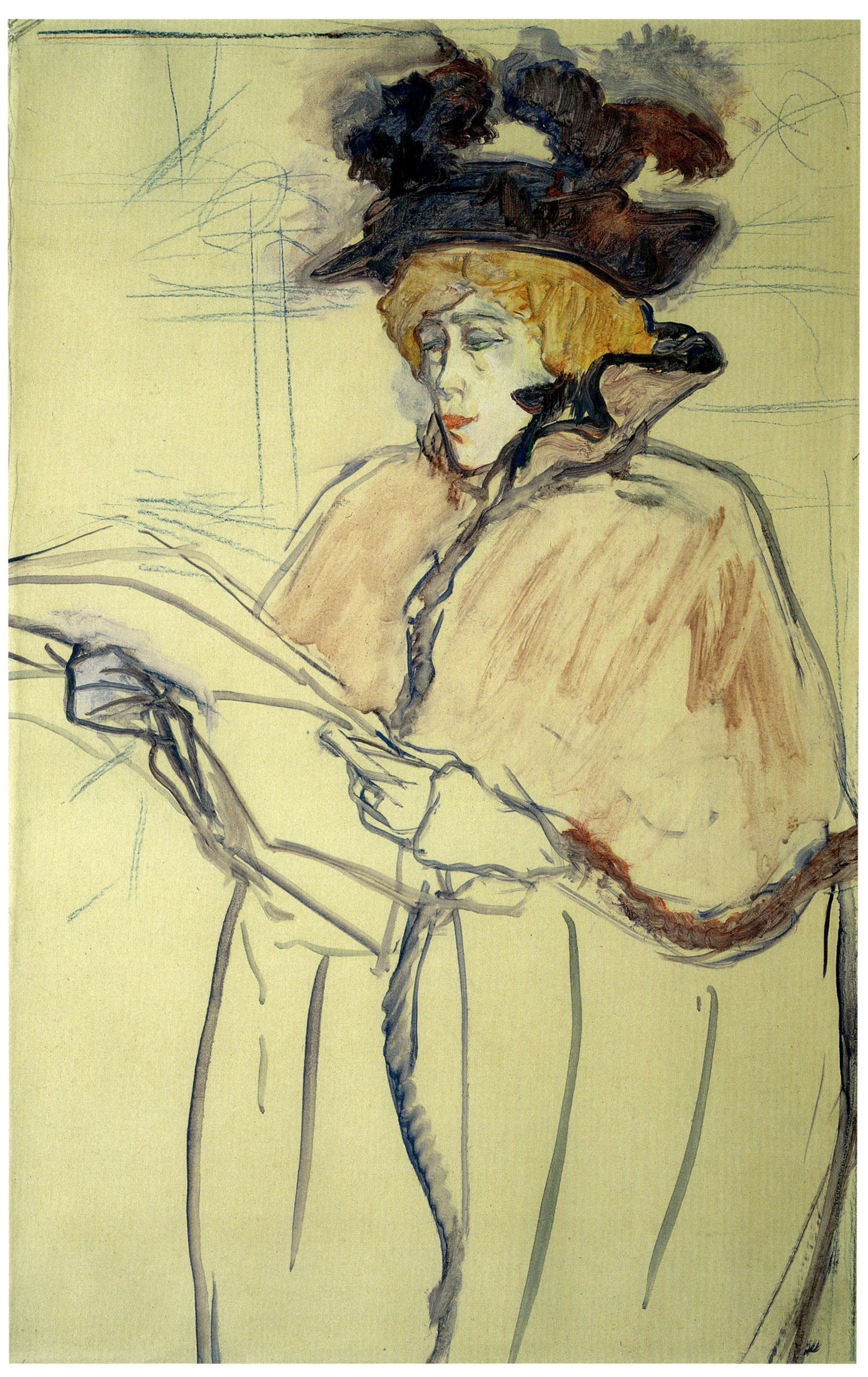

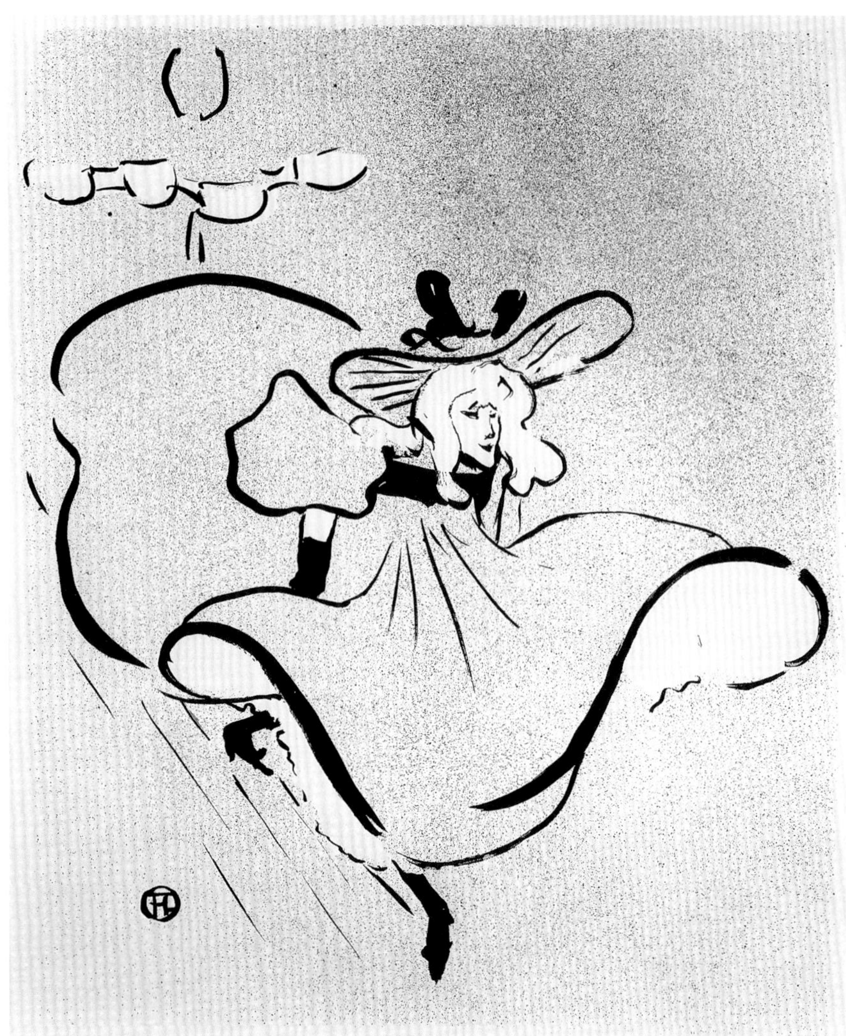

FIG. 44 Henri de Toulouse-Lautrec, *Jane Avril*, 1893, lithograph, 10⅜ × 8⅛ in. (26.2 × 20.4 cm). National Gallery of Art, Washington, Rosenwald Collection

The Bloch painting is most probably a study for a lithograph representing Jane Avril in the workshop of the master printer Le Père Cotelle, of the printing firm of Édouard Ancourt (fig. 45). The interdependence of the artist, performer, and printer as translators of one another's work is perfectly rendered in the lithograph. It appeared on the cover of the first issue of a well-known portfolio of prints by various artists, *L'estampe originale*, published by André Marty in the early 1890s. In both the print and the study, Avril examines a trial proof (the first image of the lithographic process) that has been freshly pulled by Le Père Cotelle. Typical of Toulouse-Lautrec is the economy of line and structure in the study's execution. The richness of the pigment in Avril's hair and the subtle shades depicting the nuances of her gaze and expression are offset by the energy of bold single lines defining the space and volumes of her body. That joining of power and economy looks back to the drawings of Rembrandt as much as forward to the dynamism of Art Nouveau. Best of all is Avril's hat, which seems more a live creature than the product of millinery skill. In this painting

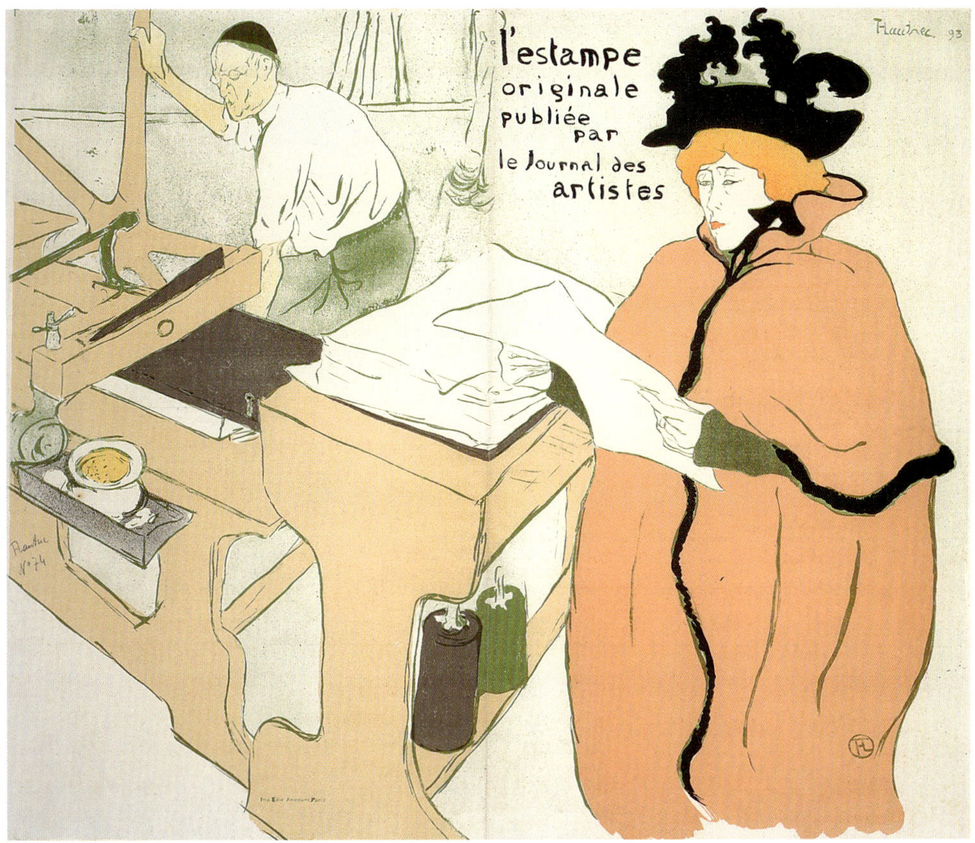

FIG. 45 Henri de Toulouse-Lautrec, *Cover for "L'estampe originale,"* 1893, color lithograph, 22¼ × 25¼ in. (56.3 × 64.2 cm). National Gallery of Art, Washington, Rosenwald Collection

Toulouse-Lautrec gives us the essence of his art and an unmatched demonstration of the power of line.

The Bloch work testifies to the relationship that tied Toulouse-Lautrec to cabaret performers and denizens of the demimonde. Often castigated as a voyeur or intruder in the world of dancers and prostitutes, Toulouse-Lautrec was in fact very much an inhabitant of that milieu. For this reason this work holds a central importance in his oeuvre. Not only does it offer a portrait of one of his favorite subjects and closest friends, but it captures the world at the margins of society in which he functioned and where he had no need to seek legitimacy from the establishment he had rejected.

—JP

Odilon Redon

French, 1840–1916

27. *The Green Vase (Le vase vert)*, c. 1900

Oil on canvas, 28¾ × 21¼ in. (73 × 54 cm), unlined; signed lower left: *Odilon Redon*

Odilon Redon is one of the most complex, perplexing, and ultimately unclassifiable artists in the history of modern art. Frequently associated with the Symbolist movement, he was often consumed by dreams and visions of the macabre, and depicted decapitated heads and floating eyeballs hovering over lugubrious landscapes. Yet the very same artist was equally fond of classic floral arrangements, as the still-life composition in the Bloch Collection testifies. After years of working almost exclusively in black and white—he produced illustrations for literary works by Charles Baudelaire, Gustave Flaubert, and Edgar Allan Poe—Redon in the late 1890s began to employ vibrant colors. In an 1894 letter to his friend Edmond Picard, he stated: "Colors contain a joy which relaxes me; besides they sway me towards something different and new."[1]

From around 1900 Redon concentrated on brilliantly colored floral still lifes such as the Bloch painting. These flower paintings were featured prominently during Redon's lifetime in two pivotal exhibitions: the 1904 Salon d'Automne and his 1906 retrospective at the Galerie Durand-Ruel. As in the Bloch still life, Redon used oil painting as if to emulate the tactile quality of pastel. This indeterminant quality to the surface of his work is somewhat reminiscent of the artist's Symbolist concerns with dreams and the irrational. The Bloch still life appears to be based equally on imagination and observable reality. On the one hand it imparts a sense of dreaminess, with the bouquet apparently detached from any real context, and on the other hand, it conveys the solidity of an apparently viable, even inhabitable space. The figures and faces, butterflies, and glorious blossoms that Redon created were not intended to represent natural truth. Redon managed to suspend his paintings between dream and reality.

The richly painted, lush, glossy turquoise vase appears to be weightless, as if suspended in space over its own shadow. But this is contradicted by a horizontal line that endows the composition with a sense of gravity and deep reality, which forbids us to think of the vase as a mere projection of the mind. This realism is reinforced by a yellow background wall that evokes a drawing-room-like space.

One contrast or opposition gives way to another. Even as the ocher of the wall anchors the composition in reality, it is immediately offset by the pale lilac shadow that emanates from nowhere, except perhaps from a dream. The entire composition hinges on oppositions, swaying between reality and dream, between actuality and imagination. This tension or blending of the

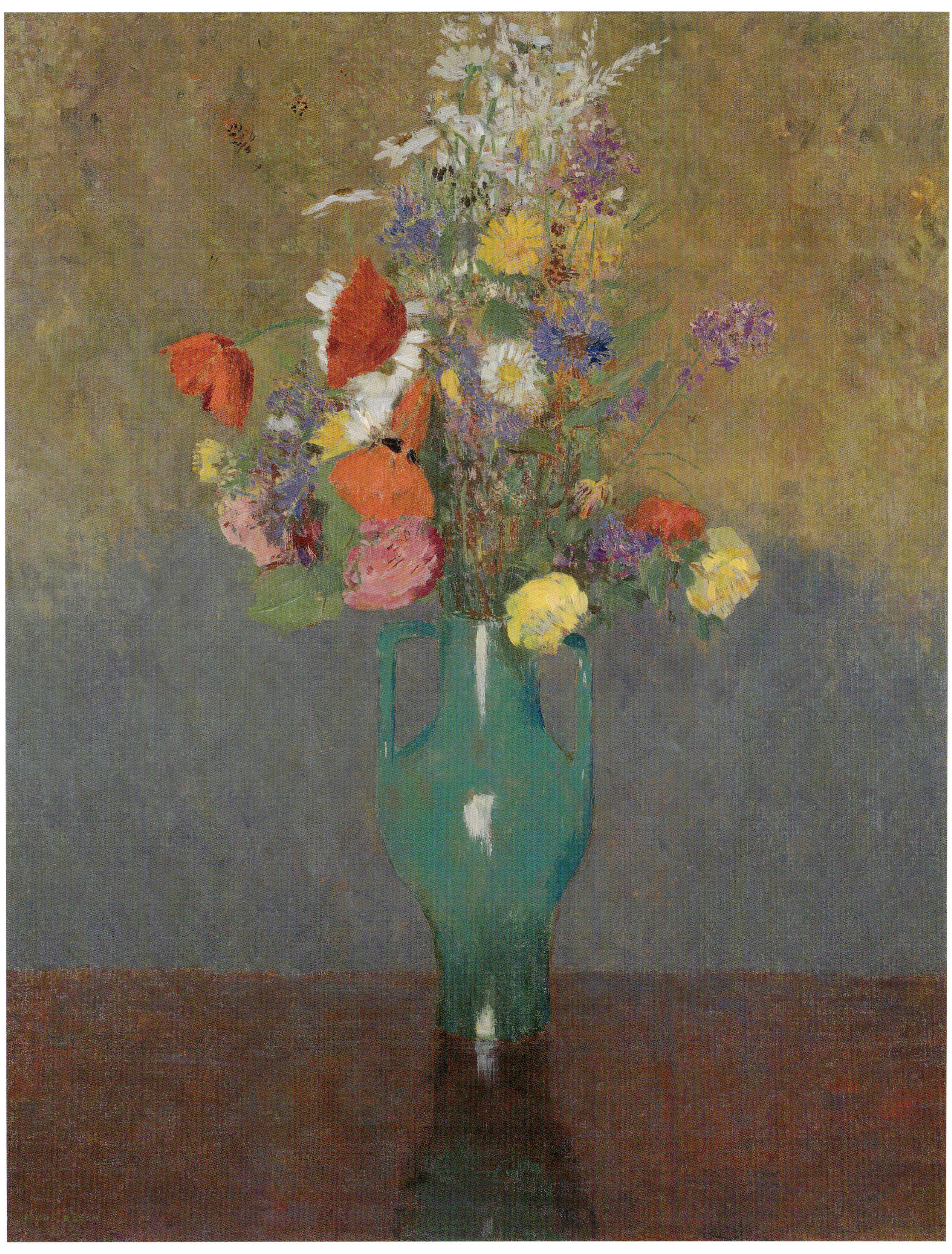

oneiric and the real epitomizes Redon's idiosyncracy and provides an extraordinarily poetic dimension to this work.

In painting floral still lifes, Redon joined a long avant-garde tradition. Scarcely an important artist of the last half of the nineteenth century failed to paint floral still lifes: Courbet, Manet, Cézanne, Pissarro, Monet, Renoir, Van Gogh, and Gauguin all had used flowers as a symbol of the artificiality of "natural" beauty. The fact that flowers had "natural" color, could be arranged as if colors on a palette, and could be enjoyed by viewers with little provocation—or knowledge—made the genre among the most personal and experimental in modern French painting. No wonder that Vuillard, Bonnard, Matisse, Picasso, and Braque all painted flowers, and that all of them looked to Redon.

—JP

NOTE

1. See John Rewald, "Odilon Redon," in *Odilon Redon, Gustave Moreau, Rodolphe Bresdin* (New York, 1961), p. 39.

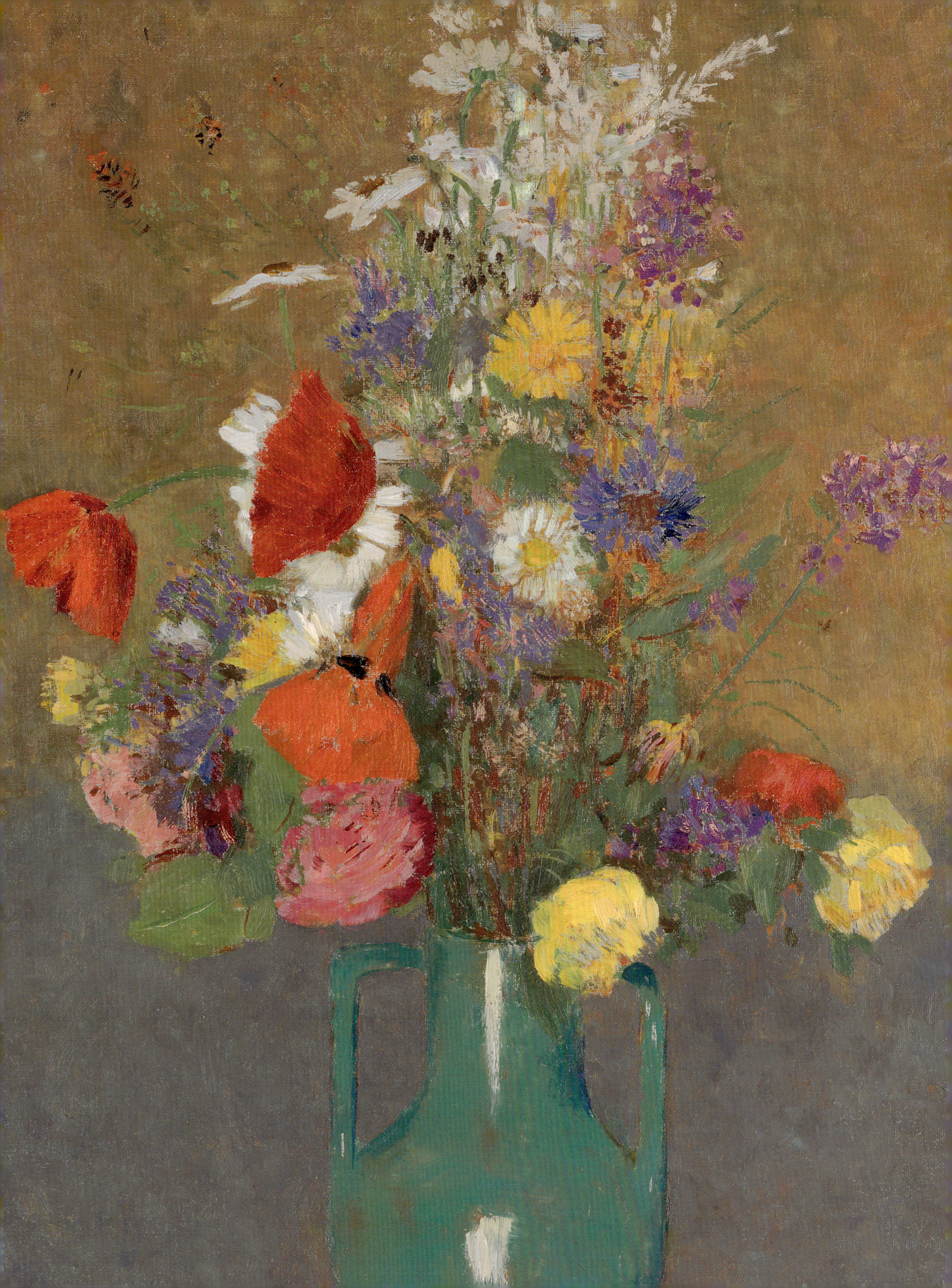

Édouard Vuillard

French, 1868–1940

28. *Woman in a Red Dress*, or *J. R. contre fenêtre*, 1899–1900

Oil on cardboard, 12⅜ × 14¾ in. (31.5 × 37.5 cm); stamped lower right: *Evuillard,*

inscribed on reverse: *J. R. contre fenêtre*

For the great writer André Gide, who wrote eloquently about the decorations of Édouard Vuillard in the early twentieth century, the artist strove, through his supremely subtle and private art, to whisper rather than to speak clearly, to exchange confidences with intimates rather than to make public declarations.[1] In this way, Vuillard moved within a small circle of friends, making works of art that represented his intimates without giving away a single of their secrets to the anonymous international collectors who purchased them. So too this small painting. It represents a glorious dark-haired woman, dressed in a red dress or, more likely, dressing gown trimmed with fur or feathers. She is seated in a large, upholstered black wood chair, her left hand seemingly arranging her hair as she looks into an unseen mirror, lighted by the warm yellow of a shaded lamp on her dressing table. She has no face, no legs, no feet, and no clear reason for being painted, and, thus, we have no idea what she is doing or who she is. A graphite inscription on the back of the cardboard on which the painting was made says "J. R. contre fenêtre" (J. R. against the window), and there does seem to be a window frame at the back left.

Many viewers of this small, unfinished painting have been completely stumped by the central figure.[2] "What is she doing?" each has asked, and one anonymous writer made his frustration clear by noting in the painting's file at the Nelson-Atkins: "It is not possible to tell what the woman is doing. Basket on the table would seem to be filled with yard or cloth, etc." Where does one go from there? If we accept the initials J. R. as correct, the likeliest subject is the famous singer Jeanne Raunay, who appeared as Iphigenia in a performance of Gluck's *Iphigénie en Tauride* at the Théâtre de la Renaissance in December 1899. Vuillard painted her in that role in a work inscribed and given to his patron Prince Emmanuel Bibesco (whereabouts unknown), and a pair of anonymous prints representing Jeanne Raunay as Iphigenia is in the collection of the Bibliothèque de l'Arsenal in Paris.[3] Perhaps, given the fact that no other female figure with the initials J. R. appears in the entire corpus of Vuillard, we may safely assume that we are viewing the singer in her dressing room, after she has donned a particularly magnificent dressing gown to greet admirers at the end of a performance. We are, it would seem, the first to arrive and have yet to interrupt her post-performance reveries. Taken together, the two Vuillard paintings of Raunay become a study in the psychology of performance, both on the stage and off.

This painting of a famous female performer was first owned by no less a figure in the Paris art world than the renowned couturiere Elsa Schiaparelli, who seems to have purchased it from

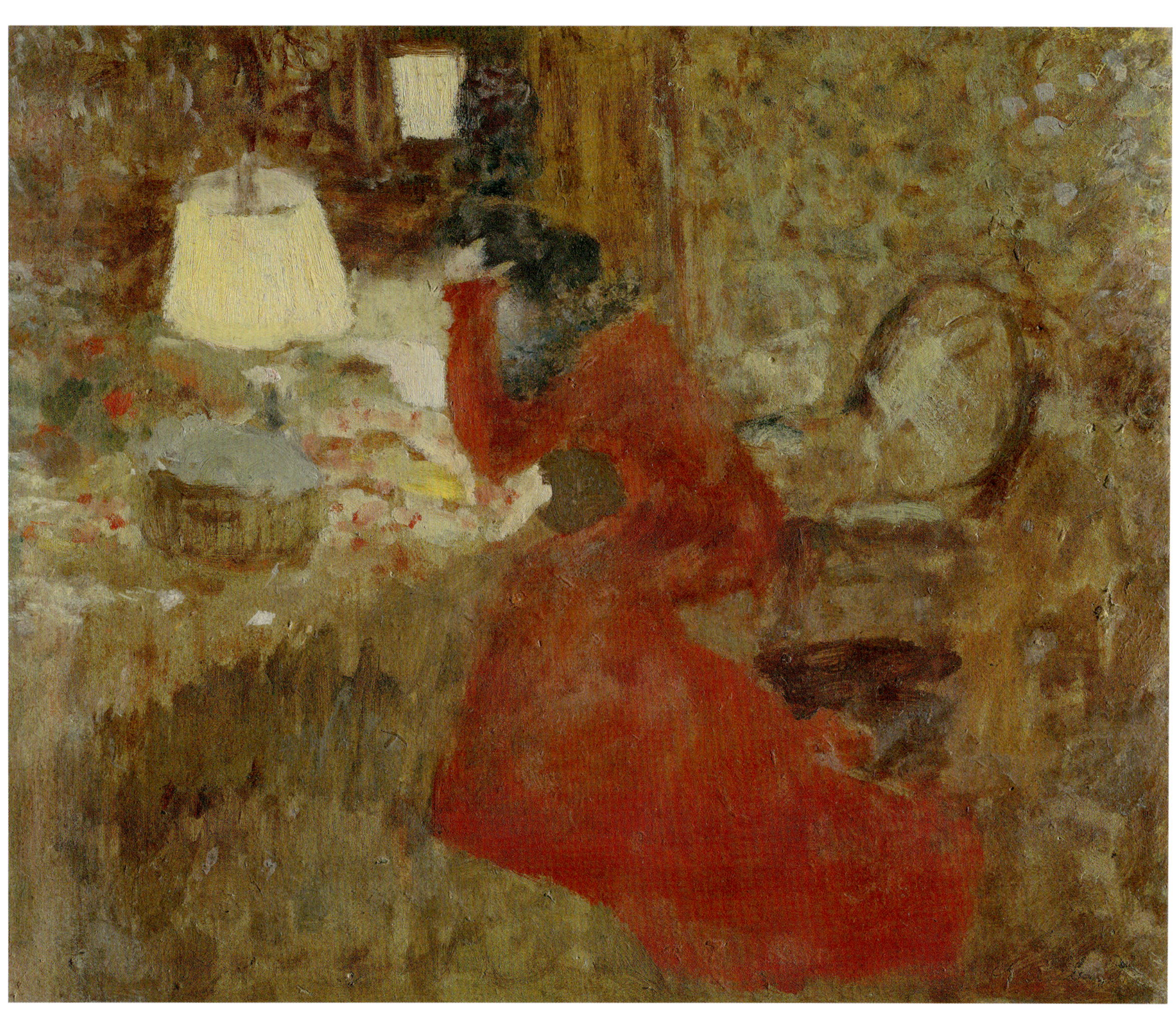

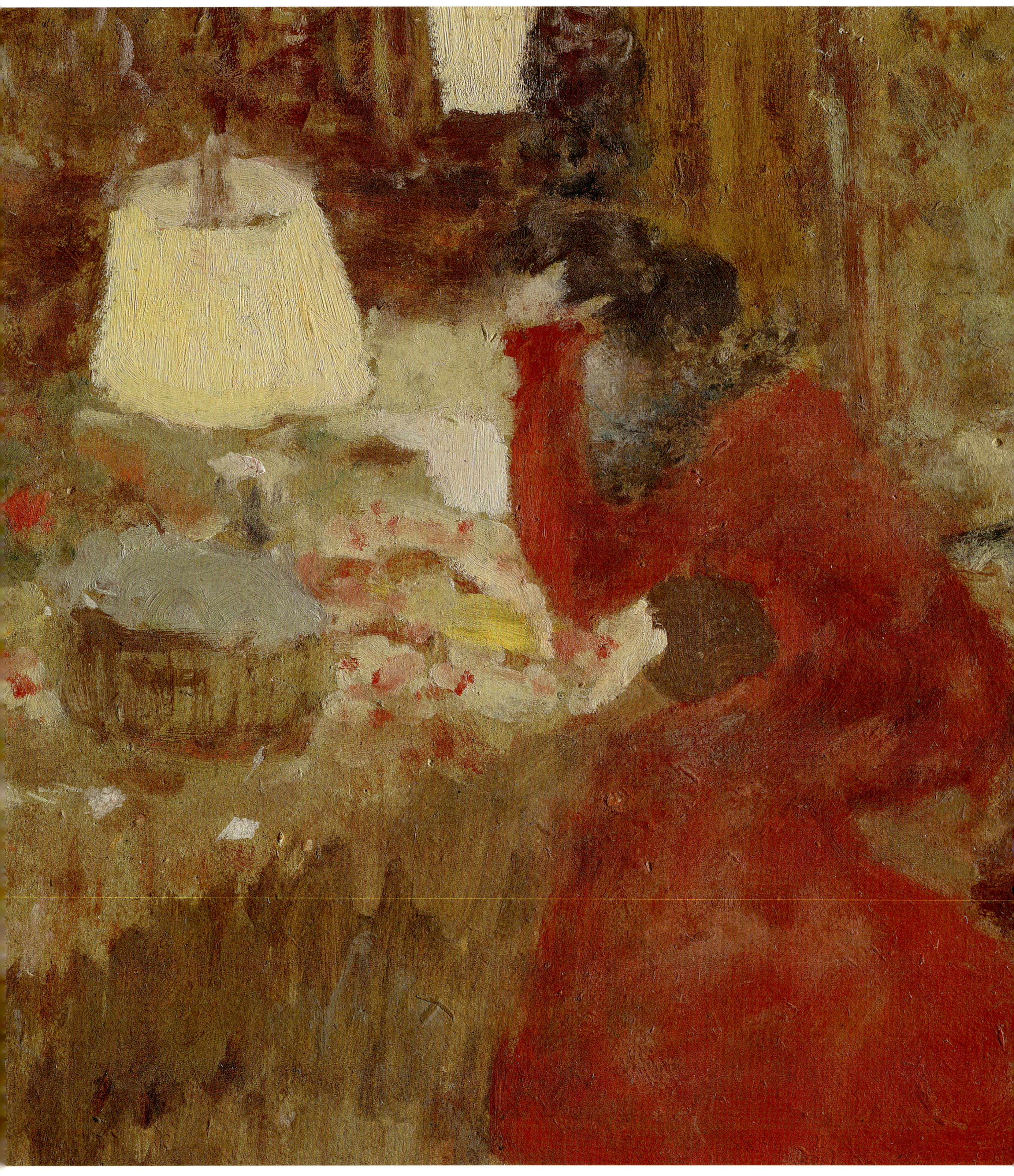

Vuillard's estate. Did she know the identity of the sitter? Unfortunately, we shall never know. Schiaparelli owned another work by Vuillard, *The Drawing Room* (private collection),[4] which represents a group of men and women together in what has been identified tentatively as the drawing room of the Lerolle family in Paris. It was painted at the very same time as the Bloch Vuillard and represents the artist's relatively recent entrée into the world of famous and successful Parisians.

—RB

NOTES

1. André Gide, "A Walk round the Salon d'Automne, 1905," in John Russell, *Vuillard, 1868–1940* (London, 1971), p. 96.

2. Unfortunately the monumental catalogue raisonné of Vuillard's paintings produced by the Wildenstein Foundation does little to help in the quest for the subject and meaning of this small painting. See Antoine Salomon and Guy Cogeval, *Vuillard, The Inexhaustible Glance: Critical Catalogue of Paintings and Pastels* (Milan, 2003), vol. 1, p. 532, VI-113.

3. Ibid., pp. 212–13.

4. Ibid., VI-113.

Pierre Bonnard

French, 1867–1947

29. *The White Cupboard (L'armoire blanche)*, 1931

Oil on canvas, 49⅜ × 36¾ in. (125.2 × 93.2 cm), unlined; signed lower right: *Bonnard*

This masterpiece represents a cupboard that formed a portion of a paneled wall in the dining room of the small house Bonnard purchased in the village of Le Cannet, above Cannes, in 1927. Bonnard immediately removed a wall between two small rooms on the ground floor, creating a single space, which served as both living and dining rooms for Bonnard, his wife, Marthe, and their visitors. Soon after he bought the house, Bonnard entertained his neighbor Henri Matisse and his faithful Swiss collectors, the Hahnlosers. Many important artists, collectors, writers, and friends had lunch or dinner in this room. Plans of the house (fig. 46), published in Michel Terrasse's wonderful *Bonnard et Le Cannet* (1987), show the room clearly and reveal that the fireplace was off-center in the room, flanked by a single paneled cupboard with two doors on the left and a group of three paneled cupboards with six doors on the right. The paneling itself effectively disguised the depth and extent of the hidden cupboards. This room and its simple paneling are clearly represented with Bonnard himself in superb black-and-white photographs by Henri Cartier-Bresson (fig. 47).

Bonnard painted this room, the largest in the house, so often that it became an entire pictorial universe, the source of almost endless motifs. Terrasse, who effectively catalogued the surviving paintings in which Bonnard represented the various rooms in the house, lists twice as many of the dining room as of any other room, including the painter's studio. Using its ample spaces, he moved the table and chairs from one part of the room to the other, depending on the light, his mood, the season, and the time of day. Certain of the paintings are primarily still lifes, focusing on the table itself (usually covered with a protective cloth of red felt) with various tablecloths, vessels, and foodstuffs. Others concentrate on the interaction of the interior space with the large garden visible from the glazed door and two ample windows facing the distant sea. Others center the pictorial world on the fireplace with its marvelously ambiguous mirror. And still others deal with the single door opposite the fireplace which led into an adjacent hall.

The Bloch painting does none of that. In composing this commanding vertical canvas, Bonnard virtually ignored the fireplace, which exists only partially on the left, and created a patterned plane of cupboards that dominates the dining table itself and its recessive still-life elements. Bonnard seemed to have been all but obsessed with pictorial grids and shadowed interior spaces. The painting is arranged with a geometric rigor rarely seen in this master of soft

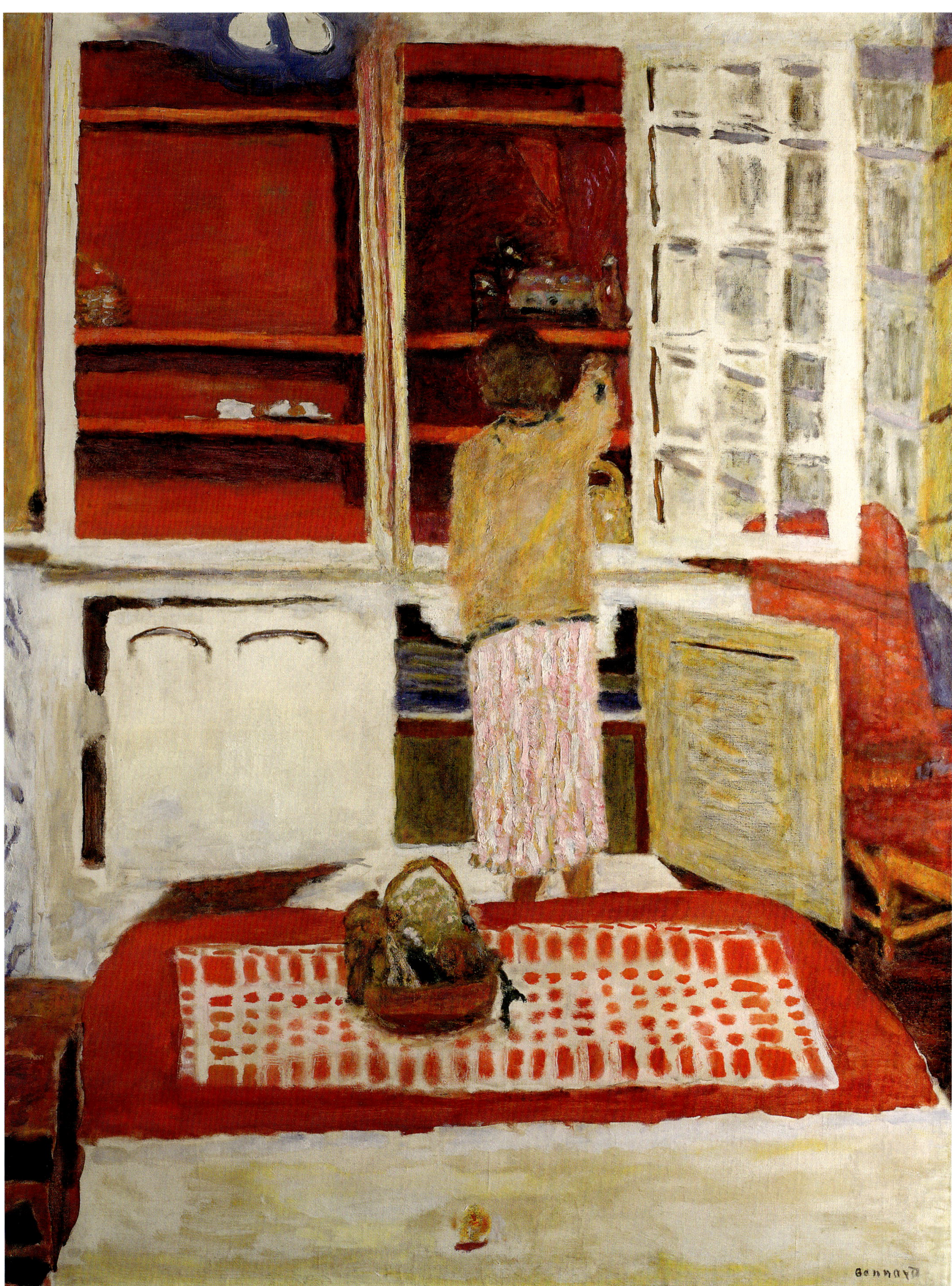
Bonnard

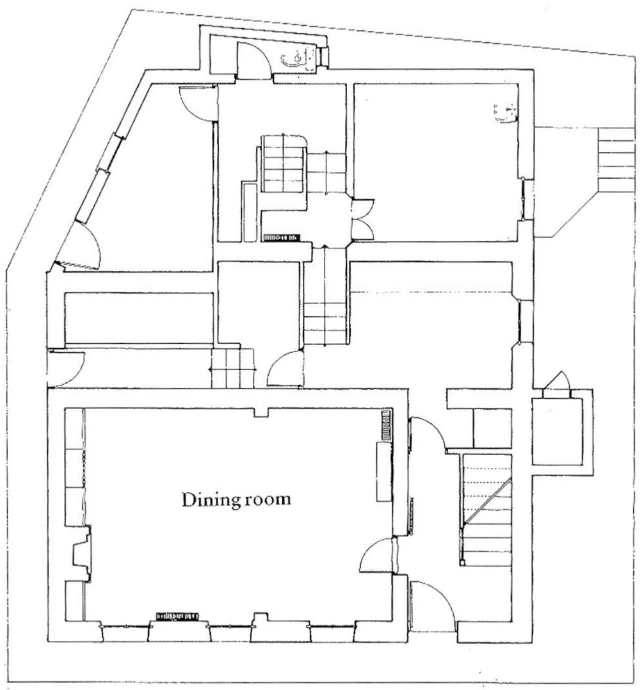

FIG. 46 Plan of the Bonnard house, "Le Bosquet," avenue Victoria, Le Cannet

chromatic masses. Its strong contrasts of dark and light, its dramatic—almost black—shadows, the strict planarity of its motif, and the gridded gingham cloth on the table make us think of the one painter then in Paris whose work is the opposite of that of Bonnard: the Dutch master Piet Mondrian. Mondrian was widely shown in Paris in the late 1920s and early 1930s, most notably in *Circle et Carré*, an exhibition of recent work held at Galerie 23 in April 1930.[1] One almost wonders whether Bonnard wandered—by mistake?—into this exhibition, seeing works such as *Composition in Red, Blue, and Yellow* (Fukuoka City Bank, Japan). Indeed, with the rather subtle exception of Marthe's pink skirt, virtually all the colors in Bonnard's paintings are the three primary hues of Mondrian's title, and Bonnard's shadowy lines are strictly horizontal and vertical, functioning pictorially in ways startlingly like those of Mondrian. It is difficult to conceive of a connection between Mondrian and Bonnard, but, if it is possible, the Bloch Bonnard is its best embodiment.

Bonnard presents us with his common-law wife and muse, Marthe, dressed in a casually fashionable skirt and jacket and arranging tableware in the cupboards. She has opened the solid door of the high cupboard on the left so that it is exactly perpendicular to the picture plane, and we see only its edge. It casts deep shadows into the cupboard with a fifteen-paned glass door in which she is working. In turn, the mullions of the glazed door create purplish shadow patterns on the white surface of the adjacent cupboard and the perpendicular yellow wall. The painting seems flooded with light, which clearly has one source—the dangling electric bulbs of the entirely functional fixture that brings blue-tinged white light into the picture from the top left. Hence this brilliantly illuminated "Mondrianesque" picture represents the room at night, when the shadows and light from the double lightbulbs were at their most intense.

It is difficult to think of Bonnard as a night painter. His love of colored masses, illuminated by the subtly varied tints of natural light, would preclude it. Yet, like his precursor Degas, who often painted at night and fetishized artificial illumination, theatrical and otherwise, Bonnard responded to the full range of natural and artificial light, and he even explored a combination of the two for its pictorial possibilities. In this he was joined by his good friend Édouard Vuillard. Both men painted in light conditions varying from dawn to the dead of night, in exteriors and interiors, lit by combinations of natural and artificial light. The artificiality of their poetry of light makes them utterly modern, and the Bloch painting shows just how up-to-date the middle-aged Bonnard was in 1931. When he painted this masterpiece, he could have been thinking of Mondrian at night!

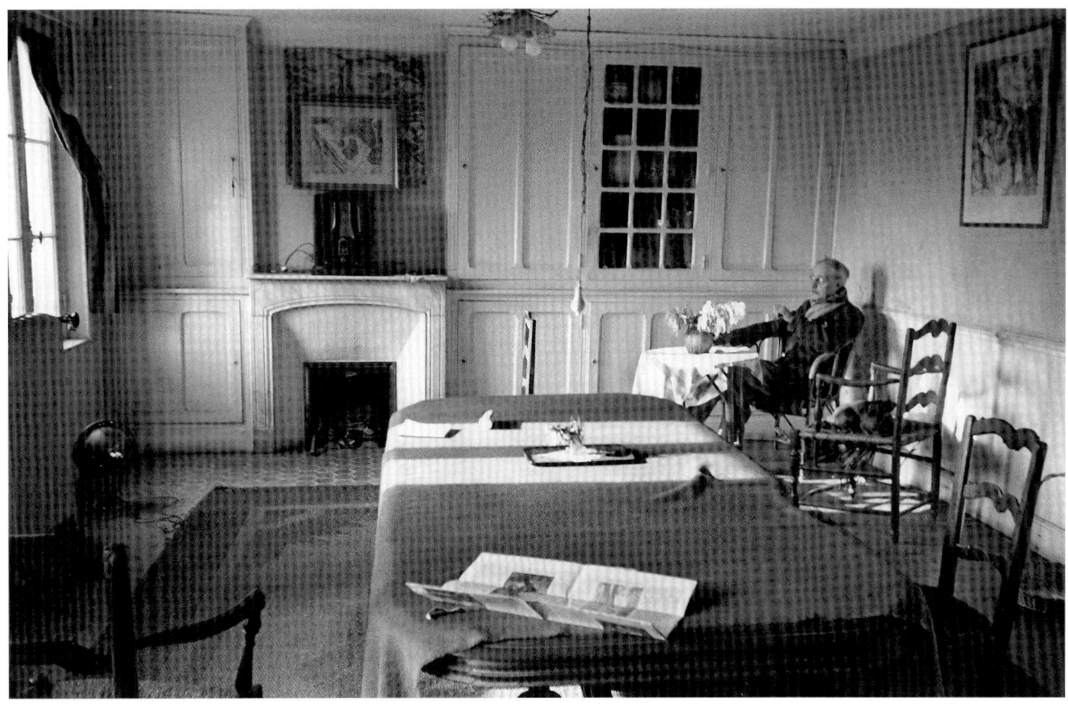

FIG. 47 Henri Cartier-Bresson, *Painter Pierre Bonnard at His Home*, 1944

The basket of figs, grapes, and other fruits that sits ceremonially on the red and white tablecloth is hardly a dominating element of this composition, and, for that reason, it has never been included in the painting's title. Yet this element is as beautifully painted and subtle as any Bonnard still life from the early 1930s. Because it is night, dinner is probably finished, and Marthe puts the dishes back into the cupboards before going upstairs to her room. Bonnard avoids any precise narrative in the painting, but he does include an enigmatic series of painted marks at the bottom center of the canvas which cry out for—yet resist—identification. Is it a plum with deep purple skin and yellow flesh that has been all but completely eaten and left on the table? Or is it simply a painted accent with no representational function? The purple and yellow bring color complements into a painting that otherwise resists them, forcing us to remember that Bonnard, like every French painter of his generation, had learned a good deal about color from Seurat, Signac, and others, and he had undoubtedly read Signac's 1899 essay, "D'Eugène Delacroix au néo-impressionisme."[2]

—RB

NOTES

1. Yve-Alain Bois et al., *Piet Mondrian, 1872–1944* (Boston, 1994), p. 59.
2. For the English translation of this essay, see Floyd Ratliff, *Paul Signac and Color in Neo-Impressionism* (New York, 1992).

Henri Matisse

French, 1869–1954

30. *Woman Seated before a Black Background (Femme assise sur fond noir)*, 1942

Oil on canvas, 21¾ × 18¼ in. (55.3 × 46 cm), unlined; signed and dated lower left: *Henri Matisse 12/42*

The Bloch Collection includes two paintings that were executed either at or shortly after a time of war and conflagration. Manet painted *The Croquet Party* (cat. no. 4) in 1871, the same year that France capitulated before the Prussian army, and Matisse made this work during World War II.

In 1942, three years after the beginning of the war, Matisse was in Nice. He spent much of his time ill in bed, recovering from surgery for cancer that was further complicated by gall bladder problems. Matisse, who recurrently referred to his close encounter with death, felt morose and upset, his personal ailment seeming to conflate with the world's problems. An abiding sense of isolation and alienation resulted from this, and the fact that he had almost no contact with old friends such as Picasso made matters worse. Matisse had not painted much since late 1941 (the glorious *Still Life with Magnolia* of October 21, 1941, now at the Musée National d'Art Moderne, Centre Georges Pompidou, Paris), and until August 1942 he concentrated instead on drawing, an activity much easier to carry out from his bed. He went back to his easel as soon as he felt up to it, starting with *Dancer in Repose* (private collection) and the famous *Dancer and Rocaille Armchair on a Black Background* (private collection) as well as a series of pictures of a woman by a French window.

The Bloch Matisse epitomizes this period of renewed physical capacity and rekindled interest in painting. As Yve-Alain Bois has described, Matisse's canvases at this point acquired a "new fluency accentuated by the thinness of the paint film and the growing role played by the aura of unpainted white surrounding the figures."[1] The black background of this particular painting carries various decorative motifs that were scratched into a film of wet paint with the tip of a brush. The drawing of these patterns is the result of antipainting (scratching paint off the surface of the canvas), a process Matisse had used earlier in *Woman in Blue* (fig. 48), executed in Nice in 1937, and seen again in *Dancer and Rocaille Armchair on a Black Background* (September 1942) and in *Tulips and Oysters on a Black Background* (February 1943; fig. 49).

This painting displays the technical opposition between painting and antipainting, between color and line, that characterizes Matisse's late works. This particular painting, however, does more: it also embodies a symbolic moment in Matisse's life when, despite the ongoing war, the artist was beginning to come out of darkness and regain an interest in life. The warm colors of

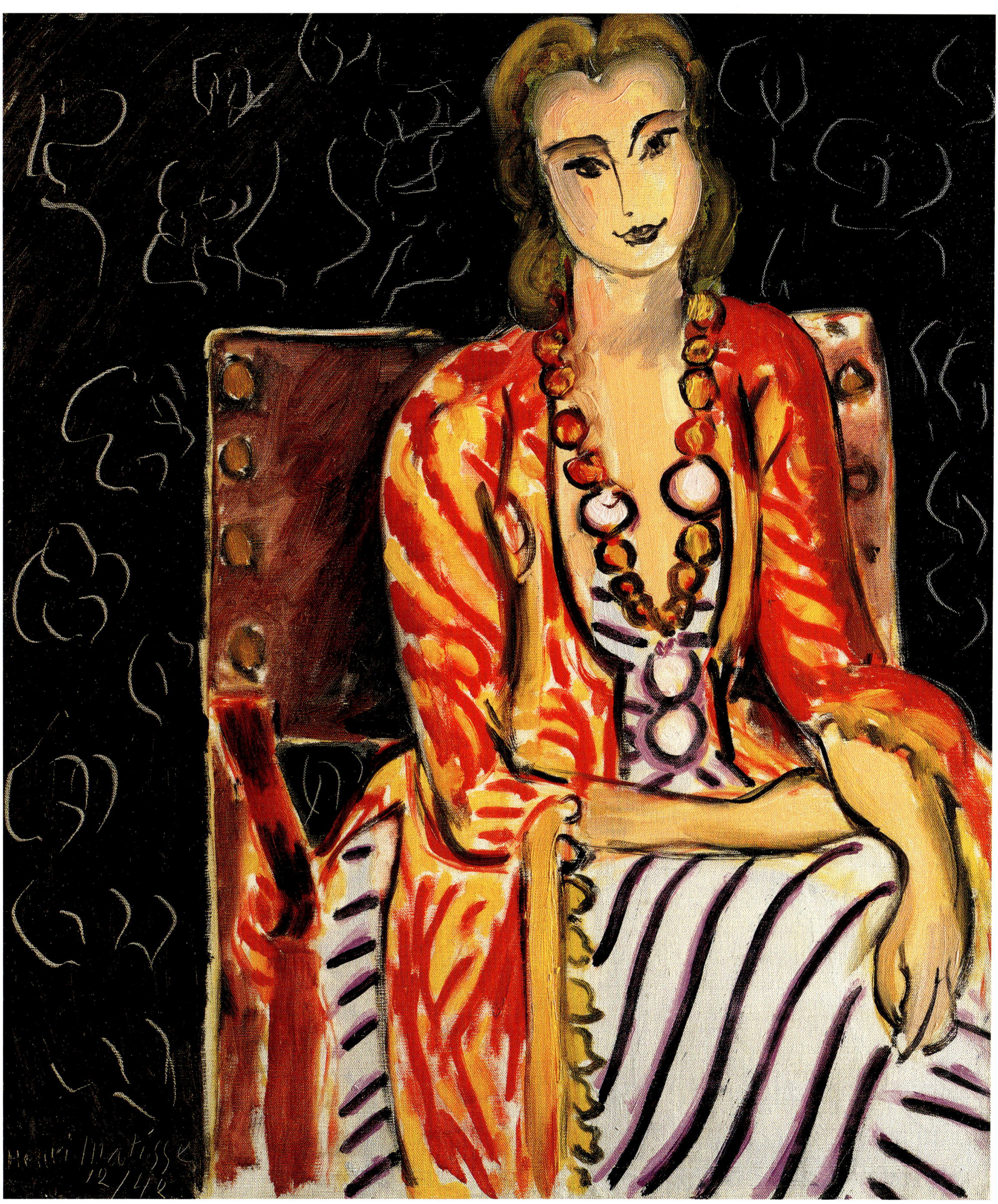
Henri Matisse
12/42

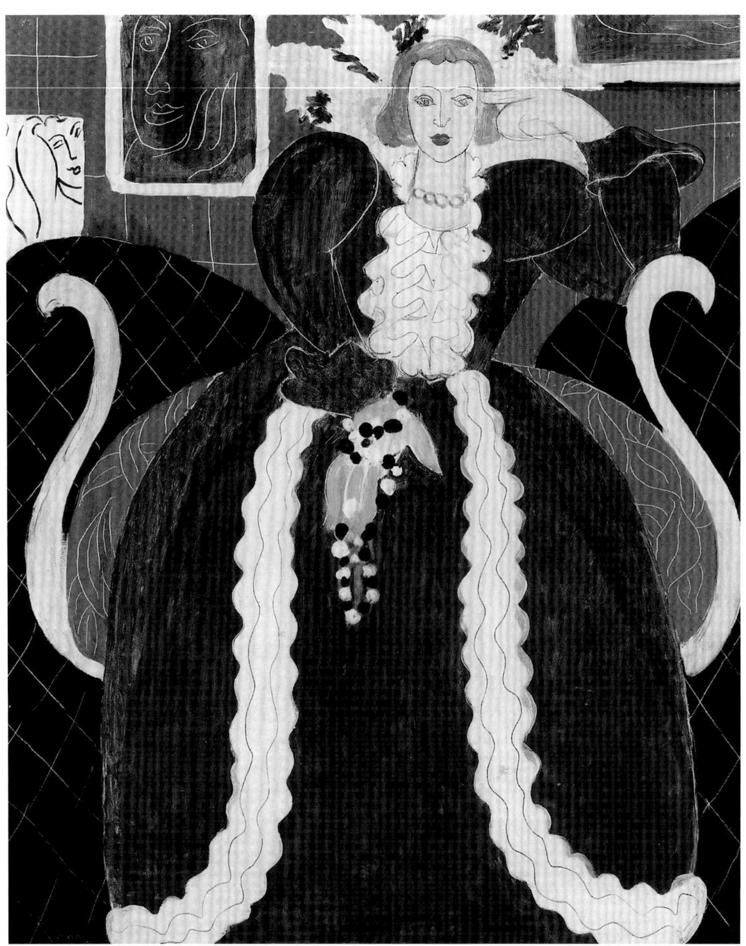

FIG. 48 Henri Matisse, *Woman in Blue*, 1937, oil on canvas, 36½ × 29 in. (92.7 × 73.7 cm). Philadelphia Museum of Art, gift of Mrs. John Wintersteen, 1956

the model's wrap and her bright face jump out of the black background and strongly suggest that brightness prevails over darkness—indeed, over all else.

As in many paintings Matisse executed during the 1930s and 1940s, *Woman Seated before a Black Background* manages to produce a very deep expressive content from a remarkable economy of means. Everything revolves around the dark, almost dazzlingly black background. This, in turn, was embellished not by adding but by subtracting paint with the tip of a brush. The resulting forms are reminiscent of abstract formulas, of arabesques taken from Matisse's sketchbooks. The overall strategy of the composition is astonishing: the background itself consists of a simple layer of black paint whose patterned drawings were created by scratching paint off the surface. From these starkly simple means and contrasts come a lyrical, melodious sequence of arabesques and abstract forms, making a decor for the seated woman that is almost, but not quite, overwhelming. How did Matisse do this, passing from "too little" to "too much"? This is the question this work directs at us.

Just like its pictorial means, the composition itself is simple and belies its opposite: an abundance of visual luxury. A woman is seated in an armchair, nothing more, yet such simplicity

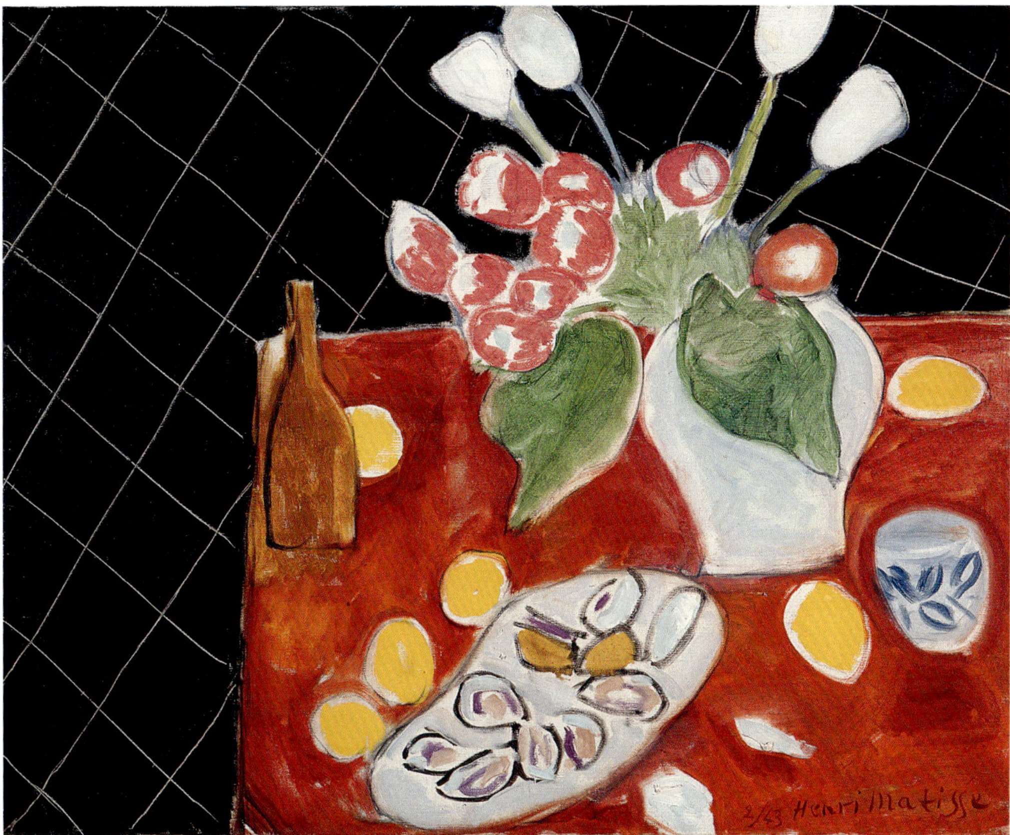

FIG. 49 Henri Matisse, *Tulips and Oysters on a Black Background*, 1943, oil on canvas, 24 × 28¾ in. (61 × 73 cm). Musée Picasso, Paris

yields extraordinary results. One can focus, for instance, on the leather-covered armchair, its backboard decorated by studs. These circular forms, seen against a flat pink and purple surface, are precisely echoed by the circular rings that form the necklace the model wears. Simplicity calls for luxury; the mundane calls for rarity; nails echo the shape of jewels.

Those circular rings, however, are offset by a succession of parallel linear patterns in the woman's dress, with its purple-pink lines, and in her shawl, with its more ornate, complex red lines against a yellow background. Here again the modesty of these devices belies the rich, colorful sensuality that imbues the entire painting. This opposition between the simplicity of means and the rich pleasurable marks of sensual color might just be the very subject of the painting. Very much like Manet's painting of the croquet party, this picture conveys the oppositions and tensions Matisse grappled with as he faced his easel again after months of physical weakness. Ironically these formal artistic tensions compounded by personal travail yielded beautiful paintings such as this. It invites us to empathize with the artist and share his thought: out of this dark era, all hope is not dead.

—JP

NOTE

1. Yve-Alain Bois, *Matisse and Picasso* (New York, 1998), p. 142.

Documentation

1. Édouard Manet
The Croquet Party (La partie de croquet), 1871

PROVENANCE: 1871 inventory of Manet's work; sold by Manet in 1879; Gustave Caillebotte, Paris; bequeathed by Caillebotte to the Musée du Luxembourg but rejected by the Conseil des Musées Nationaux, 1894; Martial Caillebotte, Paris; Mme Caillebotte, Paris, c. 1931; Chardeau, Paris; Peugeot family, France; Juan de Bestegui, Switzerland; Margo Pollins Schab, Inc., New York; Bloch purchase from Margo Pollins Schab, January 15, 1986

EXHIBITIONS: 1884, Paris, École des Beaux-Arts, *Exposition posthume Manet*, no. 73; 1886, New York, National Academy of Design, *Works in Oil and Pastel by the Impressionists of Paris*

REFERENCES: Étienne Moreau-Nélaton, *Manet raconté par lui-même* (Paris, 1926), vol. 1, p. 135, fig. 149, and vol. 2, p. 111, no. 141; Paul Jamot and Georges Wildenstein, *Manet. Catalogue critique* (Paris, 1932), no. 197; Adolphe Tabarant, *Manet et ses oeuvres* (Paris, 1947), p. 191, no. 180; Denis Rouart and Sandra Orienti, *Tout l'oeuvre peint d'Édouard Manet* (Paris, 1970), no. 151; Denis Rouart and Daniel Wildenstein, *Édouard Manet. Catalogue raisonné* (Lausanne and Paris, 1975), vol. 1, pl. 173; Juliet Wilson-Bareau, *Manet by Himself* (London, 1991), no. 147; Juliet Wilson-Bareau and David Degener, *Manet and the Sea* (Philadelphia, 2003), pp. 72–73, illus. p. 135

2. Édouard Manet
White Lilacs in a Crystal Vase
(Lilas blancs dans un vase de cristal),
1882 or 1883

PROVENANCE: Purchased from Manet by M. Pertuiset, Paris; Mme Chocquet, Paris; Chocquet sale, Galerie Georges Petit, Paris, July 1–4, 1899, no. 68; Comtesse de Béhague; Comte André de Ganay, Paris; Lefevre Gallery, London; Bloch purchase from Lefevre Gallery, September 3, 1987

EXHIBITIONS: 1884, Paris, École des Beaux-Arts, *Exposition posthume Manet*, no. 101; 1932, Paris, Musée de l'Orangerie, *Manet*, no. 83; 1940–41, San Francisco, De Young Memorial Museum, *The Painting of France after the French Revolution*, no. 68; 1941, Chicago, The Art Institute, *Masterpieces of French Art*, no. 98; 1941, New York, The Metropolitan Museum of Art, *French Painting from David to Toulouse-Lautrec*, no. 83; 1951, Paris, Galerie Charpentier, *Natures mortes françaises de XVII*[e] *siècle à nos jours*, no. 106; 1956, Paris, Galerie Alfred Daber, *Peinture et impressionisme de Géricault à Monet*, no. 16; 1958, Stockholm, National Museum, *Fem Sekler Fransk Konst*, no. 145

REFERENCES: Théodore Duret, *Histoire d'Édouard Manet et de son oeuvre* (Paris, 1902), no. 320; Étienne Moreau-Nélaton, *Manet raconté par lui-même* (Paris, 1926), p. 93, fig. 328; Paul Jamot and Georges Wildenstein, *Manet. Catalogue critique* (Paris, 1932), no. 511; Adolphe Tabarant, *Manet et ses oeuvres* (Paris, 1947), p. 462, no. 435; John Rewald, "Chocquet and Cézanne," *Gazette des Beaux-Arts* (July–August 1969), pp. 64, 75; Denis Rouart and Sandra Orienti, *Tout l'oeuvre peint d'Édouard Manet* (Paris, 1970), no. 417E; Denis Rouart and Daniel Wildenstein, *Édouard Manet. Catalogue raisonné* (Lausanne and Paris, 1975), vol. 1, no. 418; Robert Gordon and Andrew Forge, *The Last Flowers of Manet* (New York, 1986), p. 15, illus. p. 35

3. Eugène Boudin
The Beach (La plage), c. 1865

PROVENANCE: Cadart and Luquet, Paris; Hembert Collection, Paris; Galerie Schmit, Paris; Bloch purchase from Galerie Schmit, March 26, 1981

EXHIBITIONS: 1981, Paris, Galerie Schmit, *Regards sur une collection, XIX–XX siècles* (May 13–July 18), no. 5 (*Sur la plage de Trouville*).

4. Eugène Boudin
Trouville, Beach Scene (Trouville, scène de plage),
1874

PROVENANCE: Bullier Collection; Madeleine Jarry; by descent to Pierre Jarry; Richard Green, London; Bloch purchase from Richard Green, November 13, 1985

REFERENCES: Robert and Manuel Schmit, *Eugène Boudin, 1824–1898. Catalogue, deuxième supplément* (Paris, 1993), p. 28, no. 3919

5. Eugène Boudin
Boats Decorated with Flags in the Port of Deaville
(Bateaux pavoisiers dans le bassin, Deauville), 1895

PROVENANCE: Allard et Noël, Paris; Stephen Hahn, New York; private collection, Virginia; Martha Parrish, Inc., New York; Bloch purchase from Martha Parrish, April 1, 1993

REFERENCES: Robert Schmit, *Eugène Boudin, 1824–1898. Catalogue* (Paris, 1973), vol. 3, no. 3554, illus. p. 356

6. Camille Pissarro
Banks of the Seine at Port Marly
(Au bord de la Seine à Port Marly), 1871
formerly known as *Weir on the Seine at Bougival*

PROVENANCE: Georges Feydeau; Feydeau sale, Hôtel Drouot, Paris, April 4, 1903, no. 39, illus.; Raphael Gérard, Paris; Étienne Bignou; bought by Paul Cassirer, Amsterdam, from Étienne Bignou, October 1933; sold by Paul Cassirer to R. Maas, July 1934; private collection, Zurich; bought by Marlborough Galerie, Zurich, from the above in 1967 and sold to Thomas D. Neelands, Jr., New York; Thomas D. Neelands, Jr., estate sale, Parke-Bernet, New York, April 26–27, 1972, no. 6, illus.; Wildenstein and Co., New York; Bloch purchase from Wildenstein, May 20, 1987

EXHIBITIONS: 1959, New York, Wildenstein and Co., *Contrasts in Landscape: 19th and 20th Century Paintings and Drawings* (from October 31), no. 11; 1975, New York, Wildenstein and Co., *Nature as Scene: French Landscape Painting from Poussin to Bonnard* (October 29–December 6), no. 48; 1996–97, Washington, The Phillips Collection, *Impressionists on the Seine: A Celebration of Renoir's "Luncheon of the Boating Party"* (September 21–February 9), no. 5

REFERENCES: Ludovic R. Pissarro and Lionello Venturi, *Camille Pissarro, son art—son oeuvre* (Paris, 1939), vol. 1, no. 125, p. 97, and vol. 2, pl. 26, fig. 125; Parke-Bernet, New York, *Important 19th and 20th Century Paintings: Drawing and Sculpture* (April 26, 1972), lot 6, illus. p. 23; Ralph E. Shikes and Paula Harper, *Pissarro: His Life and Work* (New York, 1980), illus. p. 97; Hayward Gallery, London, *Pissarro* (1981), p. 86, cited under no. 19; Joachim Pissarro and Claire Durand-Ruel Snollaerts, *Pissarro: Critical Catalogue of Paintings* (Paris, 2005), vol. 2, p. 173, no. 203

7. Camille Pissarro
Chestnut Grove at Louveciennes
(Bois de châtaigniers à Louveciennes), 1872

PROVENANCE: Félix Gérard, Paris; Arthur Tooth and Sons, London; sold by Arthur Tooth and Sons to A. K. Charlesworth, November 9, 1937; jointly purchased by Sam Salz, New York, and Arthur Tooth and Sons, August 1950; sold by Sam Salz to Mr. and Mrs. Alexander M. Lewyt, New York, March 3, 1952; Bloch purchase from Christie's, New York (Lewyt Collection), November 11, 1997, lot 119

EXHIBITIONS: 1937, London, Arthur Tooth and Sons, *"La Flêche d'Or": Important Pictures from French Collections* (November 11–December 4), no. 8; 1965, New York, Wildenstein and Co., *Loan Exhibition, C. Pissarro* (March 25–May 1), no. 9, illus.; 1968, New York, Acquavella Galleries, *Four Masters of Impressionism* (October 24–November 30), no. 6, color illus.; 1981, Boston, Museum of Fine Arts, *Pissarro* (May 19–August 9), no. 18, illus. p. 85; 1994–95, Jerusalem, The Israel Museum, *Camille Pissarro: Impressionist Innovator* (October 11–January 9), no. 40, illus. p. 113

REFERENCES: Ludovic R. Pissarro and Lionello Venturi, *Camille Pissarro, son art—son oeuvre* (Paris, 1939), vol. 1, p. 100, no. 148, and vol. 2, pl. 30, no. 148; John Rewald, *Camille Pissarro* (London, 1963), p. 82, illus. p. 83; John Rewald, *The History of Impressionism* (New York, 1973), illus. p. 295; Christopher Lloyd, *Camille Pissarro* (Geneva, 1981), pp. 52–53, 145, illus. p. 53; Joachim Pissarro, *Camille Pissarro* (New York, 1993), pp. 66–67, 69–70, illus. p. 67; Joachim Pissarro and Claire Durand-Ruel Snollaerts, *Pissarro: Critical Catalogue of Paintings* (Paris, 2005), vol. 2, p. 191, no. 233

8. Camille Pissarro
Rue Saint-Honoré, Sun Effect, Afternoon
(La rue Saint-Honoré, effet de soleil, après-midi),
1898

PROVENANCE: Bought by Durand-Ruel from artist, May 2, 1898; sold by Durand-Ruel, New York, to Josef Stransky, New York, February 20, 1917, and bought back by Durand-Ruel on April 20, 1917; sold by Durand-Ruel, New York, to Henry D. Hughes (Pennsylvania), September 23, 1920; Marie Sterner Gallery, New York, c. 1934; Sam Salz, New York; bought before 1956 by Gladys

Lloyd Robinson and Edward G. Robinson, Los Angeles; Acquavella Galleries, New York; bought by Alex Reid and Lefevre, London, from Acquavella Galleries, 1973; sold by Alex Reid and Lefevre to Cynthia Wood, Santa Barbara (Calif.), December 1976; Bloch purchase from Cynthia Wood, December 30, 1982

EXHIBITIONS: 1898, Paris, Galerie Durand-Ruel, *Oeuvres récentes de Camille Pissarro* (June 1–18), no. 22; 1904, Paris, Galerie Durand-Ruel, *Camille Pissarro* (April 7–30), no. 110; 1908, Paris, Galerie Durand-Ruel, *Pissarro* (March), no. 7; 1917, New York, Durand-Ruel Galleries, *Paintings by Pissarro* (February 3–17), no. 5; 1934, San Francisco, California Palace of the Legion of Honor, *French Painting from the XVth Century to the Present Day* (June 8–July 8), no. 132; 1956–57, Los Angeles County Museum (September 11–November 11) and San Francisco, California Palace of the Legion of Honor (November 30–January 13), *The Gladys Lloyd Robinson and Edward G. Robinson Collection*, no. 42, illus.; 1973, London, Lefevre Gallery, *Important XIX and XX Century Paintings* (November 1–December 22), no. 13, illus. p. 28

REFERENCES: Ludovic R. Pissarro and Lionello Venturi, *Camille Pissaro, son art—son oeuvre* (Paris, 1939), vol. 1, no. 1021, p. 97, and vol. 2, pl. 204; John Rewald, *Camille Pissarro* (London, 1963), pp. 44, 150; Richard Brettell and Joachim Pissarro, *The Impressionist and the City: Pissarro's Series Paintings* (New Haven and London, 1992), p. 87, no. 61; John Rewald, "Pissarro's Paris and His France: The Camera Compares," *Apollo*, no. 5 (November 1992), illus. p. 294; Joachim Pissarro and Claire Durand-Ruel Snollaerts, *Pissarro: Critical Catalogue of Paintings* (Paris, 2005), vol. 3, p. 751, no. 1199

9. Claude Monet
Snow at Argenteuil (Neige à Argenteuil),
c. 1874–75

PROVENANCE: Galerie Georges Petit, Paris, until 1892; bought by Boussod, Valadon et Cie, Paris, from Petit, October 19, 1892; bought by Mr. and Mrs. H.O. Havemeyer, New York, from Boussod, Valadon, April 15, 1898; the Havemeyers until 1907; Mrs. H.O. Havemeyer, New York, 1907–29; her sale, American Art Association, New York, April 10, 1930, no. 85; bought at sale by H.E. Russell for Ruth S. and David M. Heyman; the Heymans until 1984; sale, Christie's, New York, May 16, 1984, no. 8; Alex Reid and Lefevre, London, 1988; Bloch purchase from Susan L. Brody Associates, New York, June 8, 1988

EXHIBITIONS: 1945, New York, Wildenstein and Co., *Monet* (April–May), no. 10

REFERENCES: *The H.O. Havemeyer Collection: Catalogue of Paintings, Prints, Sculpture and Objects of Art* (Portland, Maine, 1931), p. 504; Daniel Wildenstein, *Claude Monet. Biographie et catalogue raisonné*, vol. 1, *1840–1881* (Lausanne and Paris, 1974), p. 262, no. 349; Alice Cooney Frelinghuysen et al., *Splendid Legacy: The Havemeyer Collection* (New York, 1993), p. 363, no. 397; Charles S. Moffett et al., *Impressionists in Winter: Effets de Neige* (Washington and London, 1998), p. 96, illus.

10. Alfred Sisley
Rue de la Princesse, Winter
(La rue de la princesse, l'hiver), 1875

PROVENANCE: Purchased by Galerie Durand-Ruel, Paris, April 4, 1899; Jean d'Alayer, Paris; M. Clifford Michel, New York; Bloch purchase from William Beadleston, Inc., New York, April 16, 1979

EXHIBITIONS: 1899, Paris, Galerie Durand-Ruel, *Monet, Pissarro, Renoir, et Sisley* (April), no. 168; 1922, Paris, *Cent ans de peinture française* (March 15–April 20), no. 155; 1933, Paris, Galerie Durand-Ruel, *Monet, Pissarro, Renoir, et Sisley* (January 14–January 31), no. 40; 1934, Paris, Galerie Durand-Ruel, *De Corot à Van Gogh* (May 11–June 16), no. 60; 1937, Paris, Palais National des Arts, *Chefs d'oeuvres de l'art français*, no. 417; 1949–50, London, Royal Academy, *Landscape in French Art* (December 10–March 5), no. 256; 1970, New York, Wildenstein and Co., *One Hundred Years of Impressionism: A Tribute to Durand-Ruel* (April 2–May 9), illus. no. 26

REFERENCES: Théodore Duret, *Histoire des peintres impressionistes* (Paris, 1939), illus. p. 81; John Rewald, *The History of Impressionism* (New York, 1946), illus. p. 321; Gotthard Jedlicka, *Sisley* (Berne, 1949), pl. 19; Lionello Venturi, *De Manet à Lautrec* (Paris, 1953), p. 116, fig. 85; François Daulte, *Alfred Sisley. Catalogue raisonné de l'oeuvre peint* (Lausanne, 1959), no. 168

11. Alfred Sisley
The Lock of Saint-Mammès
(L'écluse de Saint-Mammès), 1885

PROVENANCE: Purchased from Sisley by Galerie Durand-Ruel, Paris, 1887; Erwin Davis, New York; Galerie Durand-Ruel, New York (purchased from Erwin Davis, April 14, 1899); Sam Salz (purchased from Durand-Ruel, New York, February 1, 1943); Georges Gregory, New York; private collection, New York; Bloch purchase from Richard Feigen and Co., London, November 8, 1994

REFERENCES: François Daulte, *Alfred Sisley. Catalogue raisonné de l'oeuvre peint* (Lausanne, 1959), no. 605

12. Jean-Baptiste-Armand Guillaumin
Landscape, Île de France
(Paysage d'Île de France), c. 1876–77

PROVENANCE: Saussure Collection, Paris; Galerie Schmit, Paris; acquired by Barbara and Robert Bloch in 1978

EXHIBITIONS: 1974, Bordeaux, Musée des Beaux-Arts, *Naissance de l'impressionisme*, no. 92; 1978, Paris, Galerie Schmit, *Aspects de la peinture française XIXème et XXème siècles* (May 10–June 30), p. 33, no. 31

13. Gustave Caillebotte
Boat Moored on the Seine at Argenteuil
(Bateau au mouillage sur la Seine, à Argenteuil), c. 1884

PROVENANCE: Martial Caillebotte; acquired by Jean Blum during the retrospective exhibition at Galerie Durand-Ruel, Paris, 1894; Galerie Durand-Ruel, Paris; Wildenstein and Co., New York; George Friedland, USA, 1967; Bloch purchase from Sotheby's, New York, May 14, 1985

EXHIBITIONS: 1894, Paris, Galerie Durand-Ruel, *Exposition rétrospective d'oeuvres de Gustave Caillebotte*, no. 24 (dated 1891); 1951, Paris, Galerie des Beaux-Arts, *Rétrospective Gustave Caillebotte*, no. 68; 1968, New York, Wildenstein and Co., *Gustave Caillebotte, for the Benefit of the Alliance Française of New York*, no. 61

REFERENCES: Marie Berhaut, *Catalogue: La vie et l'oeuvre de Gustave Caillebotte* (Paris, 1951), no. 256; Marie Berhaut, *Caillebotte l'impressioniste* (Lausanne, 1968), pl. 23; Marie Berhaut, *Caillebotte. Sa vie et son oeuvre, Catalogue raisonné des peintures et pastels* (Paris, 1978), p. 202, no. 360, frontispiece

14. Hilaire-Germain-Edgar Degas
Dancer Making Points
(Danseuse faisant des pointes), 1879–80

PROVENANCE: Galerie Durand-Ruel, Paris; Collection X . . . [sold at Galerie Georges Petit, Paris, May 30, 1927, lot 26]; Galerie Durand-Ruel, Paris; Georges Levy, Paris; private collection (heirs of the previous owner); Peter Findlay Gallery, New York; Bloch purchase from Susan L. Brody Associates, October 19, 1993

REFERENCES: Camille Mauclair, *Degas* (Paris, 1941), p. 141; P. A. Lemoisne, *Degas et son oeuvre* (Paris, 1946), vol. 2, no. 558; Lilian Browse, *Degas Dancers* (London, 1949), no. 140

15. Hilaire-Germain-Edgar Degas
Grande Arabesque, Third Time
(Grande arabesque, troisième temps)

PROVENANCE: Galerie Max Kaganovitch, Paris; Mr. and Mrs. Adolphe A. Juviler, Palm Beach; Parke-Bernet Galleries, New York, October 25, 1961, lot 9; Mrs. Philip D. Sang, Chicago; Sotheby's, New York, May 15, 1984, lot 14; Mrs. Peggy Joan Amster, New York; Bloch purchase from Sotheby's, New York, May 7, 1991

REFERENCES: John Rewald, *Degas's Complete Sculpture* (San Francisco, 1990), pp. 116–17, no. XXXIX; Sotheby's New York, *Impressionist and Modern Paintings, Drawings, and Sculpture, Part I* (May 3–7, 1991), no. 1; Joseph S. Czestochowski and Anne Pingeot, *Degas Sculptures: Catalogue Raisonné of the Bronzes* (Memphis, 2002), pp. 238–39

16. Pierre-Auguste Renoir
Woman Leaning on Her Elbows
(Femme accoudée), 1875–85

PROVENANCE: George Richard; Knoedler and Co., New York; Bloch purchase from Knoedler, February 10, 1976

REFERENCES: Nicholas Wadley, *Renoir: A Retrospective* (New York, 1987), p. 191

17. Pierre-Auguste Renoir
The Flowered Hat (Le chapeau épinglé), 1890–95

PROVENANCE: James Vigeveno Galleries, Los Angeles; George Friedland, Philadelphia; John and Paul Herring and Co., New York; Bloch purchase from Herring, October 27, 1976

EXHIBITIONS: 1965, Philadelphia Museum of Art (short-term loan until March 1, 1966)

REFERENCES: John Rewald, *Renoir Drawings* (New York, 1946), no. 68, illus.; François Daulte, *Renoir Retrospective* (New York, 1971), no. 64, illus.

18. Berthe Morisot
Under the Orange Tree (Sous l'oranger), 1889

PROVENANCE: Julie Manet-Rouart, Paris; Françoise Rouart, Paris; Galerie Hopkins-Thomas, Paris; private collection, USA; Galerie Hopkins-Thomas, Paris; Bloch purchase from Susan L. Brody Associates, New York, November 26, 1990

EXHIBITIONS: 1896, Paris, Galerie Durand-Ruel, *Berthe Morisot*, no. 95; 1902, Paris, Galerie Durand-Ruel, *Rétrospective Berthe Morisot*, no. 15; 1907, Paris, Salon d'Automne, *Rétrospective Berthe Morisot*, no. 32; 1936, London, M. Knoedler and Co., no. 20; 1941, Paris, Musée de l'Orangerie, *Berthe Morisot*, no. 81; 1951, Geneva, Galerie Motte, no. 11; 1952, Limoges, Musée Municipal, no. 10; 1957, Dieppe, Musée de Dieppe, no. 42; 1958, Albi, Musée Toulouse-Lautrec, no. 47; 1961, Paris, Musée Jenisch, no. 54; 1961, Paris, Musée Jacquemart-André, *Berthe Morisot*, no. 66; 1962, Aix-en-Provence, Galerie Lucien Blanc, no. 19; 1987–88, Washington, National Gallery of Art, *Berthe Morisot, Impressionist*, no. 80, illus. opp. p. 140; 1990, New York, Eastlake Gallery

REFERENCES: Marie-Louise Bataille and Georges Wildenstein, *Berthe Morisot. Catalogue des peintures, pastels, et aquarelles* (Paris, 1961), no. 237, fig. 255; Jean Dominique Rey, *Berthe Morisot* (Paris, 1982), p. 86; Alain Clairet, Delphine Montalant, and Yves Rouart, *Berthe Morisot, 1841–1895. Catalogue raisonné de l'oeuvre peint. Collection le Catalogue* (Paris, 1997), no. 241; Robert Hopson, *The Symbolist Portraiture of Berthe Morisot* (Ann Arbor, 2002), fig. 67

19. Georges-Pierre Seurat
The Channel at Gravelines, Petit-Fort-Philippe (Le chenal de Gravelines, Petit-Fort-Philippe), 1890

PROVENANCE: the artist until 1891, posthumous inventory, panel no. 138; Maximilien Luce, Paris; Sotheby's, London, December 6, 1978, lot 216; Bloch purchase from Sotheby's, New York, May 1, 1996, lot 34

EXHIBITIONS: 1905, Paris, Grandes Serres de la Ville de Paris, *XXIe Salon des artistes indépendants* (March 24–April 30), no. 43; 1908–9, Paris, Galeries Bernheim-Jeune, *Retrospective Georges Seurat* (December 14–January 9), no. 78; 1932, Paris, Galerie d'Art Braun, *Le néo-impressionisme* (February 25–March 17), no. 22; 1933–34, Paris, Galerie des Beaux-Arts, *Seurat et ses amis* (December–January), no. 64; 1985, Tokyo Metropolitan Teien Art Museum and Kyoto Municipal Art Museum, *Exposition du pointillisme*, no. 20; 1988, Tokyo Metropolitan Teien Art Museum, *Exposition for the Family*, no. 7; 1990, Indianapolis Museum of Art, *Seurat at Gravelines: The Last Landscapes*, no. 5

REFERENCES: Henri Dorra and John Rewald, *Seurat—L'oeuvre peint, biographie et catalogue critique* (Paris, 1959), p. 266, no. 204; Cesar M. de Hauke, *Seurat et son oeuvre* (Paris, 1961), vol. 1, no. 207, illus. p. 187; André Chastel and Fiorella Minervino, *Tout l'oeuvre peint de Seurat* (Paris, 1973), no. 208, illus. p. 116; Richard Thomson, *Seurat* (Oxford, 1985), p. 171, illus. p. 190; Anne Distel, *Seurat* (Paris, 1991), no. 15, illus. p. 155; Michael F. Zimmermann, *Seurat and the Art Theory of His Time* (Antwerp, 1991), p. 432, illus. no. 577

20. Paul Signac
Portrieux, The Bathing Cabins, Opus 185 (Beach of the Countess) (Portrieux, les cabines, Opus 185 [Plage de la comtesse]), 1888

PROVENANCE: Given to Paul Merme, Paris, by the artist; Dikran G. Kelekian, New York; Rains Galleries sale, New York, January 18, 1935, lot 36; Molly Netcher Brango; Richard L. Feigen and Co., Chicago, 1959; Jerome K. Ohrbach, Los Angeles, 1959; Sotheby's, New York, September 12, 1990, no. 10; Bloch purchase from Richard Feigen, New York, November 8, 1994

EXHIBITIONS: 1890, Paris, Pavillon de la Ville de Paris, Champs-Élysées, *Exposition de la Société des artistes indépendants*, (March 20–April 27), no. 741; 1930, Amsterdam, Stedelijk Museum, *Vincent Van Gogh en zijn tijdgenoten* (September 6–November 2), p. 98, no. 280

REFERENCES: Françoise Cachin, *Signac. Catalogue raisonné de l'oeuvre peint* (Paris, 2000), p. 188, no. 169

21. Vincent van Gogh
Restaurant Rispal at Asnières
(Le restaurant Rispal à Asnières), 1887

PROVENANCE: Theo van Gogh, Paris, by 1887; Johanna van Gogh-Bonger, Amsterdam, by 1891; V.W. van Gogh, Laren, by 1925; purchased by Charles Beechman, London, at Leicester Gallery, London, 1926 (£545); Galerie Bernheim-Jeune, Paris; Mr. and Mrs. Hugo Moser, Heemstede, near Haarlem, and New York, by 1939; Bloch purchase from Sotheby's, New York, November 7, 1979, lot 541

EXHIBITIONS: 1905, Amsterdam, Stedelijk Museum, *Vincent van Gogh*, no. 79; 1920, New York, Montross Gallery, *Vincent van Gogh*, no. 58; 1924, Basel, Kunsthalle, *Vincent van Gogh*, no. 18; 1925, Paris, Galerie Marcel Bernheim, *Retrospective Vincent van Gogh*, no. 15; 1925, The Hague, Pulchric Studio, *Vincent van Gogh*, no. 20; 1926, London, Leicester Gallery, *Vincent van Gogh*, no. 13; 1930, London, Arthur Tooth and Sons, *Modern French Masters*, no. 18; 1943, New York, Wildenstein and Co., *The Art and Life of Vincent van Gogh*, no. 19, illus. p. 61; 1948, Cleveland Museum of Art, *Vincent van Gogh*, no. 6; 1955, New York, Wildenstein and Co., *Vincent van Gogh*, no. 26, illus. p. 41; 1988, Paris, Musée d'Orsay, *Van Gogh à Paris*, no. 45, illus. p. 128

REFERENCES: Jacob-Baart de la Faille with Abraham M. Hammacher, *The Works of Vincent van Gogh: His Paintings and Drawings* (Amsterdam, 1970), no. F355, illus. p. 166; Paolo Lecaldano, *Tout l'oeuvre peint de Van Gogh* (Paris, 1971), vol. 1, p. 117, no. 395

22. Paul Gauguin
The Willow Tree (Le saule), 1889

PROVENANCE: Ernest Cros; Mme Étienne May, née Cros, Paris; M and Mme Mathieu-Georges May, Paris (heirs of the previous owner); Lefevre Gallery, London; Bloch purchase from Susan L. Brody Associates, June 12, 1984

EXHIBITIONS: 1906, Paris, Salon d'Automne, *Oeuvres de Gauguin*, no. 215; 1926, Paris, Association Paris-Amerique Latine, *Gauguin*, no. 7; 1936, Paris, Gazette des Beaux-Arts, *La vie ardente de Gauguin*, no. 77; 1949, Paris, Musée de l'Orangerie, *Gauguin*, no. 17; 1961, Paris, Musée Jacquemart-André, *Les trésors des collections françaises*, no. 79; 1983, London, Lefevre Gallery, *Important XIXth and XXth Century Works of Art* (June–July), no. 6

REFERENCES: Robert Rey, *Gauguin* (London, 1924), no. 5, illus.; Lee van Dovski, *Paul Gauguin* (Olten, Switzerland, 1950), p. 345, no. 174; Georges Wildenstein, *Gauguin* (Paris, 1964), vol. 1, no. 347, illus. p. 133; Daniel Wildenstein, *Gauguin, A Savage in the Making: Catalogue Raisonné of the Paintings (1873–1888)* (Paris and Milan, 2002), vol. 2, p. 346

23. Paul Cézanne
Quarry at Bibémus (Carrière de Bibémus),
1895–1900

PROVENANCE: Ambroise Vollard, Paris; Galerie Pierre, Paris; Ragnar Moltzau, Olso; Galerie Beyeler, Basel; Sam Spiegel, New York; Bloch purchase from Sotheby's, New York, May 11, 1987, no. 5

EXHIBITIONS: 1956, Zurich, Kunsthaus, *Paul Cézanne*, no. 78; 1956, Basel, Galerie Beyeler, *Maîtres de l'art moderne*, no. 17; 1957, Zurich, Kunsthaus, *The Moltzau Collection from Cézanne to Picasso*, no. 17; 1977–78, New York, Museum of Modern Art (also Museum of Fine Arts, Houston, and Grand Palais, Paris), *Cézanne: The Late Work*, no. 15, pl. 34; 1980, Washington, National Gallery of Art, *Post-Impressionism: Cross-Currents in European and American Painting, 1880–1906*, no. 17, illus.; 2006, Washington, National Gallery of Art, *Cézanne in Provence*, no. 84, illus. p. 203

REFERENCES: Lionello Venturi, *Cézanne, son art—son oeuvre* (Paris, 1936), vol. 1, p. 232, no. 778, and vol. 2, pl. 257 (*Carrière de Bibémus*); Alfonso Gatto and Sandra Orienti, *L'opera completa di Cézanne* (Milan, 1970), no. 208, illus. p. 116;

John Rewald, in collaboration with Walter Feilchenfeldt and Jayne Warman, *The Paintings of Paul Cézanne: A Catalogue Raisonné* (New York, 1996), vol. 1, no. 839, pp. 502–3, and vol. 2, p. 293

24. Paul Cézanne
Man with a Pipe (L'homme à la pipe), 1890–92

PROVENANCE: Ambroise Vollard, Paris (no. 3526, *Étude d'homme debout fumant sa pipe*); purchased from Vollard by Galerie Bernheim-Jeune, Paris, September 21, 1905 (no. 15116, *Le petit fumeur*); purchased from Galerie Bernheim-Jeune by Louis Bernard, March 8, 1907; bought back from Louis Bernard by Galerie Bernheim-Jeune, September 29, 1916 (no. 20632, *Le fumeur*); purchased from Galerie Bernheim-Jeune (Lausanne branch) by Auguste Pellerin, Paris, December 31, 1917; René Lecomte and Mme Lecomte, née Pellerin, Paris; private collection; Bloch purchase from Christie's, London [Pellerin Collection], November 30, 1992, no. 16

EXHIBITIONS: 1954, Paris, Musée de l'Orangerie, *Hommage à Cézanne* (July–September), no. 58; 1993, Kansas City, The Nelson-Atkins Museum of Art, short-term loan (February 24–April 1)

REFERENCES: H. von Wedderkop, *Paul Cézanne* (Leipzig, 1922), p. 135, no. 2; Lionello Venturi, *Cézanne, son art—son oeuvre* (Paris, 1936), pp. 186–87, no. 563, pl. 257; Maurice Raynal, *Cézanne* (Paris, 1936), pl. XXXVII; Robert Rey, "Cézanne," *La Revue des Arts*, no. 2 (June 1954), illus. p. 77; Alfred Neumeyer, *Cézanne Drawings* (New York, 1958), p. 47; Alfonso Gatto and Sandra Orienti, *L'opera completa di Cézanne* (Milan, 1970), no. 631, illus. p. 115; Theodore Reff, "Painting and Theory in the Final Decade," in *Cézanne: The Late Work* (New York, 1977), p. 21; Theodore Reff, "Cézanne's Cardplayers and Their Sources," *Arts Magazine* 55, no. 3 (November 1980); John Rewald, in collaboration with Walter Feilchenfeldt and Jayne Warman, *The Paintings of Paul Cézanne: A Catalogue Raisonné* (New York, 1996), vol. 1, p. 443, no. 705, and vol. 2, illus. p. 242

25. Henri de Toulouse-Lautrec
General Séré de Rivières
(Le Général Séré de Rivières), 1881–82

PROVENANCE: Mlle Séré de Rivières (the general's daughter); private collection; Wildenstein and Co., New York; Waterloo Fine Art, London; Bloch purchase from Sotheby's, New York, November 14, 1990, lot 101

EXHIBITIONS: 1954, Nice, Musée des Ponchettes, *Toulouse-Lautrec*, no. 299; 1956, London, Wildenstein and Co., *The Art of Drawing*

REFERENCES: *Burlington Magazine* (July 1956), p. 251, illus. no. 29; M. G. Dortu, *Toulouse-Lautrec et son oeuvre*, vol. 3, *Supplément au catalogue des peintures* (New York, 1971), p. 496, no. A.193, illus. p. 497; Sotheby's, New York, *Impressionist and Modern Drawings and Paintings* (November 14, 1990), lot 101

26. Henri de Toulouse-Lautrec
Jane Avril Looking at a Proof
(Jane Avril regardant une épreuve), 1893

PROVENANCE: P. Viau; Wildenstein and Co., New York; private collection, New York [Mr. and Mrs. David Rosenthal, USA]; Bloch purchase from John and Paul Herring, New York, October 6, 1977

EXHIBITIONS: 1935, Kansas City, The William Rockhill Nelson Gallery of Art and Mary Atkins Museum of Fine Arts, *One Hundred Years, French Painting, 1820–1920*, illus. exh. cat. cover; 1946, New York, Wildenstein and Co., *Toulouse-Lautrec*, no. 19, illus. p. 28; 1948, New York, Wildenstein and Co., *Six Masters of Post-Impressionism*, no. 28, illus. p. 45; 1955–56, Philadelphia Museum of Art (also Art Institute of Chicago), *Toulouse-Lautrec*, no. 42, illus.; 1956, New York, Museum of Modern Art, *Toulouse-Lautrec: Paintings, Drawings, Posters and Lithographs*, no. 21, illus. p. 12; 1985, New York, Museum of Modern Art, *Henri de Toulouse-Lautrec: Images of the 1890s*, no. 13, illus.

REFERENCES: M. G. Dortu, *Toulouse-Lautrec et son oeuvre*, vol. 3, *Supplément au catalogue des peintures* (New York, 1971), no. A.206, p. 502, illus.; Gabriele Mandel Sugana, *The Complete Paintings of Toulouse-Lautrec* (London, 1973), p. 108, no. 334

27. Odilon Redon
The Green Vase (Le vase vert), c. 1900

PROVENANCE: private collection, Sutherland, U.K., c. 1920–95; Bloch purchase from Thomas Gibson Fine Art, London, July 18, 1995

EXHIBITIONS: 1994, London, Thomas Gibson Fine Art, *19th and 20th Century Masters and Selected Old Masters*, p. 16, color illus. p. 17 (*Le vase vert*)

REFERENCES: Robert H. Hubbard, *European Paintings in Canadian Collections* (Toronto, 1962), vol. 2, p. 156; Alec Wildenstein, *Odilon Redon. Catalogue raisonné de l'oeuvre peint et dessiné* (Paris, 1996), vol. 3, no. 1440, illus. p. 69

28. Édouard Vuillard
Woman in a Red Dress, or *J. R. contre fenêtre*, 1899–1900

PROVENANCE: artist's studio; Elsa Schiaparelli, Paris; Marquise Cacciaputi, Paris; sale, Palais Galliera, Paris, March 31, 1977, lot 126 (illus.); Wildenstein and Co., New York; Bloch purchase from Wildenstein, July 14, 1983

EXHIBITIONS: 1981, Greenvale, New York, C.W. Post Center of Long Island University, Art Gallery, *Madame in Her Boudoir: 1870–1940: Paintings, Sculpture, Graphics, Furnishings* (October 4–November 20), illus.

REFERENCES: A. Salomon and G. Cogeval, *Vuillard, The Inexhaustible Glance: Critical Catalogue of Paintings and Pastels* (Paris, 2003), vol. 1, VI–113, p. 532

29. Pierre Bonnard
The White Cupboard (L'armoire blanche), 1931

PROVENANCE: acquired from Bonnard by Galerie Bernheim-Jeune, Paris; Charles Pomaret collection; private collection, Aix-en-Provence; Wildenstein and Co., New York; Bloch purchase from Wildenstein, April 30, 1979

EXHIBITIONS: 1933, Paris, Galerie Bernheim-Jeune, *Bonnard* (June 15–23), no. 15; 1937, Paris, Petit Palais, *Les maîtres de l'art indépendant, 1895–1937* (June–October), no. 18, illus. (*Le buffet*); 1955, Nice, Musée des Ponchettes, *Bonnard* (August–September), p. 31, no. 37; 1965, Nice, Palais de la Méditerranée, *Douze jeunes peintres autour de Bonnard* (February 5–March 14), no. IX

REFERENCES: Jean and Henry Dauberville, *Bonnard. Catalogue raisonné de l'oeuvre peint*, vol. 3 (Paris, 1973), p. 375, no. 1476, illus. p. 374; Sasha M. Newman, *Bonnard: The Late Paintings* (New York, 1984), p. 259; Michel Terrasse, *Bonnard at Le Cannet* (New York, 1988), p. 124

30. Henri Matisse
Woman Seated before a Black Background (Femme assise sur fond noir), 1942

PROVENANCE: Galerie Beyeler, Basel; Bloch purchase from Christie's, New York, November 19, 1986, lot 53

EXHIBITIONS: 1980, Basel, Galerie Beyeler, *Matisse* (June–September), no. 34, illus.; 1981, Tokyo, National Museum of Modern Art, *Henri Matisse* (March–May), no. 90, illus. p. 213, color illus. p. 115 (and Kyoto, National Museum of Modern Art, May–July 1981); 1984–85, Stockholm, Moderna Museet, *Henri Matisse* (November–January), no. 66, illus.

Index

Page numbers in italics refer to illustrations.

Photo credits
Art Resource, NY: figs. 16 (Jörg P. Anders / Bildarchiv Preussischer Kulturbesitz), 20 (Scala), 23 (Nimatallah), 28 (Daniel Arnaudet and Jean Schormans / Réunion des Musées Nationaux), 37 (Erich Lessing), 49 (R. G. Ojeda / Réunion des Musées Nationaux); Dean Beasom: fig. 45; Bob Greenspan: fig. 2; Pernille Klemp: fig. 24; Jacques Lathion: fig. 38; Robert Lorenzson: figs. 26, 41; Mark McDonald: figs. 1, 3; Mel McLean: fig. 17; Jamison Miller: figs. 6, 8; Peter Schälchli, Zürich: fig. 22; E. G. Schempf: fig. 32; Patrice Schmidt: fig. 35; Graydon Wood: fig. 48